BRANCATO

"Mafia Street Boss"

THE STORY OF FRANK BRANCATO

2-23-16

FRANK MONASTRA

Mike

Enjoy the story of the Cleveland mafia

PUBLISHED
BY
BRIGHTON PUBLISHING LLC
435 N. HARRIS DRIVE
MESA, AZ 85203

BRANCATO

"MAFIA STREET BOSS"

THE STORY OF FRANK BRANCATO

FRANK MONASTRA

BRIGHTON PUBLISHING LLC
435 N. HARRIS DRIVE
MESA, AZ 85203
WWW.BRIGHTONPUBLISHING.COM

COPYRIGHT © 2013

ISBN 13: 978-162183-136-5
ISBN 10: 1-621-83136-1

PRINTED IN THE UNITED STATES OF AMERICA

First Edition

COVER DESIGN: TOM RODRIGUEZ

TABLE OF CONTENTS

DEDICATION

In loving memory of my parents,
Jennie & James Monastra.
We continue to love and cherish you and all the wonderful
memories we have of being together as a family.

SPECIAL THANKS

To my acquisitions editor, Don McGuire, and the editors and staff from Brighton Publishing, you are truly a remarkable group of dedicated individuals. I cannot thank you enough.

I would like to thank my lovely and dear wife, my best friend, Judy, for all of her faith, and love, and for her total support while spending hours on end writing this story of my grandfather's life. To my three children, Carrie, Tanya, and Daniel, my five-grandchildren, Corey, Nathan, Alexis, Abby, and Harley, I love you all dearly. I hope when you read this, you will have a better understanding of our family's history.

To my brother and sisters, as well as our complete family on the Brancato side, for your compassion and the continued love we all share and the support of our families over the years. We may not have been the closest of cousins over the years because of the miles between where we lived, but our hearts have always been close in spirit with the love for one another that our grandfather taught us.

To Miss Jennifer Rigby who introduced me to her grandmother the lovely Mirella Britton. Mirella Britton and Jennifer both currently live in England. Mirella is the daughter of Frank's sister Rosaria Ferraccioli! Mirella has been very instrumental in helping me a great deal to fill in many of the hidden mysterious questions of my grandfather's family history and their lives in Italy that so many people never knew.

Most, if not all, of this information on our grandfather is new to everyone, but I wanted to share his complete life story, the life of our grandfather, Mr. Frank Brancato, in an honorable and true fashion.

ACKNOWLEDGEMENTS

To Mr. Rick Porrello and his books on organized crime, *The Rise and Fall of the Cleveland Mafia, To Kill the Irishman,* and *Superthief,* his web site AmericanMafia.com, and several articles inside. His first two books mentioned my grandfather, and it helped to give me the spark—the catalyst—that I needed to research and write the life story of Frank Brancato.

To Allan May, who has become a trusted friend—a well-known Mafia historian and the author of *Mob Stories, Gangland Gotham,* his third book was, *Welcome to the Jungle Inn,* the story of the famous gambling clubs, and his fourth, *"Crime Town USA"* The story of the Mahoning Valley Mafia.

Allan has contributed articles in Rick Porrello's America Mafia web site, along with Jerry Capeci's *Gangland News* and *Crime Magazine.* I have cherished Allan's expert knowledge, along with our friendship, which grew as we worked on this project together. I cannot thank you enough.

From Youngstown, Ohio, American Mafia historian Charles Molino, a.k.a. Moose, for his expert advice and editing, which helped me greatly. His knowledge helped in developing the title for this book. I cherish our new friendship, and will never forget you.

The book *The Encyclopedia of Organized Crime in the United States* by Robert Kelly.

The Cleveland Killer Celebrities web site

Information from Cleveland Magazine, August 1978; "Cleveland's Mafia."

From the FBI files and the Freedom of Information Act (FOIA) I have obtained 1,862 pages of information on my grandfather, Frank Brancato, as well as his many friends. Listed in the reports were names of over twenty FBI agents from Ohio, New York, Hawaii, Los Angeles, Las Vegas, and West Virginia. I have left their names out to protect their identities.

I spent many days and over thirty hours inside the Michael Schwartz Library, located at Cleveland State University, and the Cleveland Project, whose Special Collections division was most helpful. Thanks especially to Lynn Bycko, who was there to help me any way she could. There were hundreds of different newspaper articles I researched and collected from the archives division of the *Cleveland Press* and *Cleveland Plain Dealer*, along with hundreds more newspaper articles on microfilm.

All the Photographs of Frank Brancato, his friends and gambling clubs are courtesy of Cleveland State University Special Collections Library.

Pictures of Jim Monastra and Jennie Brancato's wedding are courtesy of James and Jennie Monastra and family.

PREFACE

Since the beginning of civilization, man has fought for what he truly believes in. We all fight for one reason or another: a cause or a passion that is near and dear to our heart.

A caveman fought for food and to stay alive when predators tried to eat him.

A person who serves in our military fights for the freedom of his country and to preserve the lifestyle he has in the United States. These privileges he holds sacred as he keeps his country safe from outside forces that wish to do him harm.

A politician fights for power. He desires to serve the citizens in his community or state, to keep the ideals and the laws of our country sound for the betterment of mankind.

A firefighter fights to save the lives of people he does not even know, or protects a home that could house a lifetime of dreams and memories for a family, or possibly a building that is the workplace for hundreds in the community.

A police officer dreams of making a difference by fighting crime in his community and being a person who places his life on the line daily while keeping others safe from harm.

An attorney fights for the rights of his clients, whether they are criminals or victims of a crime. They fight to uphold the laws of our country.

A priest, rabbi, or a minister fights because he believes with his whole body and soul in his church and his religion. He fights to keep his parishioners informed and strong in their faith when the world around them seems to be breaking down.

This story is a compilation of the facts on the life of my grandfather, Frank Brancato, who lived in Cleveland, Ohio, for more than fifty years. What you are about to read may seem like an old-fashioned fictional script that the best of the Hollywood screenwriters and producers could not have thought of or imagined in their wildest dreams. Remember, the truth is still stranger than fiction.

The life of Frank Brancato was presented in the newspapers of Cleveland, as well as the Washington press reporters, for many years. The FBI compiled daily observation reports of his criminal activities and routines for many years.

Frank Brancato respected the oath of *omertà* he took so many years ago. He never went against or betrayed his friends and fellow associates. Frank stood by his friends in good times and in bad; just as they had done for him for so many years. They supported one another from early in his career, which started in Ohio with Frank Milano and his brother, "Old Man" Tony Milano, and continued with "Big Al" Polizzi and his good friend John Scalish, the last Don in Cleveland.

> *"However mean your life is, meet it and live it; do not shun it and call it hard names. It is not so bad as you are. It looks poorest when you are the richest."*
>
> *~ Henry David Thoreau*

Frank Brancato 1940

CHAPTER ONE

Semenoro Murder

1970

April 1970 was not going to be a banner month in northeast Ohio.

Early that month, the area became ground zero in the ongoing battle with the nationwide air controller's "sick out" movement. Famed attorney F. Lee Bailey arrived in Cleveland on April 4 to hold a news conference, where he stated that judicial pressure could cause mass resignations across the country. United States District Judge Thomas D. Lambros had promised days earlier that heavy fines would be imposed against air controllers who continued to call in sick.

That same week, Cleveland Director of Public Safety Benjamin O. Davis announced that blanket police protection would remain in effect in the Collinwood section of the city, backed by Ohio National Guard units on standby alert. This was due to recent racial tensions at Collinwood High School, which, after a hastily called spring break, had been closed for two days due to fights between black and white students.

By mid-April, Ohio Teamster leader William Presser, Vice President of the International Brotherhood of Teamsters and President of Joint Council 41, had his hands full, holding strategy meetings around the state, trying to get striking truckers back to work. In Cleveland, Common Pleas Judge Herbert R. Whiting ordered the strikers not to picket or loiter near or in the vicinity of freight company terminals. The order was directed at Teamsters Local 407 drivers, of which 6,000 had walked off the job on April 1. As the wildcat strike continued, vital raw materials were cut off from the city and the economic life of Cleveland was said to be choking.

Presser upset the membership when he claimed that Communists within the union were directing the strike. Later, Presser appeared on the WEWS-TV show *Inner Circle*, hosted by legendary news journalist Dorothy Fuldheim. Presser declared "many of the elected business agents are incompetents who spend most of their time boozing with the members in an attempt to get re-elected, rather than processing grievances." He suggested that Local 407 and others should clear out the incompetents. On May 3, after a thirty-three-day strike, the dissident members of Local 407 returned to work.

Finally, Governor James A Rhodes ordered a stoppage of all commercial fishing in Lake Erie, due to the high levels of mercury pollution in the lake. He called upon Secretary of the Interior Walter Hichel for a complete investigation of the mercury problem.

While all this was going on in northeastern Ohio, the entire world was held spellbound by two events. The first was the ill-fated flight of Apollo 13 and its miraculous return to earth. The seventh manned-mission in the Apollo Space Program blasted off on April 11 on its way to land on the moon. An oxygen tank exploded two days into the journey. The mission was aborted and the lives of the three astronauts on board were in jeopardy. The exceptional work of engineers at Mission Control in Houston, combined with the incredible ingenuity performed under extreme pressure by the flight crew, allowed the capsule to make a safe splash-down on April 17.

The second event was the escalation of the war in Vietnam, with American troop incursions into Cambodia. The result of President Richard Nixon's decision to expand the war into Cambodia at the end of April caused unrest at college campuses across the nation. It also led to one of the darkest hours in northeastern Ohio, the shooting deaths of four Kent State University students by the Ohio National Guard.

No, April 1970 was certainly not a banner month in northeast Ohio.

In organized crime activity during the month, Angelo A. Amato and Jack Lubin, described by the newspapers as "two widely known Cleveland rackets figures" were indicted for tax evasion. Amato had a lengthy arrest record and was a longtime associate of Frank Brancato, who was listed by the FBI as the number-three man in the Cleveland Mafia. Lubin was a close associate of Cleveland Mafia Boss John T. Scalish. Lubin's wife and Scalish's wife were sisters.

Later that month, Daniel J. "Danny" Greene pleaded guilty to falsifying union records. Greene, the former president of Local 1317 of the International Longshoreman's Association, was looking at a year in federal prison and a $10,000 fine. A few years later, Greene's ambitions would lead to a destructive bombing war which, in the end, cost him his life and eventually led to the destruction of the Cleveland Mafia Family by the mid-1980s.

Before the month was over, a federal grand jury indicted Frank Brancato and four of his associates for conspiring to extort money from two Youngstown, Ohio, businessmen. The indictments were the result of a new crime tool being used against organized crime in America called the Strike Force. Indicted with Brancato was a brash thirty-two-year-old hood from New Jersey, Carmen Thomas Semenoro.

It didn't appear as if the underworld was having a banner month either in northeastern Ohio.

John T. Scalish had been the boss of the Cleveland Mafia Family since the mid-1940s, when he took over from Alfred "Big Al" Polizzi. Scalish did his best to keep a low profile, operating from the offices of the Buckeye Cigarette Service, later known as the Buckeye Vending Company, a vending machine supplier. His one time in the national spotlight came when he was arrested as one of the attendees of the notorious Apalachin Summit, held in upstate New York, in November 1957.

Involved with the vending company were Milton "Maishe" Rockman and Angelo "Big Ange" Lonardo. Both were brothers-in-law of Scalish, who seemed to keep an all-in-the-family approach to both his legitimate and underworld business. In addition to the vending machine business, Scalish played an important role in helping to call the shots for the Teamsters' Union, both locally and nationally. He helped control loans issued by the union's Central State's Pension Fund, and maintained the reins over Cleveland union heavyweights Bill Presser and Louis "Babe" Triscaro.

The top people in Scalish's inner circle, in addition to his brothers-in-law, were Frank Brancato and John DeMarco. On Sunday mornings they would hold meetings in a barbershop on Kinsman Road, until the neighborhood changed, and then they switched the venue to a barbershop on Chagrin Boulevard.

One of the criticisms of Scalish over the years was that he failed to initiate new members. The reason given for this was that the elite of the Cleveland Mafia Family did not want to share their illegal profits with any new members. This would lead to big problems for the Family years later, when Scalish passed away. This practice may also have been the reason Frank Brancato went outside the Family to look for new muscle in 1969 to handle collections for him and his associates.

The man brought in by Brancato was Carmen Semenoro, who moved his wife and young son into an apartment complex in Warrensville Heights, Ohio. Located just outside of Cleveland on the southeast side, many of the city's underworld members chose this area of Cuyahoga County as their home. On his FBI record, Semenoro was officially listed as a salesman for the Munroe Lighting Company of Cuyahoga Falls, for which he earned a salary of $200 a week. Selling light bulbs, however, was not the reason Semenoro was asked to come to Cleveland.

Shortly after his arrival, stories began making the rounds about Semenoro, spread mostly by himself. Word had it that he was a member of New York's Gambino Crime Family and that he had been sent here because the heat was on him in that city. He once bragged, "I had to kill this guy in New York, and then when I found out there was a witness, I had to kill the witness." He reputedly told the same story so many times that it got back to the FBI, who checked it out and found it to be false.

Working with Brancato, Dominic Lonardo, Michael Romeo and Francis B. Ross, Semenoro was used to intimidate people from whom the group was attempting to extort money. Lonardo would introduce Semenoro as "a killer for hire." One of the Youngstown businessmen, from whom the group obtained $545, was told by Semenoro that he was going to break his legs. During the initial meeting with the businessmen, held at the Highlander Motor Inn in Warrensville Heights in December 1969, Semenoro told one of the men he would cut off his leg and throw it in the driveway outside the man's home.

While making payments, the businessmen went to the FBI and informed them about what was happening. Word that the FBI was investigating must have leaked out, because on April 13 an official bureau teletype advised that *"SUBJECT SEMENORO PLANS TO FLEE THE CLEVELAND AREA EVENING OF APRIL FOURTEEN."* The next morning Semenoro was arrested by FBI agents after leaving his apartment and entering a 1964 Chevrolet Chevelle, not his usual 1968 red Cadillac Coupe de Ville with the black vinyl top, in which he tooled around.

Semenoro was arraigned before a U.S. commissioner, who set his bond at $100,000. Over the next two weeks, the strike force presented testimony to a federal grand jury, while an attorney provided by Brancato tried in vain to get Semenoro's bail reduced. On April 28, the grand jury handed down indictments on the five men.

On May 15 Brancato, Romeo and Semenoro were arraigned before Federal Judge Thomas Lambros. The strike force attorney described Brancato as the brains of the operation, but exposed that Semenoro made the threats. Bail was set at $10,000 for Brancato and Romeo and each was soon released, but the judge continued Semenoro's $100,000 bail and he was returned to jail.

Semenoro sat in jail for two and a half months. The long wait could not have made him happy with his new crime boss and associates, who were all free and on the outside. On the last day of June, Judge Lambros unexpectedly lowered the bond to $25,000. The judge had ordered a special probation report on Semenoro and found out his only crime as an adult was a charge for beating his wife. Semenoro posted the bond and was allowed to leave.

In the weeks that followed his release there were reports of Semenoro making enemies in the area, mostly due to his womanizing at various mob hangouts in the East Side suburbs. One story involved a heated argument at a lounge where Semenoro was hitting on a married waitress.

All of these stories were brought to the attention of Brancato, Semenoro's sponsor into the Cleveland underworld. At one point it was reported to the FBI that, "Brancato contacted the New York people about Semenoro and they indicated to Brancato that Semenoro was nothing and they could not care less about him."

In addition, Brancato was taking heat from inside the Cleveland Mafia Family on two fronts: those that were reportedly incensed with him for allowing himself to become associated with Semenoro; and those who were furious because of his failure to disassociate himself from him. Brancato was well aware of the danger Semenoro posed as being a co-defendant in the upcoming extortion trial. But what concerned Brancato the most were the whispered rumors that Semenoro had become a stool pigeon.

While Brancato contemplated what had to be done, Semenoro seemed to be waiting to see what was going to be done. He told a young custodian at his apartment, "Take my word for it, and don't wind up like me. I got in with the wrong crowd and my life isn't worth anything now."

Semenoro's prophecy was quick to come true. The night before his death he saw Brancato at a clam bake. Any conversation the two men may have had is lost to history. The following night, September 23, 1970, Semenoro spent with his wife and son. Late that evening he was painting a ceramic lamp in his basement-level apartment. At 10:15, a telephone with an unlisted number in the bedroom began ringing. Sharon Semenoro went into the bedroom to answer it with her son Kevin following her. When Sharon picked up the phone and said hello, the only sound she heard was someone hanging up on the other end.

In the living room, Carmen Semenoro could be seen through the thin window drapes from outside the apartment. He was hunched over, concentrating on his work, when the first of three shotgun blasts were fired. All three hit Semenoro in the head and face, killing him instantly.

Few people familiar with "Uncle Frank Brancato" wasted time wondering who could have ordered the hit. Brancato knew what had to be done and didn't hesitate to order the killing. Although it would take almost a year and a half, the charges against him and the remaining three defendants would be dismissed. At the age of 73, Brancato had dodged another bullet.

CHAPTER TWO

Sicilian Heritage

"You must fully understand the past before you can begin to understand the present, and only God knows what He has in store for the future."

~ Anonymous

Before we can get involved with the life story and history of Frank Brancato, we must first understand his culture and the way of life of all Sicilians.

For Frank Brancato it all started in Licata, a city and community located on the sunny southern coast of Sicily at the mouth of the Salso River, about midway between the towns of Agrigento and Gela. Licata was a major seaport at the turn of the twentieth century, shipping sulfur Mining, asphalt, and at times shipping cheese.

"Other things may change us, but we start and end with family."

~ Anthony Brandt

Frank loved his Sicilian heritage and was very proud of it; he raised his children to believe in God and to love their Catholic faith, their family, and foremost, their history as Sicilians.

"To have seen Italy without having seen Sicily is to not have seen Italy at all, for Sicily is the clue to everything."

~ Goethe

Sicily is the largest island in the Mediterranean Sea, comprising an autonomous region of Italy. Several smaller minor islands surrounding it, such as the Aeolian Islands, are part of Sicily.

Throughout much of its history, Sicily has been considered a crucial strategic location, due in large part to its importance for Mediterranean trade routes.

Sicily, like all regions of Italy, has its very own rich and unique culture, especially with regard to the arts, music, literature, cuisine, architecture, and language. It has given birth to some of the greatest and most influential people in our history.

The Sicilian economy is largely based on agriculture; this same rural countryside has attracted significant tourism in the modern age, as its natural beauty is highly regarded.

The main agricultural products are oranges, lemons, olives, olive oil, almonds, grapes and wine. Hundreds of livestock farms in many parts of the island can be found, which include cattle, mules, donkeys, and sheep. Because the island is surrounded by the Mediterranean Sea, fishing is a major part of the economy as well; there are many tuna and sardine fisheries and processing plants that service the world market today.

In addition to wonderful tasting wine, Sicily manufactures a full assortment of processed food, chemicals, refined petroleum, fertilizers, textiles, ships, leather goods, and forest products. There are petroleum fields in the southeast, and natural gas and sulfur are also produced. Improvements in Sicily's road system have helped to promote industrial development throughout the region.

The people of Sicily are very proud of their island and their heritage. It is not uncommon for people to describe themselves as Sicilian before the more national description of Italian.

Sicilians tend to closely associate themselves with other southern Italians, with whom they share a common history. Today the island of Sicily itself has a population of approximately five million, and there are an additional ten million people of Sicilian descent around the world, mostly located in North America, Argentina, Australia, and other European countries. Like the rest of southern Italy, immigration to the island is very low compared to other regions of Italy, because workers tend to head to northern Italy instead, due to better employment and industrial opportunities.

The villagers have a tradition of working very hard and helping needy neighbors with food. They thrive on the traditional Mediterranean diet of foods based on the livestock, fishing and agriculture of their region, which has a long growing season and rather mild climate. Some have suggested that the Mediterranean diet was rooted in some way in regional poverty, but in fact, ancient Rome and medieval Sicily were Europe's most prosperous regions. It so happens that most cheeses made from sheep's milk are lower in cholesterol than those made from cow's milk, while olive oil, with its monounsaturated fat, is healthier than cholesterol-laden butter. Mediterranean peoples historically consumed fish, poultry, game, lamb, and kid rather than beef. The meat of sheep, goats, and even chickens contains some fat, of course, but Mediterranean's usually consumed less meat than their northern European neighbors. Wine, which has certain cholesterol reducing effects, is a staple of the Mediterranean diet. Freshly grown fruit and vegetables were almost always in season, and became a strong part of their daily diet, as well.

Sicily's sunny, dry climate, scenery, cuisine, history, and architecture attract many tourists from mainland Italy, Europe, America, and abroad. The tourist season peaks in the summer months, although people visit the island all year round. Popular destinations include Mount Etna, the beaches, the archeological sites, and the two major cities of Catania and Palermo.

The Catholic Church is an important fixture in Sicilian lifestyle. Most public places are adorned with crucifixes on their walls, and most Sicilian homes contain pictures of saints, statues, and other religious relics. Each town and city has its own patron saint, and the feast days or festivals are celebrated and are marked by gaudy processions through the streets with marching bands and displays of fireworks.

ITALIAN MARRIAGE CUSTOMS

Most Sicilian weddings are lavish, expensive, and traditional by nature. They are normally held in their local church, the center of their Catholic upbringing.

The day of the wedding, the groomsmen try their hardest to make the groom as uncomfortable as possible by saying things like, "Maybe she forgot where the church is," or, "She did not want to marry you, anyway."

In some parts of Italy, a party known as a serenade is thrown outside of the bride's home by the groom. His family and friends come and wait for the bride, entertaining themselves until she appears. The groom then sings to his bride to further seduce her. Once his song is sung, the party ends.

It is also traditional for the groom's family to give a dowry to the bride and to provide the engagement ring. The bride's family is then responsible for receiving the guests of the wedding in their home for a

9

reception afterward.

The color green is very important in the Italian wedding. In Italy, the tradition of something blue is replaced with something green. This color is thought to bring good luck to the married couple.

The veil and bridesmaids also were important in an Italian wedding. The tradition began in Ancient Rome, when the veil was used to hide the bride from any spirits that would corrupt her. The bridesmaids were to wear similar outfits, so the evil spirits would be further confused.

An old Roman custom was that brides threw nuts at rejected suitors as they left the ceremony.

After dessert, more dancing commences, gifts are given, and the guests eventually begin to leave. In southern Italy, as the guests leave, they hand envelopes of money to the bride and groom, who return the gift with a wedding favor or gift, a small token of his appreciation.

Today, daughters usually remain at home with their parents until they decide to marry, which tends to occur later now than in previous decades. In the past, many Sicilian marriages were pre-arranged by their parents when the daughters were still very young. Frank Brancato's three daughters were all married by the time they were eighteen. Couples back then would expect to have five to eight children. Today they have fewer children than before, yet babies and children are much revered in Sicilian culture and almost always accompany their parents to social events as a total family unit.

Frank Brancato believed that his family was the heart and the soul of his Sicilian culture and lifestyle, just as it had always been for generations. Even today, this pride is passed along from generation to generation. To keep the family close together and strong is often a motto. Family members often live close to each other, sometimes in the same housing complex, street or city.

About 5.5 million Italians immigrated to the U.S from 1820 to 2004. The greatest surge of immigration occurred between 1880 and 1920. That period alone brought more than four million Italians to America.

About eighty percent of the Italian immigrants came from the southern regions, especially from Sicily and Naples. This region was mainly rural, overpopulated and economically underdeveloped, little benefiting from the industrialization process that characterized the northern part of the country. The Italian government even encouraged emigration of landless peasants to relieve economic pressures in the south.

Once in America, the immigrants faced great difficulties. Usually with no knowledge of the English language and with little education, many of the immigrants were compelled to accept the poorest-paying and most undesirable jobs, and were frequently exploited by the middlemen who acted as intermediaries between them and the prospective employers.

Many sought housing in the older sections of the large, northeastern cities in which they settled, which became known as "Little Italies," often in overcrowded, substandard tenements, living with relatives until they could get a job and live on their own.

During the period of mass immigration to the United States, like so many others, Italians suffered widespread discrimination in housing and employment. They were often victims of prejudice, economic exploitation, and sometimes even violence, notably in the South.

Italian stereotypes abounded as a means of justifying this maltreatment of the immigrants. The print media greatly contributed to the stereotyping of Italians, with lurid accounts of secret societies and criminality. From 1890 to1920, Italian neighborhoods were often stereotyped as violent and controlled by criminals.

The destinations of many of the Italian immigrants were not only the large cities of the East Coast in New York and New Jersey; many also migrated to remote regions of the country like Ohio, Florida, Illinois, and California, to name just a few. Italians were drawn to the different regions by opportunities in agriculture, mining, railroad construction, lumbering and other activities under way at the time. Many of the immigrants had contracted to work in these areas of the country as a condition for payment of their passage. In many cases, especially in the South, the immigrants were subject to economic exploitation, hostility, and sometimes even violence.

Many of the Italian laborers who went to these areas were later joined by their wives and children, which resulted in the establishment of permanent Italian-American settlements in diverse parts of the country.

While the vast majority of Italian immigrants brought with them a tradition of honesty and hard work, others brought a very different old-world custom. This criminal element preyed on the immigrants of the Little Italies, using intimidation and threats to extract protection money from the wealthier immigrants and shop owners, and were also involved in a multitude of other illegal activities. When the Fascists had come to power in Italy, they had made the destruction of the Mafia in Sicily a high priority. Hundreds of these men had fled to America in the 1920s and '30s to avoid prosecution of their crimes.

From the earliest days of the movie industry, Italians have been portrayed as violent criminals and sociopaths. This trend has continued to the present day. The stereotype of Italian-Americans is the standardized mental picture which has been fostered by the entertainment industry, especially through movies like *The Godfather*, *Goodfellas* and *Casino* and TV programs such as *The Sopranos* and *Vegas*. These have been a thorn in the side of many Italian-Americans, who resent how the films and TV shows portray their countrymen, focusing on a very few men—maybe one percent in all—who took a different avenue when coming to America. This is not the way the other proud ninety-nine percent live and behave.

A highly publicized protest from the Italian American community came in 2001 when the Chicago-based organization AIDA (American Italian Anti-Defamation Association) unsuccessfully sued Time Warner for distribution of HBO's series *The Sopranos* because of its negative portrayal of Italian Americans.

CHAPTER THREE

Birth in Italy, New Start in America
1897-1924

Francesco Brancato was born on September 27, 1897, in Licata. There were a total of 8 boys and 6 girls in their large Brancato family. Francesco was the middle of five sons of Ninfa (Vecchio) and Giuseppe Brancato. Giovanni was three years older and Giuseppe two years older, while Salvatore and Samuel were three and four years younger, respectively. Two sisters; Antoinette, Rosaria (Known as Mary or Sara.)

Frank's parents were not poor by any means, like many others in their small community, they were actually quite wealthy. They owned a large grocery store in the heart of the town, which sold the community every food items they could possible need.

There was the town's Post Office, located inside the store that Giuseppe (Francesco father) operated while Ninfa his mother managed the store, she was quite a business woman for the time. The proud couple owned a good size factory that salted sardines and made them into anchovies. They owned an old-fashion Tuscan style, but attractive large size home for the area and where proud owners of an assortment of horses and carriages were many other families in the community only had a mule or one-horse.

The Brancato's had the wealth to hire a woman who helped with the household choirs and another as a nanny for the smaller children. Both women lived with the Brancato's full time as there was also a woman who would do their laundry when both husband and wife worked at their business. Mr. Giuseppe Brancato hired a man who managed and operated the factory and was happy to have many of the town's people working for them.

By the 1940's at the ago of 60, Giuseppe Brancato became quite ill and was diagnosed with cancer. Ninfa, the formidable business woman that she was, did not wish to waste time fighting the terrible illness, since her husband did not have much time left to live. She then became upset and was not satisfied with the doctors in their town and for the poor care and treatment of her beloved husband was not receiving. They decided to sell their home, store and factory, below the highly expected market value of all three and moved the remaining family to Rome. This included their other younger children still living at home; Nunzio, Vincenzo, Carmela, Elena and Angelina (known as Lina). Mr. Giuseppe Brancato died within a year of moving to Rome. The senior Mr Brancato would be buried in Rome, where his heart would always be. Soon after his death, the family would start to loose their financial fortune.

By the late 1880s nearly two generations of southern Italians had grown up in poverty. Still, they were part of a tight-knit community whose residents knew one another and helped each other, whether it was on their farmland or in a crisis, such as a fire or the death of a loved one.

With no promise of improvement on the horizon, members of the Brancato family did what thousands of southern Italians had done before them; they decided to create a new life for themselves in America. Francesco and his brother Giovanni were the first to venture forth to the land where the streets were paved with gold.

Coming to America was taking a big chance for Frank Brancato. He was taking a leap of faith that he would end up in a better place to live and to raise his future family, with more opportunities and growth for all.

Francesco was 5'6" tall and weighed 135 pounds, with a lighter complexion and light blue eyes. He was skinny youth, but would get darker from all the sunny and hot days in Sicily. Giovanni was taller by two inches and weighed 175 pounds. He, too, had light blue eyes and the same light completion.

After saving money for their cruise across the Atlantic, the boys made arrangements to stay with relatives once they arrived in New York City. Giovanni booked passage on the *Martha Washington* out of Palermo and arrived in New York City on September 8, 1913.

Eight months later, Frank booked his passage on the SS *Laura*, which departed from the port of Palermo during the second week of May 1914. On May 25 he arrived in New York Harbor.

The SS Laura, the ship that Frank took to come to America

Both brothers endured their thirteen-day voyages with very little food, water, or sleep.

Like his brother several months before, Frank Brancato found himself in extremely long lines for hours on end, waiting to be processed through Ellis Island, just as hundreds of thousands of other European immigrants from around the world before them. Francesco was given the Alien Registration Number 2544646.

Both men in turn ferried to Manhattan or Brooklyn, where they were greeted by their Aunt Josephine and her husband Gino before setting out for the Little Italy section of Brooklyn, where their relatives resided and from where both brothers would begin their new lives.

One of the first things the brothers experienced in their new environment was the Americanization of their first names. Francesco soon became known as Frank and Giovanni became known as John. They were proud to report their progress to their family back in Licata, and it would not be long before they were joined in America by other family members. Over the next few years, brothers Giuseppe (Joseph), Salvatore, and Samuel arrived, as would their sisters Mary and Antoinette.

John remained in the Brooklyn area, but after a short period of time, Frank left New York for Ohio to meet up and live with his cousin Giuseppe DaManti, who lived on Orange Avenue in Cleveland. He stayed there for a short period of time before deciding to move back to

Brooklyn.

It would not take long for Frank and John to find out that making a living in New York City was not as easy as they had envisioned it would be in their dreams. They found themselves in need of money to help support their aunt and uncle's family, a tradition followed by many of the other young immigrants in the small community. Their dinners consisted of a few potatoes, rice, bread and water.

They were hampered by the lack of an education and by the fact that they spoke only a little broken English. Frank found work selling newspapers on the street corners for a few pennies, or sometimes for a nickel on special occasions. The more young men hustled to sell their papers, the more money they received. But with the multitude of newspapers in the city, and newsboys swarming on every corner, there was seldom enough money to be made.

Frank would often supplement his income by delivering groceries for the local Italian grocer in the neighborhood. It did not take long to see that this was not what he wanted to do for a living, as he desired more money to buy himself whatever he wanted.

When Frank was eighteen years old he found work on the massive New York City docks, working as a longshoreman. New York Harbor was the largest and busiest in the world. The loading and unloading of these massive ships requires knowledge of how to operate the equipment. Longshoremen need to possess strong arms and legs, but more importantly, a strong back, and they had to know the proper technique for lifting and stowing cargo, which included many different materials, from grains and coal to barrels of chemicals and fabric.

For the next seven years, Frank handled the backbreaking work of loading and unloading ships in any kind of weather and at any hour of the day or night. Frank never grew taller than 5'6" tall, and he did not fit the normal profile of the burly longshoremen, most of whom were much taller and more powerfully built than he was. He struggled to get recognized during the "shape up" hiring process used on the docks, being passed over many times due to his smaller size.

On the days Frank was not called upon during the shape up, he stayed and watched the others work, hoping to be called when the next ship arrived in port. During this free, time he observed the techniques of the other longshoremen. Frank learned at an early age it was better to watch how people worked than to just open up his mouth and talk; he could always learn more this way. It was a lesson he would pass along to his children.

On some days, Frank was assigned to work inside the massive holding hulls of a vessel. Sometimes it would take hundreds of men to empty the ship's load. The temperatures inside the cargo holds could reach as high as ninety degrees on most days, and even hotter during the summer months. On these days, working in this environment, Frank could lose as much as six pounds before his work was through.

He found himself in a battle to prove himself against the other workers, but by the end of the day, he outlasted many men bigger and stronger than himself. This caught the eye of the boss on the dock. He began to get noticed as a man who got things done. From that time forward, Frank was called upon to work many of the ships arriving in the dock.

Frank learned about the garbage hauling industry on the streets of New York and became very interested, not only in how they operated, but more importantly, how they earned their money, hauling trash from restaurants and homes. This knowledge would later help him in Cleveland.

Like many of his co-workers, Frank started smoking. His brand of choice was Lucky Strikes. It began as a pack-a-day habit, but would grow to two packs a day a few years later.

When he first started working in America, Frank was trying to earn a few dollars to help his aunt and uncle with their bills and to put food on the table, but like so many other young people, as he grew older, his desire for more money increased. He was envious of some of the finer things that others owned and he wanted them for himself: items like tailored suits, hats, and dresses for the women in his life. Coming from a very poor background, Frank desired this more prosperous lifestyle for himself and his future family.

Frank was not satisfied with the money he was earning. He didn't like having to kick back money each week to his hiring boss. He was determined not to live in poverty like his parents did back in Sicily. Frank wanted more out of his life—the chance to earn more and allow his children to have a better life than he did growing up. Truly, that was the American dream for all, and Frank wanted it!

While living in the Brooklyn area, Frank had met and fallen in love with his only wife, Vicenza "Virginia" Balsamo, who was born on May 16, 1903. Frank had stayed in Cleveland near the Sandusky area for over a year, but was still in love with Virginia and wanted to marry her, so he went back to Brooklyn and married the girl he loved on April 16, 1922, in the best royal fashion, based on the Sicilian marriage customs, that their families were able to afford.

Frank's wedding was a small affair compared to some, with only the Balsamo family and a few of the Brancato family, along with his aunt and uncle to witness the event.

On January 12, 1923, Frank and Virginia were blessed with the birth of their first son, Joseph. As it is an Italian tradition to name children after the parents, they both decided to name their son after Frank's father in Sicily and after St. Joseph the Worker, who was the spouse of Our Lady and adoptive father to Our Lord Jesus Christ. Tradition teaches us that he was a carpenter by trade, and known as the patron saint of many causes, including all laborers and families.

By the end of 1923, Frank and V, as he called his lovely and devoted wife, had settled in the small east side town of Cleveland near East Thirty-Ninth Street between Woodland and Scovill Avenues. They would later have four more children.

It did not take Frank long before he met up with several men who could help him support his new family.

CLEVELAND, 1924-1930

The City of Cleveland was just like many of the other major cities across America, where the men who held the power and the money believed it was good business to help take care of their own people. In Cleveland, the successful Italians helped their fellow countrymen get a start on a new and a better life in their new country.

Many of the immigrants who had taken this journey of a lifetime found that they did not have enough money to live on or to feed their families in their new city. Often they would find themselves down to their last few dollars. Many tried to live with family members or other relatives.

Unlike the plots found in some of the popular mob movies, these powerful men in Cleveland did not take money to protect their own people or their businesses. They helped them by paying their rent, or giving them some money for food, or often just having some food delivered to their home by a local grocer. They knew that the Italian community was a major part of their heart and soul and they did whatever they could to help their fellow Sicilians.

PROHIBITION

The Eighteenth Amendment, prohibiting the sale, production, and transportation of alcohol, was ratified on January 16, 1919, and went into effect on January 16, 1920. The act did not actually prohibit the consumption of alcohol. Many people actually stockpiled wines and liquors for their own use in the latter part of 1919, before sales of alcohol became illegal the following January.

Prohibition would become the catalyst to spark a new line of moneymaking opportunities: bootlegging and rum-running, which helped to launch many major organized crime families in the United States.

Section 29 of the Volstead Act allowed the making at home of wine and cider from fruit (but not beer). Up to two hundred gallons per year could be made.

Home brewing became very popular in many communities in Cleveland and around Ohio. Some vineyards grew grapes for home use

The Lonardos helped their clients with building their own homemade stills, and then supplied them with the sweetener called corn sugar that they needed to make the liquor. At this time it took six pounds of sugar to make one gallon of whiskey.

Frank began delivering the corn sugar that was needed to make whiskey to the warehouse located on Woodland Avenue.

Frank met up with a young guy from Wheeling, West Virginia, named Bill Lias. After talking for a while over a cup of coffee at a truck stop, Lias asked Frank if he could deliver whiskey to him in Wheeling. It is unsure how much money Lias offered him, but Frank took Lias up on his offer and the two men became friends in business.

One of Frank's friends, Charlie Colletto, who was the cousin of Little Angelo Sciria, helped him as they made their weekly visits to Canada. The runs would be made with boats full of whiskey from Windsor, Canada. They would go past Cedar Point and into Sandusky Bay, where they would then transfer their whiskey into large cargo trucks for distribution to many of their friends, bars and social clubs in the east and west side of Cleveland.

A rum-running captain could make several hundred thousand dollars a year by piloting his boats out of harm's way and escaping the Coast Guard.

These huge rewards meant the rum-runners were willing to take on big risks as often as they could. They would run without lights at night or in fog, risking life and limb to deliver their hundreds of boxes of whiskey.

Oftentimes, the shores of the north coast could be seen littered with bottles from a rum-runner who had sunk after hitting a sandbar or a reef in the dark night at a high speed. Most of the captains would destroy the remaining bottles, since they had no way of carrying them away. The men had to save themselves first and foremost; they could always get more whiskey to sell and could make another run another day.

The rum-runners were faster and more maneuverable than the other ships. Rum-runners would often keep cans of used engine oil handy on the deck to pour on hot exhaust manifolds, in case a smoke screen was needed to escape the revenue ships or Coast Guard vessels.

The men in their new Italian families of friends learned the first and most important rule to their chosen profession: the code of *omertà*, known as silence. Omertà is a popular attitude and code of honor common in areas of southern Italy, such as Sicily. It also exists to a lesser extent in certain Italian-American communities where the Mafia has influence.

The Little Italy section of Cleveland was established around 1885, when the stone and marble cutters arrived from Italy and found employment making the headstones and monuments for Lake View Cemetery, located on a small hill along what is now known as Mayfield Road.

By early 1920s two brothers, Frank and Tony Milano, had started a social club to help their Italian friends. The club became known as the Italian-American Brotherhood Club, or IAB Club. The club also held the Milano Brotherhood Loan Company, a legitimate business venture that provided loans to the Italian community that other banks may not have approved, at a reasonable rate, to help their fellow countrymen grow and prosper in America. This gave the community a sense of unity and strength, as they all worked hard and struggled to make a living and to raise their families in peace and harmony.

Frank and Tony Milano started a grocery store on Mayfield Road that later became known as Mayfield Imports, which specialized in importing items from their home country, Italy. By doing this, they helped the Italians in the community to be able to enjoy the food that they had grown up with, including homemade pastas, olives, and olive oil.

For Frank, this was a settling-in period, during which he would meet many of the men with whom he would have a long relationship, including Frank and Tony Milano and some of the men from the Lonardo and Porrello's, as well, who were starting to get involved with importing corn sugar for making whiskey.

Frank Brancato was a smart man and a quick learner and became a good student of the Milano brothers, who by this time were rising in popularity inside the Italian community and would become the future leaders of the Mayfield Road Gang.

One fall day back in 1978, I was visiting my Uncle Nasher at his restaurant known as Heller's, located on the west side of Cleveland on Lorain and Dover Center Road. After dinner we were enjoying a few drinks and talking about my grandfather and the old days. I asked him, "How did Grandpa get started in the gambling rackets?"

He informed me, "Grandpa went to Atlantic City to visit and to learn the gambling business from a man named Nucky." Then my uncle dropped the conversation and we moved on to other current family topics.

At that time, I did not fully understand the importance of the man named Nucky, or that his last name was Johnson, until I started the research for this book.

By late 1923, Frank visited an Irishman known as Enoch "Nucky" Johnson, a man he had heard about in Atlantic City, New Jersey, who was becoming a major player in prohibition on the East Coast and who was being recognized by many of the top men in New York families. The story of Nucky Johnson's career is currently a very popular HBO series named *Boardwalk Empire*.

At this time Atlantic City was becoming a popular tourist destination, and the city leaders knew that its success as a vacation resort completely depended on providing an exciting vacation for its visitors with everything they wanted. What many tourists wanted was the ability to drink, gamble and have sex without the government bothering them. City leaders realized that permitting a vice industry would give the city an edge over its competitors in the travel and tourism business in major cities like New York, Buffalo and Niagara Falls. The city dubbed itself "The World's Playground."

Nucky Johnson provided alcohol on Sundays in many restaurants (at this time it was prohibited in the state of New Jersey). Gambling and prostitution were allowed in exchange for the payment of protection money to his organization. Support of this popular industry thrived under Nucky Johnson's control.

Johnson also controlled other forms of corruption that included kickbacks on government contracts to city officials. Most of Johnson's income came from the percentages that he took on every gallon of illegal liquor sold, as well from his gambling and prostitution operations within Atlantic City that he oversaw with great pride. Johnson once said:

"We have whiskey, wine, women, song, and slot machines. I won't deny it and I won't apologize for it. If the majority of the people didn't want them, they wouldn't be profitable and they would not exist. The fact that they do exist proves to me that the people want them."

After spending several months with Nucky, he and Frank became good friends. They had a mutual respect, even though Nucky was of Irish decent and Frank was Sicilian.

Frank Brancato had opened up the communication lines for Cleveland with this new friend in Atlantic City, in case the time ever came when they needed to buy whiskey to help drive their growing business in Cleveland.

Frank then came back to Cleveland and worked closely with the Milanos for their own business of making money for their friends and families.

Because of Around 1924, the Woodland Avenue district of Cleveland was known as Big Italy. It had come into existence in the 1890s. Their illegitimate occupation, the Milano brothers taught Frank to do his best to stay as low profile as possible and to keep out of the interest of the police.

All these men made various charitable contributions, and helped their fellow Italians using the money they made from their illegal activities. They were viewed by many to be saviors to some people in their neighborhoods.

One of the community causes they became known for was helping to sponsor the annual Feast of the Assumption Festival, a very popular Italian event each year in the heart of the Little Italy neighborhood. This feast, normally held on August 15, is the focal point of the Catholic year for these cities It commemorates the death of Mary and her assumption into heaven. The feast includes live Italian music, a spectacular procession and street fair that takes place for four days. The festival attracts visitors of all ages from all over the greater Cleveland area and the money that is made helps the financial interests of the Catholic Church and the Italian community.

During this time period, with financial help from the Milanos, the festival included carnival games and rides, along with fireworks for the children at the end of the day. For the adults there were casino-style games run by Frank Brancato (from which these men took a small profit).

According to an FBI file, in 1924 Brancato reported that he was working as a street vendor selling fruit near his home on East 39th Street.

On April 19, 1924, Frank and V were blessed with their first daughter. They named her Ninfa after Frank's mother, who still lived in Sicily. Frank's mother was originally from the northern part of Italy. Like many children born in Italy, both Ninfas had a lighter Italian complexion with bluish eyes and reddish- blonde hair.

About this time, Frank's younger brother Samuel came to America from Sicily in the same fashion as Frank and his brothers John and Joseph had done years earlier, arriving by ship in New York City and staying in Brooklyn for a short time. Samuel would later settle in Mackinaw Island. Sam was a barber by trade and never got involved with organized crime like his older brothers. Samuel later would die of cancer in 1940.

CHAPTER FOUR

Cleveland

1925-1927

In March of 1925 August Rini was becoming a popular local politician in Cleveland who enjoyed importing alcohol from his friends in Buffalo, New York. Rini was friendly and popular with other Italians in the community. Rini was asked by his friends to stop getting his whiskey from Buffalo and to use local distributors. Rini refused, and within a few months he cornered the whiskey market in Cleveland area.

By May, Rini had a large stockpile of whiskey. In June, his trucks were hijacked three different times. Many barrels were stolen from railroad cars coming in from Buffalo.

Rini's office was located in the Twenty-fifth Street district of Woodland Avenue, close to the Lonardos' warehouse. One day in June, August Rini left his home for his office. When he arrived, he was gunned down at close range by three men. It was speculated that Rini was visited and killed by Lonardo and possibly other men. Frank Brancato was believed to have been involved, but no one was ever arrested for the murder. After a brief investigation by the Cleveland police, the case was closed.

The Murray Hill area was quickly becoming the focal point for all the Italian-Americans in Cleveland. In the summer months, street vendors would set up daily, selling their homemade bread and pastries. Grocery stores like Mayfield Imports would sell fresh Italian meats, such as freshly made Italian pork sausage (either hot or sweet), pepperoni, capicola (an Italian spiced ham) with aged Provolone, fresh garlic along with fresh mozzarella balls, Romano and Parmesan cheeses. There would be a selection of homemade Italian pastas and cheeses, along with fine wines from the vines in Italy and Sicily, and a vast assortment of olives and olive oil imported from Italy. The olives would sit in large fifty-five gallon wooden barrels laid open for the patrons to taste. They would select a few of each as they mixed them together. There were also fresh fruit and vegetables from local growers.

The city streets would have a wonderful aroma of fresh Italian bread baking in an open oven from either Presti's, LaPuma, or Corbo's bakeries. The intoxicating fragrance of fresh Italian pastries, second to none, wafted around the streets of Little Italy, calling everyone into their shops to come and buy.

Many of the older Italians would first go to Holy Rosary Church on Mayfield Road daily for early morning mass. Then they would leisurely walk up and down the hill, seeing friends and relatives and relaxing the day away. They felt like they were home in Italy.

Many friends would enter into the IAB club, owned by Frank and Tony Milano, for coffee or espresso. They would visit with their friends for hours at a time, playing pinochle or canasta and talking about their current life and the old days as children in Italy. Frank Milano would soon open up The Venetian Restaurant on Murray Hill. The restaurant had a wonderful reputation for homemade Italian foods. For many years, it was a popular dining spot for the citizens of Cleveland.

1926

In 1926, working hard on the streets of Cleveland, Frank Brancato found himself in the middle of a citywide war between his friends. Joe Porrello had left the employ of the Lonardos to start his own sugar wholesaling sugar cane business. Porrello and his six brothers pooled their money together and eventually became successful corn sugar dealers headquartered in the upper Woodland Avenue area near East 110th Street. Frank decided to stay with the Milanos and the Lonardos.

Frank was only arrested once that year, for bootlegging; he was fined $100. When he was arrested, he had $3,050 in cash in his pocket. He gladly paid his small fine, smiling as he left the police precinct. That $3,050 in his pocket was the equivalent of $38,314 today. Noted in the FBI files, this was the first known arrest for Frank Brancato. How long could he be lucky and stay out of jail? That was a question that would only take a few years to be answered.

With few competitors, corn sugar dealers and bootleggers were mysteriously dying violent deaths. The Lonardos' business flourished as they gained a near-monopoly on the corn sugar business in Cleveland. Their main competitors were now their old friends the Porrellos.

In late 1926, "Big Joe" Lonardo, now at the height of his wealth

25

and power, left Cleveland for Sicily to visit his mother and other relatives. Lonardo left his closest business partner and brother John in charge of their empire. Unexpected raids by the police on many of the Lonardos' home-still operators brought undue pressure on the Lonardo clan. Hijacking of sugar cane and whiskey ran rampant around the city during Big Joe's six-month absence. Lonardo lost much of his $5,000-a-week profits (the modern equivalent of $62,810) to the Porrellos, who took full advantage of John Lonardo's lack of business skills and the assistance of a disgruntled Lonardo employee.

Big Joe returned and business talks began between the Porrellos and the Lonardos. Lonardo urged the Porrellos to return their lost clientele.

On May 26, 1926, Frank and Virginia were blessed with the birth of another daughter. They named her Isabella after V's aunt in Italy.

Virginia's brother Charles (a.k.a. Chito) Balsamo also moved to Cleveland at this time from Brooklyn, New York. Balsamo, a well-known chef in Brooklyn, would later open a very popular Italian restaurant named Da Vinci's, located on the west side of town on Hilliard Road in Rocky River. That restaurant remained a local fixture until the end of the 1980s.

Rumors were coming out of Washington D.C. and filtering around the country in the newspapers that Prohibition could be ending soon, but no one seem to know when that would occur. This caused the men in organized crime great concern. A repeal would cost mobsters thousands of dollars, if not hundreds of thousands, of income in many cities across America.

1927

In June of 1927, Salvatore Vella was becoming a leader in the community. He operated his own small-time bootlegging business and was also known as an informant who would often tell the police stories about the Lonardos' business transactions.

One day, Vella parked his car in front of Piunno Funeral Parlor on Woodland Avenue, waiting for a friend to meet with him. Another car pulled up next to his car and stopped. Vella looked at him through his window. The driver smiled back at Vella with a nod of his head that seemed to say hello. Vella then smiled back, not knowing the man.

Then, without any warning to Vella, another man walking slowly on the sidewalk next to Vella's parked car paused and looked into the driver's window. Vella's face was only a few inches away. Shots were fired into the car, hitting Vella. Panicking, Vella tried as hard as he could to get out of his car. Several more shots hit him, fired by the man he never saw coming beside of his car. The killer ran into the street and jumped into the waiting car, which quickly sped away.

A few days later, police were actively looking into possible suspects and picked up several men for questioning in connection with Vella's murder. These men included Frank Brancato, along with Antonio Lando. Frank was a known as a friend of both the Lonardos and Porrellos—competitors of Vella's. Frank was released before the end of the day, for lack of evidence.

According to the FBI files concerning Frank's arrest on June 13, this was the second recorded arrest for Frank Brancato.

Lando was later convicted of the shooting, since the police had an eyewitness who had recognized Lando. Lando was later acquitted of the charges against him; after the eyewitness became less than one hundred percent sure it was him standing next to the car door firing the shots into Vella.

The police believed Frank was the driver in the other car, but again, no one could identify him.

Frank made sure he visited Lando's wife each week while his friend was in jail. He gave her some money to help support her young family while her husband was behind bars.

According to the book *The Rise and Fall of the Cleveland Mafia*, by Rick Porrello, in the early evening of October 13, Big Joe and John Lonardo went to the Porrello barbershop to play cards and talk business with Angelo Porrello as they had been doing for the past few weeks. After entering the back room and hanging up their coats, the men could hear music in the background coming from Luna Park, located nearby.

As they sat down at their normal table in the corner of the room, ready to talk and play cards, two guns poked out of the doorway. Suddenly, all that could be heard in the room was the sound of shots being fired, one after another. The room was filled with gray smoke and blood. Big Joe Lonardo was shot three times; once in his head and twice in his chest. John Lonardo was luckier; he was hit only once in the stomach and twice in the leg, but would die shortly.

News quickly spread that one of the top crime bosses had been killed in the city of Cleveland. The police brought in over twenty known criminals for questioning in their investigation, as they usually did. Frank Brancato, along with his friends Colletto, Lupo, Sciria, and all of the Porrello brothers, were arrested as being suspicious persons in this crime. Later, all the men were released after police questioned them and searched their homes for any evidence that would connect them to the murders of Big Joe Lonardo and his brother.

"Black Sam" Todaro, who had been the Lonardos' financial advisor for many years, was thought to have been the mastermind of the two murders, but later only Angelo Porrello was charged with the Lonardo brothers' murders. The police tried very hard to obtain the proper evidence against him, but the charges were later dropped for lack of evidence.

Joe Porrello would succeed the Lonardos as corn sugar baron. He later appointed himself capo of the Cleveland Mafia.

FBI file reports that Frank Brancato was arrested on December 11, 1927, along with an undisclosed associate, in connection with a robbery case; both men were released later that same day.

1928-1929

The deaths of Big Joe Lonardo and his brother John brought about changes for the organized crime world in Cleveland. Both Joe Porrello and Frank Milano were now in charge in Cleveland—Porrello in the Woodland area and Milano in the Little Italy area on Mayfield Road.

According to the *Cleveland Press*, in late May, Larry Lupo was working in his headquarters, which the Lonardos just happened to own. Two men pulled up and Lupo, who was a well-known beer baron and gang leader, got into the car, and was "taken for a ride." Charlie Colletto was in the passenger seat, while Chuck Polizzi was driving. Lupo trusted these men, since they had worked together before on several occasions around the city. Ten minutes, later Lupo was found dead, with five bullets in his head. His body was found on Orange Avenue and East Thirtieth Street.

Within hours, over ten men were arrested by the Cleveland police for questioning in connection with Lupo's murder. One of those men is believed to have been Frank Brancato.

A few days later, the police had an eyewitness who said that

Charles Colletto was in fact the murderer. Somehow, an unnamed photographer was able to get a picture of the witness and then proceeded to run it in the Cleveland News, a local paper.

At the trial, the witness recanted his earlier statement and said he never knew or saw the driver, who the police claimed was Chuck Polizzi or Charles Colletto; nor did the witness see the other man in the car. He claimed the police made up the crazy story and he went along with it to get his name in the newspapers.

The charges against the men were instantly dropped due to lack of evidence; the case was later dismissed. This has never been documented, but it was strongly believed by the police that Frank Brancato had visited the witness and mentioned to him that it would not be in his best interest or good for his health to testify against his two friends. If he wished to stay alive, the witness needed to decide not to testify.

Frank Milano and his Mayfield Road Gang were now planning for the future.

Milano knew that the gaming business was a very good way to expand his growing income and profits. He looked into the legitimate slot machine business that was being controlled in Cleveland by Nate Weisenberg.

A campaign of intimidation began against Weisenberg. His home was later bombed. Big Al Polizzi, John Scalish, Frank Brancato and Chuck Colletto were brought in for questioning by the Cleveland police, but all were later released.

Milano's gang had successfully muscled their way into the lucrative slot machine business and now enjoyed a large portion of the profits. It has been noted that as high as fifty to sixty cents on a dollar bet in the machines is profit.

1929

It is speculated that on a spring day in 1929, Frank Brancato, John DeMarco and John Scalish all received a message they had been waiting for. Their boss, Big Al Polizzi, told them to meet in a smaller room behind the main hall at the IAB club by 11:00 that night in Little Italy.

They entered the dark, smoke-filled room. Inside was a table with two lighted candles and six chairs normally used for a private card games. When the three close friends walked into the room, Frank and Tony Milano, along with Big Al Polizzi, were already in the room having a drink and a cigar. Standing near the bar area, they were laughing and having a good time.

"Come in," Big Al told his men. They all greeted each other and Al gave the three men a drink.

Frank asked, "We're here, Al; what can we do for you?"

The Milano brothers and Al just laughed once again, looking at one another and the three men in front of them.

With a smile, Big Al told his friends, "Tonight, guys, you will become made. You have all proven yourselves to be stand-up guys and good moneymakers for our family. You have all contributed over the past few years, so we cannot deny you membership into our family any longer."

The three friends were overjoyed. They had the look of shock and happiness at the same time; they had been waiting for this moment.

A made man, also known as a wiseguy, made guy, goodfella, man of honor, or Mafioso (plural: Mafiosi), is someone who has been officially inducted into the Sicilian or American Mafia (Cosa Nostra).

Traditionally, in order to become a made member of the Mafia, the inductee had to be a male of full southern Italian blood, preferably of Sicilian descent. Today, it is believed that this requirement has been loosened so that males of half Italian descent through their father's line can also be inducted. Other sources say that a half-Italian through his mother's line can also be acceptable if he has an Italian surname.

An associate of a crime family who was once in the police force or attended a police academy cannot become a made member of the Mafia.

Before being inducted, a potential made man is required to carry out a contract killing. Any murders committed for personal reasons do not count in this respect. Committing one's first contracted killing is referred to as making your bones.

When introducing one made man to another, the phrase "a friend of ours" is used, indicating that he is a member and business can be discussed openly with him. If the person being introduced is an associate or civilian to whom business should not be mentioned, the phrase "a friend of mine" is used instead.

Made men are the only ones who can rise through the ranks of the organization, beginning as a soldier to *caporegime* (captain, or "capo" for short), *consigliere*, underboss, and then the boss.

The sponsor knows the associate very well and vouches for his good character, abilities and devotion to their family. Although a capo or other senior member will determine the prospective member's credibility, ultimately the decision lies with the boss of the family into which he will be inducted.

When the crime family "opens the books" (i.e., accepts new members), an associate will get a call telling him to get ready and dressed. He will then be picked up and taken to the room where the ceremony will take place with the other accepted candidates.

An inductee will be required to take the oath of omertà, the Mafia code of silence. Though the ceremony varies from family to family, it usually involves the pricking of the trigger finger of the inductee, then dripping blood onto a picture of a saint, typically St. Francis of Assisi or the Virgin Mary, which is then set on fire in his hand and kept burning until the inductee has sworn the oath of loyalty to his new family, saying "As this card burns, may my soul burn in hell if I betray the oath of omertà," or "As burns this saint, so will burn my soul. I enter alive and I will have to get out dead."

After the ceremony, the inductee is then a made man and a full member of the Mafia hierarchy. Inducted as a solider, he is given certain responsibilities and privileges. The made man now enjoys the full protection and backing of the Mafia establishment as long as he remains in favor and earns enough money, of which a percentage is passed farther up the ladder to his bosses.

To attack, let alone kill, another made man for any reason without the permission of the Mafia boss higher up in the organization is seen by the mob as a cardinal sin, which will normally be met with severe retaliation and possibly death. This is often the case regardless of whether the perpetrator has a legitimate grievance.

The made man was traditionally seen as untouchable by the law as well as by his fellow criminals—a man to be respected and feared.

About this time, on March 6, 1929, Frank and Virginia Brancato introduced their second son, Ignatius, to the world. He became known as Nasher by his friends and family. Ignatius was named after the saint who wrote a series of letters which have been preserved as an example of very early Christian theology. Important topics addressed in these letters include the sacraments and the role of bishops.

By now the Porrellos were having major problems of their own with the Cleveland police and with several of the major stills being destroyed within the city. The police raided the homes of two operators and destroyed their major stills, one with over a 500-gallon capacity, and another with a 300-gallon capacity. By now the Milanos, along with Polizzi, Scalish, DeMarco, and Frank Brancato, were supplying northeastern Ohio and Pennsylvania with good tasting alcohol to enjoy whenever and wherever the citizens wanted it.

Cleveland, like other major cities across the country and the world, suffered the effects of the Great Depression in the decade preceding World War II. The timing of the Depression varied across nations, but in most countries it started in 1929 and lasted until late 1939 or the early 1940s. It was the longest, most widespread, and deepest emotional and financial depression of the twentieth century.

In the twenty-first century, the Great Depression is commonly used as an example of how far the world's economy can decline. The Depression originated in the U.S. starting with the fall in stock prices that began around September 4, 1929, and became worldwide news with the stock market crash of October 29, 1929 (known as Black Tuesday). From there, fear quickly spread to almost every corner in the world.

By this time, Frank Milano and his brother Tony had purchased and remodeled The Venetian restaurant on Mayfield Road in Little Italy. The boss of the Mayfield Road Mob would often meet his top two capos, Big Al Polizzi, John Scalish, and on occasion, Frank Brancato and John DeMarco, in a rear room set up for private meetings, just off the kitchen area. The men would meet nightly to review the day's activities and to make plans for the next day or the next week. Sometimes they met just play cards and relax. Soon the men would begin meeting in neighborhood barbershops on Sunday afternoons.

Before the end of this year, Frank Brancato went to the Immigration Board in downtown Cleveland and took the required exam to become an American citizen. In doing so, he willingly gave up his Italian citizenship. Brancato needed statements from several American citizens to testify that he was of good moral character, held a steady job, and was not a criminal.

Frank passed the test and took the Oath of Allegiance on November 15, 1929, and became a United States citizen. His wife Virginia had been born in the United States, so she was a citizen by birth.

CHAPTER FIVE

Alessi Murder

1930

With his new American citizenship papers, Frank Brancato visited Italy and Sicily for several months. His devoted wife Virginia was by his side, along with their four children. This would be the first and only time "V" saw the birthplace of her parents, and it was Frank's first and only visit back to the old country since he had arrived in America.

In Rome, the family would stay with Frank's Mother Ninfa and Father Gusieppe and attended his sister Rosaria's wedding on January 8, 1930 to Emerillo Ferraccioli. Frank's young family enjoyed the two months' time in the city of his birthplace, Licata. Most of the homes are built on the gorgeous mountainsides, giving the families a wonderful scenic view of the countryside. Prior to the wedding and his visit to Licata, Frank had sent over enough money to pay for his younger sister's wedding and their grand honeymoon.

Frank showed Virginia the historic sites around the city, including the old stone churches with their amazing statues of saints. They enjoyed the wonderful colors and the beauty of the mountains of his country and the romantic, rustic beauty of the villages. But more important to Frank was getting to see his family and experience the allure of Sicily that it offered to its guests. Best of all were the friends and the close-knit families who still lived in the community, and how they all loved and cared for one another.

Still very popular in America was the numbers game, better known as the policy racket or Italian lottery. The game is an illegal lottery played in mostly the poorer neighborhoods in the communities throughout the United States. A bettor attempts to pick three numbers to match those that are randomly drawn the following day. The gambler places his bet with a man called a bookie, normally at a bar or tavern or another location that serves as a betting parlor. A person, often a young boy (known as a runner) would then carry the money and the betting slips to the local headquarters, called a numbers or policy bank.

As documented in the FBI files, the 1930s were disturbing years for the friends of Frank Brancato. On January 10, 1930, John Scalish was arrested in Lorain, Ohio, as a person of interest in a crime in Cleveland, Ohio. He was later released.

John DeMarco was first arrested on July 31, 1930, in Cleveland, Ohio, as a suspicious person in a crime; he was released on August 1.

Frank Visconti was first arrested by Cleveland police on January 29, 1931, as a person of interest in a crime. He was released the next day.

Angelo Amato, cousin to Frank Brancato, was first arrested on October 2, 1936, in Cleveland, Ohio, under one of his aliases, Enzo Bruno. Amato was arrested for Internal Revenue law violations. The charges were dropped on October 3.

Gamblers from around the state of Ohio and other neighboring states knew they could come to Cleveland to do their gambling in some of the best nightclubs. Moe Dalitz, with the help of Tommy McGinty, ran several social clubs. One club, named the Thomas Club, was located on Dunham Road in Maple Heights. Another was The Mounds Club, which was located on Chardon Road and was known for attracting the elite society in Cleveland, and the Arrow Club located in Geauga County. Years later, it would be raided several times and finally closed down by the police and fire departments in July of 1949 for liquor law and fire code violations.

The Harvard Club was another very popular club in Cleveland. Other major clubs in Ohio were the Jungle Novelty Inn, located just outside the city limits of Youngstown, and the Ohio Villa, located on Highland Road in Richmond Heights.

Gamblers would enjoy playing the slot machines, craps, roulette and poker all night long, or as long as their cash held out, in a very upscale environment. Walls were either painted in bright colors or had wallpaper on them to enhance the decor. There were wooden dance floors for the girlfriends and wives to enjoy themselves, and a band stage area that would hold from three to ten musicians. It was place fashionable people would go to see friends for a glamorous dinner, then to gamble and enjoy the evening out with the hope of winning some big money.

Another popular club was the Harvard Club, located in Newburg Heights, Ohio, which would see anywhere from 500 to 1,000 customers nightly inside their club. The Harvard Club would stay open until 1941, when a court shut them down after a lengthy grand jury investigation. These clubs would be the first of many in Ohio.

The very popular Mounds Club was set up similar to the Harvard Club. It was located on east side of town. The mob had less influence with the police and judges in Lake County, which made it very difficult to stay open for business long, but it offered good food, plenty of top-notch alcohol, and some of the best local and regional performers, who played there often for the guest to enjoy.

Both men and women enjoyed the slot machines. The price ranged from nickel and dime machines to some quarter and even fifty-cent machines for the bigger gamblers. Chuck-a-luck started at ten cents per bet, while poker and craps bets ranged from $1 to $5. There were some big games called "the sky's the limit," where any dollar amount could be placed.

For some of the women who enjoyed gambling in a smaller fashion, bingo games started at one dollar per card, per night, for a fifteen- or sixteen-game evening of entertainment. Additional cards cost from ten cents to a quarter, depending on the winning pot size for the night.

Many of the gambling joints attracted women by offering a grand prize to draw them into the club: this could be a refrigerator or possibly an oven—items that all women desired to have in their homes.

Of course, all the gambling houses provided off-racetrack betting rooms for their customers, who enjoyed playing the ponies from different racetracks around the country.

Frank Brancato was now growing in status as a made man. He was becoming known as the street boss, watching over the gambling business on the streets of Cleveland and throughout Ohio.

By this time, Milano and his Mayfield Road Mob, a gang based in Cleveland's Little Italy, had replaced the Porrellos as the Cleveland area's premier Mafia group.

On Wednesday June 11, 1930, eighteen-year-old Angelo Lonardo and Dominic Sospirato were convicted in the revenge murder of Black

Sam Todaro, who was shot five times. Todaro had organized the murder of Angelo's father, Big Joe. Their sentence, sent down by Judge Ruhl, would be life in prison in the Ohio State Penitentiary for both men, which was unheard of at the time and would be fought in an appeals court for the next few years.

As he has done before, Frank Brancato once again made sure that the families of his friends in prison would receive money weekly to support them while they were away.

In July 1930 after the large funeral for both Joe Porrello and Sam Tilocco. Sam worked as a Lieutenant for the Porrello brothers. He was known to be in the cigar shop on October 13th when "Big Joe" Lonardo was shot to death. Sam and Angelo Porrello where then charged with the murder of "Big Joe" Lonardo on 1928, but were later found "not guilty" at the end of the trial. In June 1930 both Sam Tilocco and Joe Porrello would be shot to death inside Frank Milano's "Ventian" Restaurant located on Murry Hill inside the heart of Little Italy, after Joe Porrello refused to pay Milano for protection.

Frank Milano was finally located by police in his Lyndhurst home on the east side of town. He was arrested for the murder of both men. Bond for Milano was set at only $25,000.

After months of investigation into the murders by Police Inspector Cornelius W. Cody, he was unable to find a witness or enough evidence to tie in Big Al Polizzi, Colletto, Angersola or Frank Brancato to these murders.

According to the *Cleveland Press*, Frank Alessi was the brother-in-law of Black Sam Todaro, a Porrello associate. Alessi was a known racketeer in Cleveland. Alessi was a reputed gunman and an alleged member of the Lonardo clan. He was credited by Cleveland gangsters as having been the man who pointed out Frank Lonardo in the card game where he was killed. Alessi had been arrested on October 20, 1929, in connection with the murder of Frank Lonardo, and was then released.

On August 19, 1930 Alessi, who was thirty-seven, was playing cards inside the Novario Bowling Alley with six other men inside an east side gambling room at East Ninth Street. After a long night of drinking and playing cards, the game finally broke up at 3 a.m. and the men left for home.

Alessi was walking toward his car across the cold, dark Scoville Avenue district (known as the heart of Cleveland's organized crime region) and was surprised by two men waiting in a car parked next to his. Within an instant, both of the men opened fire, hitting Alessi with four shots. Alessi tried to stagger to his car and drive away. Both gunmen ran away as Alessi's friends, who had heard the shooting, came running out of the building to his aid. One of his friends drove him to St. Vincent Charity Hospital in downtown Cleveland to get medical attention.

Detective Sergeant Alex Nagorski of the Cleveland police arrived at the scene. Within an hour, the police ran a check of the two license plates of the cars parked next to Alessi and found one to be owned by Frank Brancato. Lying on the ground near the crime scene between the two cars, the police found a Smith and Wesson .32-caliber revolver.

Frank was acknowledged to be one of a few men who were still loyal to the Lonardo faction in the face of this deadly war between the two families.

Police officers quickly rushed to Frank's home on East Thirty-Ninth Street, waking him up as they knocked as loudly as possible and almost kicked the door down. The noise quickly got him out of bed.

"Why did you shoot him, Frank?" one of the officers exclaimed when Brancato came to the door.

In his broken English, he replied, "Shoot who?"

"Frank," was the officer's reply.

"Frank Alessi?" in broken English, Brancato replied with a surprised look on his face, acting like he knew nothing about the shooting.

The officers quickly handcuffed Brancato and took him from his home to Charity Hospital, directly into Alessi's room. The two officers also grabbed three other men standing in the hallway, who were reporters trying to get a lead story about the shooting for the morning paper.

Looking directly into the eyes of Alessi, they asked, "Which one of these men shot you, Frank?"

Alessi replied instantly in his broken English, "He shot me," looking right at Frank Brancato and pointing his finger at him.

Alessi had broken the code of omertà. Brancato, with a strong, stern face, looked deeply into Alessi's eyes, almost like he was looking into his soul, and said, "No, no; that man is crazy; I never shot him, and I can prove it."

38

The police quickly took him out of the room. Brancato, who was still in handcuffs locked behind his back, continued to insist that he was innocent. He claimed he had been in a pool room nearby, playing cards. He said he had left his car in that lot because it wouldn't start, so he got a ride home from a friend.

The next day a doctor telephoned the police to say that Alessi was not doing well and was not going to make it much longer. Inspector Cody then sent Sgt. Charles Cavolo to the hospital to get a sworn, signed statement from Alessi to convict Brancato of the shooting before his death. When Cavolo arrived, Alessi refused to make a statement or talk to the police, much less sign a formal statement against Frank Brancato. The police were thoroughly convinced that after they had left the hospital, someone visited Alessi and reminded him of his code of omertà, or silence, and that he should not speak of it to anyone, not even the police.

Alessi died the next morning. The police quickly arrested Frank Brancato for his murder, desperately hoping that they would be able to prosecute him based on the earlier statement Alessi had made while he lay dying in the hospital room.

An FBI file states that Frank Brancato was arrested on August 21, 1930, and was charged with murder of Frank Alessi. The file states, "At 3:00 a.m. on August 19, Brancato willfully and maliciously shot Frank Alessi at point-blank range with intent to kill him. After a long surgery and a battle for his life, Alessi would later die on August 31, at 3:30 a.m." Frank Brancato was later indicted. His trial for murder would start on December 1.

On November 24, one of the two *Cleveland Press* headlines was, "Trace Gang War in Murder Trial. Prosecutors Charge Brancato Killed Alessi, Kin to Slain Todaro."

> *Gang feuds of long standing were to be probed in the murder trial of Frank Brancato, which got under way today in the Common Pleas Court with Judge Samuel H. Silbert. Brancato is charged with the killing of Frank Alessi, a reputed gambler and racketeer, on Ninth Street on August. According to police, Alessi was a relative of Black Sam Todaro, who was a lieutenant for the old Lonardo corn sugar dynasty, who was shot to death after he had reputedly turned against his former associates.*

In another *Cleveland Press* article titled "Brancato Judge Samuel Silbert Admits Murdered Man's Deathbed Statement as Evidence:"

An important point was scored by the state in the murder trial of Frank Alessi, a thirty-seven-year-old reputed gambler and racketeer. Brancato was identified by Alessi on his deathbed with several other witnesses in the room. Brancato defense attorney James Connell opposed the admission of the statement and the jury was dismissed while the point was argued in front of the judge. Connell brought up that there were two police officers who were in the room at the time, Alex Nagorski and Edward Kartisck, and heard how Frank Brancato proclaimed "No, no," shortly after he was accused by Frank Alessi.

Detective Inspector C.W. Cody explained to the court that he would make an inquiry on why the two officers did not report Brancato's statement earlier to him and to the Grand Jury. At the hospital, Brancato was taken to Alessi's room with Detective Lieutenant Kurt Gloeckner, Webster Seeley, a reporter for the Cleveland News, and reporter I. A. Nedelmar, from The Cleveland Press with Detective Frank Gronovsky and Kartlsck behind the four men. Gloeckner, Seeley and Nedelman all testified that Alessi confidently picked out Brancato and said, "He shot me." Connell aggressively protested the deathbed confession, as how it was not admissible in court.

From the *Cleveland Press* dated November 28, an article related how Judge Samuel H. Silbert earlier allowed the deathbed testimony from Frank Alessi into the murder case against Brancato, even though the police did not have a signed statement from Alessi. Judge Silbert pointed out "the law allows such evidence, if the accused man does not make an equivocal or ambiguous reply to the charges, at the time, or if he makes no reply at all."

Both the morning paper, *The Plain Dealer*, and the evening paper, *The Press*, ran an article on November 30.

Contradictions in Brancato case will send somebody to the woods. There have been many rumors going around the old court house. In this article, the defense attorney for Brancato was James C. Connell, who argued forcefully in the courtroom to get the omission of these three statements. Defense attorney James Connell tried in vain to get the deathbed statement made by Alessi thrown out of court and not admitted into evidence against Brancato, who maintains he was not in the area of the murder at the time. Judge Silbert stood firm on his earlier ruling and allowed

40

the statement anyway. During the trial, Police Detective Sergeant Alex Nagorski and Detective Edward Kartlsck reported how Brancato did in fact remark, "No, no," but they failed to report this in their earlier reports.

Brancato's attorney said the statement concerning Frank's denial was very important. According to Nagorski's earlier testimony, he did not hear Brancato say anything or deny the allegation. The judge ruled that only the jury could rule and make the decision about this new evidence during the trial.

With both Frank Brancato and Frank Milano in police custody at the same time for murder, and the passing of the city Ordinance 92.329, the Sugar Dealer Licensing Law, the police confidently felt they had the city finally under control.

Earlier in October, while waiting for his trial for the murder of Frank Alessi, Frank Brancato was in a Cleveland cell with his close friend John DeMarco, who was a cousin of the Lonardos. In their jail cell was another young man, twenty-one year old confessed slayer Tony Colletto, who was in jail awaiting trial for the murder of his eighteen-year old wife Christina Lorenzo. Christina had enjoyed being with other men and talking to her friends about the illegal activities of her husband and his friends, and that of his uncle, Chuck Colletto. The elder Colletto was a well-known racketeer and friend of Brancato and DeMarco.

The police believed that the young Colletto was given an order to kill his wife because she could not keep her mouth shut and would bring the police down on their entire organization. Being a soldier in the organization, he needed to fulfill this order given to him, or be killed himself.

One morning when the police came to get Frank Brancato from his jail cell for a court date, they were surprised to find young Tony Colletto hanging from the ceiling with his leather belt around his neck, just hours before he was to have gone on trial for his life.

Guards took Colletto's body directly to the jail hospital and worked tirelessly for over an hour to revive him, but he had died. Other guards quickly woke up both men, who were sound asleep, and began questioning them at great length. Both Brancato and DeMarco explained to the guards that they were asleep all night and did not hear anything.

The guard later called for the warden, and once again the two were questioned in depth, but both men kept to their story.

Police believed that one or possibly both of the men killed Colletto, but with no evidence and with no witnesses, they could not prove or do anything. After some deliberation the police decided that Colletto had committed suicide, since he could not live with the fact that he had killed his wife. Others speculated he could not imagine the thought of being put to death by the electric chair.

Common Pleas Judge Samuel H. Silbert at once ordered a grand jury investigation into Colletto's death. Attorneys Sara Hedrick and William Marsteller told reporters Colletto was murdered because he knew too much. Young Colletto was allegedly a witness to the gangland slaying of Joe Porrello and Sam Tilocco, who was a former corn sugar dealer. Coroner A.J. Pearse quickly ordered a complete autopsy, with a special effort to determine if the body was positioned.

Brancato was released on $1,000 bail the next day, awaiting his trial date for the Alessi murder.

Two months after Frank Milano's release, Brancato was set for his trial for the murder of Frank Alessi. His attorney was now Eddie Stanton, who helped Brancato just as he did his boss, Frank Milano, in the earlier murder case against him.

Brancato dressed in a fashionable style, wearing a well-made tailored suit from Bailey's Clothing Store, located on Euclid Avenue. He looked more like a businessman than a criminal as he sat silently day in and day out, and listening patiently to the testimony of the men who accused him of this murder.

The main focal point of the trial was that the police and prosecution had no witness who could clearly testify against Brancato, nor did they have an actual signed statement from Frank Alessi before he died.

After a long deliberation, the jury acquitted him on December 1, 1930, of the murder of Frank Alessi.

On January 6, 1931, Frank and Virginia Brancato were blessed by God once again with their fifth and last child. They named her Joanne (Jennie) Grace Brancato

In 1931, Milano joined the National Crime Syndicate with many powerful criminals around the country, such as Charlie Luciano and Meyer Lansky. Milano was now the official boss of Cleveland crime family. By 1932, Milano had become one of the top American Mafia bosses in the country and a charter member of The National Commission.

ROSOLINO VISCONTI MURDER

According to Allan May, Cleveland's Mafia historian, the last murder of the Lonardo-Porrello Corn Sugar War, before what can only be described as the grand finale, came on June 26, 1931, with the slaying of Rosolino Visconti.

The *Cleveland Press* called Visconti a "drive yourself" ride victim. Instead of being taken for a ride, this time the victim was shotgunned as he drove his own car.

Visconti's death gave credence to the old adage, "the third time's a charm." This was the third and final attempt to kill the fish peddler-turned-florist-turned-bootlegger.

Born in Sicily, Visconti was a fisherman in Palermo before coming to America and settling in Cleveland in 1913. He opened the Palermo Fish Market on East 22nd Street and ran it with his mother and three sisters. When Visconti was stricken with arthritis in 1918, he turned the business over to his son Frank, who renamed it the Fulton Fish Market and moved the store to Woodland Avenue.

As a successful businessman, Rosolino Visconti drew the attention of the Black Hand.

"The Black Hand" is another name for a mafia organization, an extortion racket practiced by Mafia members in America and Italy.

He refused their extortion demands and nearly paid the ultimate price. On September 16, 1918, Visconti and Frank Messina were sitting in an automobile outside the fish market when a gunman opened fire, hitting both men. Visconti suffered a chest wound. Both men recovered, but refused to provide any details of the attack, the assailant, or a possible motive to police. Visconti claimed the shooting was accidental.

Within weeks of recovering, Messina was murdered. The thirty-two year-old was the father of six children, the youngest being just ten days old. On December 4, 1918, Messina had left his Allen Avenue home in Big Italy and went to a grocery store to purchase milk for one of his children, who was ill. As he was returning home, walking on Allen Avenue near East Fourteenth Street, two gunmen opened fire, hitting Messina in the face and head. He died instantly.

Messina was close enough to home that his wife and children heard the shooting taking place. According to police, Messina had showed too much interest in Visconti's behalf when the latter was made the victim of a Black Hand extortion plot.

The Black Handers made a second attempt on Visconti's life on January 15, 1919. That evening, after Visconti had arrived home and parked his car in front of his East 22nd Street home, two gunmen fired at him as he walked down the sidewalk. This time Visconti was hit five times—in the head, shoulder, elbow and wrist.

Taken to Charity Hospital, where he was not expected to live, Visconti was questioned by Detective Phil Mooney. Instead of telling Mooney he was a victim of the Black Hand, he blamed the attack on a black man, claiming he was shot after refusing to hand over his watch and money. Not even the fact that eyewitnesses reported seeing a white man fleeing the scene could shake Visconti's story.

The ensuing police investigation revealed that Visconti was prominent in the affairs of the Black Hand. Visconti survived and, after recovering from this latest shooting, reportedly moved to Buffalo, where it was alleged that he was shot at in 1920 a couple of times after becoming involved in a triangle love affair.

Through the decade of the 1920s, Visconti apparently kept out of harm's way. He returned to Cleveland and opened a florist shop on Woodland Avenue. Police believed, however, that he was still involved in the liquor trade business and maintained friendly ties to the city's bootleg bosses.

In January 1931, Visconti's son Frank was arrested by federal prohibition agents on a liquor law violation. After pleading guilty before Federal Judge West, Frank Visconti was sentenced to four months in the Canton Workhouse and fined $500.

On the night of June 26, Rosolino Visconti called his wife and informed her he was on his way home for dinner. He got into his automobile and headed toward his East 143rd Street home. Driving east on Kinsman Road, Visconti was crossing a bridge over the Pennsylvania railroad tracks, just before East 87th Street, when a small coupe closed in on him from behind.

As the vehicle passed him on the right, a shotgun was aimed at Visconti's car and fired; the blast hit him on the right side of his neck. The heavy-grade pellets severed Visconti's jugular vein and spinal cord, killing the fifty-five-year-old instantly. Visconti's car swerved off the street, careened across the sidewalk, crashed through a steel guardrail, and plunged over a five-foot wall into a loading pit at the Teachout Lumber Company.

Across the street from the scene, a young man was delivering a meal to his father, a night watchman at the Ohio Varnish Company. He told arriving officers he had heard what sounded like a blowout just before seeing the automobile leave the road. He believed the man had simply lost control of the car.

When firemen arrived at the scene, they had to chop a hole in the roof of the vehicle to extract Visconti's body. It was not until they pulled him from the vehicle that they realized he had been the victim of a shotgun blast.

Fifteen minutes after the murder, police found the small coupe parked in front of a house on East 105th Street. The shotgun used in the murder was found lying on the rear seat. A check of the license plate showed it had been issued to a fictitious address. The car had been purchased in Youngstown on February 13 and to date it had only 1,800 miles on it. *The News* reported, "The coupe was new cause for the police to believe that it may have been purchased specially for the killing—a circumstance not without precedent among gangland killers." The same method had been used earlier in the James Porrello murder.

The reporting of theories in the three dailies, fueled by statements from the police, was conflicting, to say the least:

NEWS, JUNE 26:

"Visconti was a known associate of the Porrellos," Police Lieutenant Cavolo asserted. "He was always hanging around them. The shooting of Jim Porrello, Mike Lobosco and Visconti were all on the same order. I am practically satisfied that the same men who killed the first two killed Visconti."

PLAIN DEALER, JUNE 27:

"Capt. Story revealed there was nothing to connect the slaying with the Porrello-Lonardo corn sugar feud. It was reported after the murder... Visconti had been an associate of the Porrellos. Capt. Story explained, "Visconti merely knew the Porrellos, as did a great many others in that section of the city."

PRESS, JUNE 27:

"Detective Lieutenant Charles Cavolo... verified how Visconti was never in on the liquor racket 'after the money went out of it.' Cavolo went on, 'Visconti was friendly to both the Porrello and Lonardo factions and his death has no connection with the deadly feud waged by these families'."

With the contradicting reports, police needed a new theory to explain his murder. Cavolo offered up that it could be a continuance of the love affair which had caused Visconti to be used for target practice in Buffalo ten years earlier. Detectives Carl Zicarelli and Frank Herling, assigned to the case, suggested there might be a feud among flower vendors or that Visconti might have become involved with a new love locally.

Visconti's family provided no helpful information. On his body police found a .32 pearl-handled revolver. Family members implied that they never knew him to carry a weapon. Police said the presence of the revolver indicated that he may have feared vengeance by some enemy.

Police sent officers to the Canton Workhouse to bring Frank Visconti back for questioning. The son told police he knew of no one who was an enemy of his father or anyone who would want to kill him. Police then brought in several female associates of Visconti to be questioned.

Later, two men were arrested and held for questioning. One was a twenty-two year-old was believed to have been the last owner of the death car. The second man was exposed to have been in an automobile, which passed Visconti just before the fatal shotgun blast was heard. Both men were later released and no one was ever brought to trial for the murder of Rosolino Visconti.

CHAPTER SIX

Porrello Brothers Murder

1932

In several well-documented newspaper articles from the *Cleveland Press* and the *Cleveland Plain Dealer*, after the truce was formed between the Porrello brothers and Frank Milano, the Porrellos began stopping at a cigar shop owned by their friend Joe Todaro on East 111ᵗʰ Street. Inside the shop there were two tables set up for anyone who wished to play cards, relax, waste some time, and talk among friends. The Porrello brothers were known to play there almost daily, as they enjoyed these games with their friends in the neighborhood.

On February 25, 1932, the Porrello boys were playing their usual card game in the corner of the back room. They chose that table for protection, since they could easily see if anyone entered the room. They played with their friend and bodyguard Dominic (Guelli) Mangino, also known as Terra-Terra.

About twenty minutes after their game had begun, three unidentified men walked into the shop through the front door, unseen by the three men who were concentrating on their card game. A canary sang a song above their heads.

Ray Porrello suddenly looked up and to his surprise he saw what looked to be an assassin squad standing there with shotguns and revolvers in their hands. Joe Todaro dashed behind the counter as Ray Porrello jumped up, pushed his chair back, and tried to pull out his gun.

The gunmen sprayed the room with bullets. Ray fell to the floor with a bullet in his head, while Rosario stood up and was shot three times in the head. Guelli was in the middle of the room when he was shot through his brain. He refused to die for two hours. Another man was killed who just happened to be in the room; it was believed that he was killed simply because dead men tell no tales.

With their top coats and hats on, trying to cover their faces and keeping their heads down so no one could identify them, and dropping their guns to their sides, the gunmen ran out of the smoke shop. They quickly got into cars that were waiting for them with the engines running. A witness on the street told the police one of the men seemed to have been shot and was bleeding badly and holding his stomach. He seemed to be in great pain as he was helped into the car by the other men.

Inside the cigar shop was a grotesque crime scene, with pools of blood and three men lying dead on the ground. It would soon become a spectacle in the neighborhood. Hundreds of curious people in the community came running over to the cigar shop from nearby stores. Within minutes, reporters came running to snap a few photos or get the first scoop of who the dead gangsters were. By this time, the police were trying desperately to secure and to close down the crime scene so they could start their investigation.

Police blamed the murders on a renewal of the feud between the Porrellos and the Milanos. Back in late June 1930, Frank Milano, Al Polizzi, Johnny Angersola and Charlie Colletti had been accused of the murder of Joe Porrello and Sam Tilocco at Milano's Venetian restaurant on Mayfield Road. The feud was believed to be because Milano resented the Porrellos' attempt to control the corn sugar business.

Some four to five hours after the cigar-shop shooting, as darkness fell on the city, a car pulled into the parking lot of a west side hospital. The driver helped another man get out of the passenger's side of the car and walk toward the entrance. The passenger was holding his stomach and appeared to be bleeding and in great pain. The driver is believed to have been Angelo Sciria. He quickly left the parking lot with the lights still off on his car, to make sure he was not seen by anyone in the area.

Then, with a bullet deep inside his stomach, the man walked slowly and calmly into St John's Hospital.

"I have pain in my stomach," Frank Brancato told a nurse on duty at the front desk.

The nurse noticed the blood on his abdomen and brought him into a room for an examination. As they suspected, the doctor and nurse found that he had been shot. The wound had a small, inadequate dressing on it.

The emergency room doctor immediately started to treat the man.

First on his agenda was trying to stop the bleeding.

After several minutes, the doctor finally recognized the man who lay on the table in front of him from one of his many pictures in the newspapers. As soon as the doctor got the bleeding under control and the patient stabilized, he notified the police that the man he was treating was Frank Brancato.

The police wasted no time in sending over Inspector Cody to the hospital to interview Frank and to find out what had happened to him and how he had been shot. By this time, the police already suspected that Brancato had taken part in the shooting at the smoke shop earlier in the day, along with Angelo Lonardo and Dominic Sospirato. However, the murder case was still in the beginning stages and they did not know for sure who had been involved. Was Brancato one of the men involved, or had he been shot in another location?

Being very weak and having a hard time breathing, Frank struggled to tell his story in soft, broken English that was hard for the men to understand.

"I was walking down Detroit Avenue when I heard something that sounded like a car backfiring, and then I felt blood trickling down my leg," Brancato reported to Inspector Cody.

The way Brancato told his story, the police were now very suspicious about his statement. They did not believe a word he said to them and now felt certain he was, in fact, one of the men who had stormed the smoke shop and killed Raymond and Rosario Porrello and Dominic Gueli.

The emergency room doctor told the police the bullet was located deep inside Frank's intestines, and that he had very little chance of surviving the night. The doctor said he did not have the skills to do the operation to save his life.

The next morning, two other men were picked up by the Cleveland police: Angelo Lonardo and Dominic Sospirato. After several hours of in-depth questioning and interrogation by Inspector Cody and another detective, the men were released. They both stuck to their story about not knowing anything about the murder, which was one of Cleveland's most gruesome killings.

The *Cleveland Press* reported on February 26, 1932, that police continued to question and interrogate Frank Brancato, as he was under arrest at St John's Hospital, a few hours after the triple murder.

Brancato's wife Virginia appeared at the hospital and ran to Frank's bedside. She threw her arms around him and exclaimed, "Frank, Frank, tell me what happened!"

The police guard said the two whispered in English for a short while, and then they both quickly changed to Italian. Virginia then claimed to the police that Frank had been home with her that evening before he was shot.

Frank later told the police he may have gotten some medical attention from his wife, but he was too weak to recall for sure. Little hope was held for Brancato's life at this time, as he was not expected to survive the night or the upcoming surgery, scheduled for the next day to remove the bullet deep inside his abdomen.

The hospital decided to call in a surgeon who was well respected in the Cleveland community. This type of operation was his specialty. His name was Dr. Joseph Romano.

Inside the operating room the next day, Dr. Romano worked diligently for several hours to locate the bullet. However, he found it was lodged too deep for him to reach in a normal operating fashion. If he continued the procedure, Brancato would surely die from massive, uncontrolled bleeding.

Dr. Romano decided to close up Frank's stomach for the day and to review the X-rays of his stomach area once again, after he stabilized him. The weakened patient rested comfortably overnight with an IV and oxygen helping him to breathe. His wife V sat quietly at his side, praying silently.

The next morning, Dr. Romano brought Frank back into the operating room to try something different that he had thought of overnight. Romano decided first to take out Brancato's intestines in order to get to the bullet.

It was a very strange thing to try, and had never been heard of before in the operating room or in the medical community. Unsure whether it would work, Dr. Romano took his time in a five-hour surgical procedure. He patiently took out Frank's intestines and laid them on a sterile steel tray on Brancato's stomach. Dr. Romano was then able to finally locate the bullet and take it out, while repairing eight damaged areas of his stomach and intestines.

Romano then worked delicately and diligently to repair the holes in the patient's stomach linings. Dr. Romano slowly and methodically placed Frank's intestines back inside his body and hoped for the best.

The police and Inspector Cody hoped that Frank Brancato would live through the night so the City of Cleveland could prosecute him for these three murders.

Sitting quietly, V never left Frank's side over the next few days and nights. She kept saying her rosary and praying to God to save the life of the man she loved unconditionally.

After a few days of being in intensive care and in a coma, Frank slowly regained consciousness. Later that day, he was upgraded from serious to fair condition. Dr. Romano would become well-known for his surgical efforts and heroic fight to keep Brancato alive.

The police had now taken the bullet from Brancato and matched it to one of the guns used at the scene of the multiple murders. By doing this, it would now place Brancato at the smoke shop at the time of the shootings. The police strongly felt they now had one of the men responsible for the horrific shooting.

Brancato still insisted to the police that he had been nowhere near the cigar shop or the shooting of the Porrellos. He continued to maintain his innocence, claiming he was on West 65th Street and Detroit Avenue when he was hit by the stray bullet that almost killed him. The police and Inspector Cody were confident they had their man.

On the morning of March 4, a story in the *Cleveland Plain Dealer* declared Brancato was at the scene of Porrello killings. It mentioned the bullet that was taken from his stomach area, which came from one of the weapons used in the shooting of the three men.

The News and the *Cleveland Press,* another evening newspaper in the city, had similar stories daily on who the police were investigating for this triple murder in the criminal underworld. The articles said police felt very confident that they had one man on whom they could pin the triple murder: Frank Brancato.

Newspapers and people in the community speculated that the earlier attack and murder of Frank Alessi was brought about because of the loss of Frank Brancato's good friend. The police believed Brancato became involved with this murder to avenge the death of his friend Mike Lobosco, who had been shot in May of 1931, along with Jim Porrello and Rosolino Visconti (Frank Visconti's father). Lobosco was also a known close friend of Big Joe Lonardo and had been a still operator for the Porrellos.

51

On March 24, after being released from the hospital and still recovering from his major surgery, Brancato was brought back to the Cleveland Police Station to be interviewed once again, to see if he knew of any information of yet another killing, they had been investigating. They questioned him for two hours in connection with the murder of Fred Capillo.

Leaving the police station with his attorney, Frank Brancato went home to his wife and children to recuperate and gain his strength back.

Nothing was more important to Brancato at this time than his family; they were his world, and when he almost died, he realized more than ever the importance of his wife and children. He appreciated them more than ever.

CHAPTER SEVEN

Perjury Trial and Appeal

1932-1933

It was reported in the *Cleveland Press* on April 7 that the grand jury wanted to see Frank Brancato. He was escorted into the county grand jury courtroom in front of Judge Oscar C. Bell to answer questions for two hours by Inspector Cody about his stomach wound.

Brancato's attorney, Martin A. McCormack, had filed a legal motion attacking the suspicious-person warrants issued against his client by the Cleveland Police Department. Judge Bell told the men he would consider the motion.

During the trial that started on April 8, The *Cleveland Plain Dealer* and the *Cleveland Press* reported that the police had called upon D. L. Cowles, a police ballistics expert, to testify that the bullet removed from Brancato's stomach was similar to one of the bullets found at the crime scene of the triple murder on Woodland Avenue, and that it had been shot from a gun that was found on the scene, indicating that Brancato had to have been there at the time.

On April 9, The *Press* reported that Brancato would be arraigned the next day on perjury charges for his refusal to admit he was at the scene of the murders.

"Frank Brancato, a known gunman and gang member, was indicted today on perjury charges growing from the killing of Porrello brothers and their bodyguard on February 25. The perjury count is based on the fact that Brancato swore before the grand jury that his wound was suffered in a gun battle in another location and proclaimed his innocence that he was not at the scene of the killings. Confronted with the evidence after his release, Brancato refused to speak to the police and was placed on a $5,000 bail, as a suspicious person."

The reporter reminded the public that Brancato was acquitted one year earlier of gang murder of Frank Alessi, and was known to be a gunman for the old Lonardo faction.

The *Cleveland Plain Dealer* reported Judge Walther set Brancato's bail at $7,500 after he pleaded "not guilty" and was released.

According to a later FBI file, on April 9, Frank Brancato was arrested and charged with perjury on April 8, having falsely testified before the county grand jury in certain matters concerning a murder. He was placed in a jail cell next to accused killer Joe Filkowski, who was awaiting trial for a murder as well.

On April 11, The *Cleveland Plain Dealer* reported that a case was to open that morning against Joseph Filkowski, known as "the smiling gunman," who "has made monkeys out of the local police."

Guards were placed in the cell block watching Filkowski closely in three eight-hour shifts, as he continues to tell them they will not convict him. Located in the cell next to him is Frank Brancato, a known Lonardo and Milano henchman, who was wounded in a triple murder and who is currently in jail awaiting his trail for the murder of the Porrello brothers in a cigar shop on Woodland Ave. and East 110th Street. Brancato was a cellmate of Tony Colletto, the friendliest youth, found hanging in his cell more than a year ago. Colletto was on trial for the murder of his young wife Christine while Brancato ... was awaiting trial for perjury. The grand jury strongly believes that he lied last week when Brancato maintains how he was shot on Detroit Avenue, not in the cigar shop where the Porrello brothers were killed. The indictment against Filkowski charges on June 6, 1930, he shot and killed Tony Veryk in a holdup at an apartment.

According to an FBI file, on April 23, Brancato attorney Henry Levine withdrew the plea of guilty in abatement. Then, on May 11 in federal court, during a preliminary hearing, the motion to quash was overruled by Judge Bell. On May 13, after completely reviewing and thinking over the request, Judge Bell overruled the abatement proposal. On May 18, Brancato's perjury trial began in the Common Pleas Court of Judge Dempsey.

This list below was located in December 16, 1957. FBI agents examined the Common Pleas Court records of Frank Brancato, which reflected the following entries.

April 9, 1932—Waivers service

April 23, 1932—Withdrew not-guilty pleas and filed plea in abatement

May 11, 1932—Motion to quash was overruled

May 13, 1932—Defendant pleas in abatement overruled. Defendant accepts

May 18, 1932—The jury is sworn in.

May 20, 1932—Guilty verdict.

June 2, 1932—Appeals bond of $3,000 is pending error. Bond put up by his property.

July 28, 1932—Arrested as a suspicious person on general principles.

April 5, 1933—While in prison the motion to file error proceedings in the Court of Appeals was overruled.

On May 1, an article in the *Cleveland Plain Dealer* said the pistol found at the scene of the murders shown in the Brancato perjury case had a matching slug taken from his abdomen, proving he was one of Lonardo henchmen. A ballistics expert D. L. Cowles testified that the gun which was found on the scene was a .32 caliber revolver, and was one of the murder weapons used in the triple killings. The perjury trial against Frank Brancato was now set to start on May 18 in Common Pleas Court of Judge Dempsey.

On May 19, the evening *Cleveland Press* reported about the police ballistics expert's testimony linking a gun found at the scene of the brutal murders to Brancato as the perjury trial began.

The expert testified that there were three different guns fired inside the cigar room where the three men were found. However, only one revolver was found on the scene in the Woodland Avenue cigar shop where the two Porrello brothers were found murdered.

...On cross examination, Martin McCormick, the defense attorney for Brancato, recalled the famous Yorkell-Brownslein gun fiasco of several years ago in which the New York ballistic expert claimed that the two gangsters were slain by a gun which was later found to have been in a factory when the murders were committed. Frank T. Cullitan, the Chief Assistant Prosecutor for the City of Cleveland, made his closing remarks to the grand jury,

doing his best to convince the jury of Brancato's involvement.

An article dated May 20 in the *Cleveland Plain Dealer* reported Brancato's defense attorney, Martin McCormick had studied the testimony by D. L. Cowles in his client's perjury case and he decided to bring a rebuttal witness into court to defend Brancato on May 19. His ballistics expert had been with the British Royal Air Corps and spent five hours examining the bullet, with several scientific tests performed. He then determined that the bullet found inside Brancato's stomach did not match and it would be impossible to prove that they were fired from the same gun that was found on the scene of the crime, because of the damage on the bullet casing.

It is not known for sure if Frank went home after the shooting, or if the wound was treated and dressed by his wife "V" or by Angelo Sciria who drove Frank to the hospital, as they arrived about 10:30 PM.

McCormick also brought in well-known local weatherman G. Harold Noyes, who testified that at 6:40 p.m., the time of the shooting; it would have been too dark for anyone to have seen someone clearly across the street from where the shooting took place.

For several days, the grand jury in the Brancato case took their time and evaluated all the evidence brought up against him. They made their decision on May 30. The court was informed that a guilty verdict had been decided, not on the murder charge of the three men, since they had very little evidence to convict him of the murder, but on a lesser charge of perjury, since they had all agreed he was in the area of the shooting.

On June 2, The *Plain Dealer* and the *Cleveland Press* reported Frank Brancato was indicted after he swore before the grand jury that he was not present at the Woodland Avenue cigar shop when the two Porrello brothers were killed. Brancato was only convicted of perjury, as the prosecutors were not able to convince the grand jury and Judge John P. Dempsey that Brancato in fact had murdered the three men in cold blood. Brancato was given the sentence of two to ten years in the Ohio State Penitentiary.

Praying quietly and crying softly in the courtroom behind Brancato was his wife V, who was waiting patiently for the expected bad news. After the guilty verdict was read, Brancato stood up, turned around to look at V with a small grin on his face. Mrs. Brancato gave her husband a last kiss goodbye for many years. Crying, she now asked in Italian, "Frank, how am I going to buy food for the children and pay the rent on our home?"

Being a strong man Frank smiled at V and assured her, "Honey, do not worry; my friends will pay you a visit each week and take care of you. If you ever need anything ask Johnny D. or Johnny Scalish; they will help you."

Still crying, and with a sad look on her face, but trying to be strong and brave, V smiled back at her husband, knowing that she needed to take care of their five children, who at the time ranged in age from two to ten years. Brancato was not worried about doing time in prison; he knew that he would be treated well by both the guards and his fellow inmates when he got to prison.

In the book, *The Rise and Fall of the Cleveland Mafia*, written by Rick Porrello, he notes that Dr. Romano was born in 1877 and studied medicine in Palermo, Sicily, before coming to Cleveland, Ohio, in 1906, where he started his practice and became a wealthy man and a well-known surgeon in the community. Romano became the president of the Italian Red Cross in Cleveland but had a secret life that very few people knew about. He was connected to the Mafia and was said to have been a boss.

During his investigation into the Porrello murders, Inspector Cody could not understand why Frank Brancato just happened to show up at St John's Hospital on the west side of town, when there were several other good hospitals closer to his home on East 39th Street. Only Brancato's friends knew the truth: Brancato went there because he did not trust just anyone with his life. He insisted on seeing a friend of the family, Dr. Romano.

From an article in the *Cleveland Plain Dealer* on July 20:

Police have been told by their chief George Matowitz to stop and search all gangsters on sight. His order for war on all racketeers follows two policy raids in which big shots were jailed. Chief Matowitz has ordered his men to stop every known and suspected gangster on sight, search him for concealed weapons and cart him to jail and to the detective headquarters. If he refuses or he cannot give a satisfactory account of his current activities, (officers were ordered to) arrest him. This mandate follows closely on the heels of two police raids on a large front yard policy drawing game in which three men were picked up and which a total of 250 men and women disappeared into the surrounding homes. Arrested in the raid (were)... two of the city's most widely advertised outlaws, Willie Richardson the well-known policy king, and Frank Brancato.

Richardson and Brancato, both of whom are under sentence to the penitentiary for perjury in connection with different gangland-style murders, were questioned to the purposed efforts of the Mayfield Road gang in muscling in on policy rackets. Cody said "He had gained no further information from either man."

From a *Plain Dealer* article on August 10:

Alex Birns, 27, and Frank Brancato, 34, were found talking together on the curb at East 50th Street and Woodland Avenue late last night. Both men were swiftly taken to Central Police Station by Detective Sergeant James McDonald in accordance with an order issued on July 19th by Police Chief George Matowitz, calling on all police forces "To harass every suspected racketeer and muscle man." This has been the third time since the official order was issued that Brancato was brought into the headquarters for questioning. Brancato has been freed on a $5,000 bond, pending his appeal on the perjury charges against him for the Porrello murders. Sergeant McDonald said "Birns and Brancato would be held as long as possible and then would be released." Brancato's attorney, Martin McCormick, is now challenging the suspicious person law in court and (said) that his client is now being harassed by the police.

On September 15, it was reported that Judge Day upheld Chief Matowitz' order allowing the police force to pick up all known criminals in Cleveland under the suspicious person law. Later that afternoon, the suspicious person charge against Brancato was dismissed and he was released.

A *Plain Dealer* article on October 19 said:

Nick Satulla and Frank Brancato and four other men described by police as gangsters were arrested and (were) being held for questioning by detectives in the connection with the early Monday morning shooting of John (Hot Stuff) Johnson, one of the big four policy operators in Cleveland. Two brothers and another man were picked up in the vicinity of East 55th and Woodland a little later, making a total of nine arrested. None of these three men have a police record, but will be questioned in regard to their *knowledge of Brancato or Satulla. Satulla is known as Cleveland's most arrested gangster. The four other men arrested on East 36th Street were Vincent Dolonski, Joseph Artwell, James Corso and Samuel Fazzio. Police suspect that Satulla with his gang and Brancato, along with his Mayfield Road Gang, are trying to muscle their way into the policy rackets here.*

ERA OF GAMBLING DENS
1933-1937

This story was told to me by my cousin Dorothy. On one visit to the Ohio State prison by our grandmother, where they only spoke in Italian, she mentioned to her husband that she was not getting enough money to support their five children.

Frank asked, "Are the boys coming to see you every week?"

She replied, "Yes, they are Frank, thank you; but it is still not enough."

"Why, how much are you getting a week?"

"They started with only $30, but now I am getting $60." (Note: $30 in 1932 was worth $487 nowadays.)

"What did you tell them, V?" Frank just smiled, with a look of shock on his face.

"I simply told Johnny D how $30 was not enough for us, so the next week he brought me $60 from then on. It is helping us, Frank."

Harold Burton was the newly elected Mayor of Cleveland. He replaced Mayor Davis after Davis exhibited increasing incompetence in his office and the city became a haven for criminal activity.

The police department was corrupt, and prostitution as well as illegal gambling were running rampant in the city, as organized crime was operated by the powerful Mayfield Road Gang, which was still abundant in the city of Cleveland.

Following the end of Prohibition in 1933, Eliot Ness was promoted to Chief Investigator of the Prohibition Bureau for Chicago and then in 1934 for the State of Ohio. Ness was assigned as an alcohol tax agent in the Moonshine Mountains of southern Ohio, Kentucky, and Tennessee in 1934. He was then transferred to Cleveland, Ohio, in December 1935. Newly elected Cleveland Mayor Harold Burton hired him to be the City's Safety Director, which put him in charge of both the police and the fire departments. Ness made a name for himself in Cleveland by first and foremost cleaning up the corruption in the city's police department. He then modernized the outdated fire department. Ness fired corrupt, incompetent and crooked cops from the police force and replaced them with talented rookies and unrecognized veterans. He also orchestrated several raids on such notorious gambling spots as The Harvard Club and The Blackhawk Inn. In addition, Ness instituted on-the-spot drunk-driving tests. Those failing the test would be arrested immediately. With Ness at the head of the city's Safety Directorate, crime plummeted 38 percent in a single year.

In 1936 according to the book, *The Rise and Fall of the Cleveland Mafia,* by Rick Porrello, Dr. Romano, the surgeon who had saved Frank Brancato's life back in 1932, became a problem for the Cleveland Family, namely for Tony Milano and Angelo Lonardo. Romano lived on the east side of town in the city of Willoughby. One of these men felt Romano was becoming too powerful and was a threat against the Mayfield Road Gang.

On June 11, 1936, a county worker found Dr. Romano's body in a car along Chagrin River Road in Moreland Hills near his home. Dr. Romano's body would be found in the back seat of his car. His arm was broken and he had sustained a crushing blow to his head. He was shot twice in the head, and then shot four more times in the groin.

At this time, only a few men were brought in for questioning, but no one was ever convicted for the murder of Dr. Romano. It would not be until years later that the FBI would find out from a reliable informant who had committed the murder and who the responsible trigger man behind Romano's death was.

Reported in the *Cleveland Press* Brancato tried in vain to get an early parole release; once in March 1936 and once again on April 22, 1936. The parole board ruled that they would not hear another motion for an early release until April of 1938. Brancato would not have to wait two more years in prison for this third hearing.

It is believed that later that year, on December 2, Ohio Governor Martin L. Davey was visited by several friends of Brancato, asking for his early release and a complete pardon from the governor. It was reported later in the newspapers that the identity of these men was not known, nor was the exact date and time known that they had met with Governor Davey. In late December 1936, inmate 6919, Frank Brancato, walked out of the Ohio prison a free man.

At this time it was highly speculated by the newspapers in Ohio that the two men who encouraged Governor Davey to help secure Brancato's release were Al Polizzi and Tony Milano. It has never been known what these men talked about or what was possibly promised to the governor, or whether any money actually exchanged hands in that important meeting, but both men needed their good friend Brancato back on the streets helping them to make money for their Family. Governor Davey only served one term as governor in Ohio from 1935 until 1939.

Arriving safely home in late December, the family had a festive welcome-home party for Frank. Brancato had served only forty-four months in jail.

The guys often called a prison term "going to college." Since most of these men did not have a secondary or high school education, they learned what they needed to know growing up on the streets or in jail. After being released, they would celebrate the wonderful event and always have a welcome-home party. All of their friends, along with their wives and children, would celebrate this event and come to his home. Many would bring a plate of food, normally a pasta dish like baked lasagna, eggplant, fresh seafood, shrimp, clams, salads, and of course there was always fresh Italian bread and rolls, Italian pastries, cannolis or a fresh ricotta pie and cookies like biscotti.

The men would all toast their health, good fortune and friendship with Italian liquors like amaretto, frangelico, or grappa

There would always be homemade wine from a friend in the neighborhood who enjoyed making it and giving it away to his friends.

At his welcome-home party, for the first time Frank noticed that he could no longer enjoy the wonderful taste of wine or hard whiskey. He found that, since his near-fatal shot in the stomach, he now could only tolerate the taste of Scotch; this would become his drink of choice for the rest of his life.

On January 29, 1937, the *Cleveland Press* had an article about

Frank's release:

> *"An old Lonardo gangster has been out of prison for two months on the action of our own Governor Davey. Brancato, a gunman for the Lonardo clan and a known Prohibition bootlegger, has been out of the Ohio Penitentiary for two months now. Brancato's term for perjury, from the trial of killing three men, was to have been from two to ten years in prison, but he was secretly commuted by the governor after only serving a short three years and eight months in the Ohio prison system."*

By February 2, the word was out on the streets of Cleveland that Frank Brancato had received a secret pardon from Governor Davey. Reported in the *Cleveland Press* on February 1, the headlines revealed, "Brancato Freed Without a Parole Board Action: Chairman of Parole Board Insists Governor Davey Ignored the Prison Parole Group Motion in Commuting the Sentence of the Lonardo Gang Member."

Governor Davey tried to explain to the reporters how the recommendation for commuting Brancato's sentence was made to him by Charles Leasure, who formerly heard and commuted cases for the governor; Leasure had since become a member of the unemployment compensation commission.

"Davey did not follow the legal procedure" Records show only one letter from a brewing company in Cleveland recommended that Brancato should be given his freedom because of his good behavior and being a good citizen. The parole board chairman, Leland S Dugan, told reporters that he had no knowledge of Governor Davey's actions regarding Brancato's release. This was the same letter the parole board received earlier in the year and denied any action to be taken on Brancato's behalf. It was also reported that Governor Davey based his decision on only this one letter and did not inform or ask for the parole board's permission or their opinion on the matter of Brancato's early release. Governor Davey refused to explain his actions to anyone and denied that he was ever visited by friends of Brancato.

Governor Davey would take a lot of heat from the city newspapers over the next few years. This one act may have cost him his re-election in 1939.

On February 2, an article in the *Cleveland Press* reported a full report was made by Joseph Furtos, a Cleveland Investigator for the Parole Board. It stated, "Brancato was believed to be back living in the Cleveland area, but a Cleveland detective reported they have not seen him on the streets in two months since he has been secretly freed."

The *Cleveland Press* reported on February 3, there was a direct order from Safety Director Eliot Ness to Detective Inspector Joseph Sweeney, to keep an eye on the gang gunner.

> *The gang gunner he was speaking of is Brancato, who was secretly released from the Ohio Penitentiary by Governor Martin Davey. After a complete search of the City of Cleveland the police reported to Mr. Ness that they have not been able to find Brancato at any of his known hangouts, but they will continue searching for him with his former pals in the Milano and Lonardo clans. Ness informed reporters that he has no wish to argue the merits of Brancato's release from prison or why he was secretly released, but for now he is out on the streets and it will be better for Cleveland if we keep an eye on him and his activities. In Columbus it was learned that Governor Davey did not follow the recommendations of the investigator for the parole board when his criminal sentence of Brancato was quietly commuted.*

Early in 1937 an action was filed by the United States in the Federal Court for the Northern District of Ohio, seeking to cancel the naturalization of Frank Brancato on the grounds that his original petition for naturalization was not verified by affidavits of two credible witnesses, as required by the Naturalization Act of June 29, 1906. Frank Brancato filed and answered this complaint and denied the allegation, but later entered in a stipulation with the United States Attorney under which the answer was withdrawn and the allegation admitted. On April 12, 1939, the court entered a judgment that the earlier order dated November 15, 1929, "Admitted the subject Frank Brancato to his citizenship and the same is hereby vacated and said order is annulled and certified by the Naturalization Number 320057 issued by the order is canceled."

The judgment further provided that Mr. Brancato would be stopped from setting up or claiming any right or privileges of a United States citizen whatsoever by virtue of the order November 15, 1929, which had earlier admitted him citizenship. The FBI report continues by saying, "Mr. Brancato is definitely an alien and further informed that if they could prove that he ever leaves the United States for any reason or is convicted of a crime involving moral turpitude, the INS will be certain to reactivate their investigation in an attempt to deport him."

The *Press* reported on October 7 that Frank Brancato had been arrested and held for investigation as a suspected racketeer. He spent the night in jail and was released the next day.

An article in the *Cleveland Press* on November 5 stated that the federal government had started to move ahead with deportation actions against Brancato. It said, "The Federal INS department is looking to first permanently revoke his natural citizenship, and if they are successful they will then be able to work with the federal courts to deport him back to Italy."

By 1937, according to Rick Porrello's book, *To Kill the Irishman*,

Moe Daltiz and brothers Frank and Tony Milano were into the gambling rackets and closely working together. They first began opening up gambling houses, and then began muscling their way into some of the best places in Ohio. It is believed that with the help of Frank Brancato from the Milano Family, these men took over a share of the profits without putting in any money. The clubs included The Jungle Inn, The Thomas Club, The Harvard Club, The Arrow Club on Pettibone Road, which would later be opened as The Pettibone Club in 1946, and the Mounds Club. Another site was The Ohio Villa Club. It was later renamed The Richmond Country Club. This was on the property that Milanos owned in Richmond Heights. It would later burn to the ground in a fire. This site would become the Italian-American Brotherhood Club and was famous for featuring Italian singers like Perry Como.

The three men also ventured into the southern portion of Ohio and took over the Coney Island Race Track in Cincinnati and helped to rename it "River Downs." Their next step was going to the city of Chesapeake, where they operated a large casino called the Continental Supper Club.

On September 17, 1937 a Zanesville, Ohio newspaper reported that Governor Davey was developing a plan to reorganize the parole process. "I feel sure that the program we are developing will meet the expectations of all," he told reporters. The article said Governor Davey had requested the resignation of several people on the parole board, and that their activities were under investigation by Attorney General Herbert Duff. "The people of Ohio could expect a complete integrity in the forthcoming reorganization." Davey told reporters that in his three years in office, he had only granted twenty-eight outright pardons, which he said was a record low for the past Ohio governors.

The *Cleveland Press* reported in 1937 that a truck driver for the Ohio Delivery Company located on West 9th Street stepped out of his truck to report to his manager inside the building. When the driver returned several minutes later, his truck had been stolen. The driver told the police there were about 313 cases of whiskey inside. The company estimated the load was worth $11,000. The Cleveland police interviewed the list of several of their normal suspects, including Frank Brancato. After several hours, the police were positive Frank was involved in this hijacking, but once again, they had no eyewitness or credible evidence to prove he was involved in this daring daytime robbery. The case went on to become yet another unsolved hijacking in Cleveland.

John Scalish and Frank Brancato built their own empires in separate directions in the thirties and into the early forties through investments in local gambling clubs, loan sharking, pinball and vending machines—plus the money the Cleveland Mob continued to skim from the Las Vegas casinos it had helped finance years later.

Scalish stayed behind in Cleveland in the late forties when other men of his rank, such as Tommy McGinty and Moe Dalitz, left for Las Vegas. In the early fifties, Ohio Governor Frank Lausche closed the local gambling casinos in Ohio that Scalish and Brancato had operated. John Scalish, who was always a smart businessman, took his profits and invested with his wife's brother, Milton (Maische) Rockman, in the Buckeye Cigarette Service Company, a vending machine firm. The company grew over the years by muscling routes from its weaker competition.

An FBI file noted that, by the end of 1937, the U.S. District Court had filed an action to cancel Frank Brancato's naturalization and a petition for naturalization because it was improperly verified. The thirteen-page document would be reviewed by the district courts for over one year and was finally approved on April 12, 1939, taking away Brancato's U.S. citizenship.

Brancato claimed he was making his living by working at a fruit store in Akron, Ohio, and was not able to make a living any longer, so in 1937 he became the manager of the Jungle Novelty Inn on Applegate Road in Youngstown, Ohio, for six years. It was a known gambling club that had dice, cards, roulette, horse betting and bingo. He also reported to the FBI that he had sold sweaters in the downtown in Cleveland and Akron area streets.

An article written in one of the Cleveland newspapers reported:

Big time gambling in Cuyahoga County today traces its origin directly to the gangs, which controlled the lucrative beer, alcohol and corn sugar rackets when Prohibition was repealed. With millions of dollars in illicit revenue cut off, the gangsters' dynasties each turned to gambling to perpetuate the golden flow of money. Some of the clubs mentioned in the article were The Thomas Club in Maple Heights; The Harvard Club in Newbury Heights, and the most elaborate club in the city, the new Richmond Country Club (the old Ohio Villa Club) where they had spent more than $100,000 in renovations.

Helen Sciria, the daughter of Little Angelo, who was seven, and Jennie Brancato, who was now six, were playing together at yet another party. The Brancato family was having a welcome home party or celebration for a friend of Frank's who was a mob member and was coming home from college (getting out of prison). Helen never had an opportunity to meet "Mr. B." before and asked Jennie, "Who is your father?"

Jennie pointed to him talking with some other men and told Helen proudly, "That is my father, over there. I love him so much!" She ran up and kissed him and gave him the biggest hug she could. She missed him so much. Her father seemed to be always working and home very little to play with his young children. Jennie was proud to be his daughter and Helen could tell Jennie loved him very much.

In the years 1938 and 1939 the *Cleveland Press*, *Plain Dealer* and *Cleveland News* were all having a field day reporting on the gambling activities in and around Cleveland. One *News* headline read, "Three Gaming Clubs Are Sued for $54,850."

In Common Pleas court, damages for $54,850 were filed against The Thomas Club, Ohio Villa and The Arrow Club, all known to be gambling joints outside the city limits. The lawsuit was filed by Mrs. Gertrude Seaver of East 134th Street. She claims her husband lost $50,000 to these three clubs over three years and was seeking damages of another $4,850.

CHAPTER EIGHT

1940-1945

"Mistakes are part of the dues one pays for a full life."

~ Sophia Loren

The summer of 1940 was the start of an amazing yearly summer vacation for the Brancato children. That summer Jennie, the youngest child, was only eight. This was the summer that she, along with her mother, sisters Ninfa and Bella, and her brother Nasher began visiting the area of Sandusky, Ohio. In a few years, all her siblings would stop going, since they were growing up. That left just my mother, Jennie, and her mother to relax the summer away together.

They would take the causeway access road toward the Cedar Point amusement park and go in about mile or so, to a cluster of homes on the left side of the road. For many wealthier families during the early forties, these became elite vacation cottages. Families would rent them from June until the end of August so they could enjoy the amazing beachfront of Lake Erie right across the street from their cottages. On occasion, Frank would join them for a few days each week and play with his children, just like a normal father would do. My mother would often tell us her stories of playing with the other children who also came each year, relaxing and making sand castles and running on the beach. She had fond memories of the happiness that she and her siblings enjoyed together.

Every time I would go to Cedar Point with my parents and siblings, we would stop on the causeway and my mother would show us the home that they rented each year. That tradition would end for her in 1947.

In an FBI file dated November 6, it was verified that the Cleveland Police Department had furnished the Cleveland FBI office with names of the top hoodlums in Cleveland, along with their home addresses, names and ages of their wives and children, their arrest numbers, make and model of their cars, along with their license plate numbers, and a complete description of their principal illegal activities. This list included Frank Brancato (ID Number 29603), along with John Scalish and John DeMarco. The report said Brancato drove a 1940 Buick sedan and his main interests were listed as gambling and the narcotics rackets.

1941

An article in the *Cleveland Plain Dealer* dated February 9, described how county officials and the Department of Industrial Relations succeeded in closing four of the major gambling resorts in Ohio. Earlier in January the city had closed down the Arrow Gambling Club in Geauga County. The Walbridge Club was located about thirty-five miles south of Cleveland in Cuyahoga Falls, inside a large building that did not look to be anything special from the outside A *Plain Dealer* reporter stopped at a gas station and asked the attendant, "Where is the Walbridge Club?" His reply was, "Just two blocks ahead," as if the question has been asked of him hundreds of times before.

It was believed that Frank Brancato was an unnamed partner who insisted that their clubs be a "classy joint," like the Terrace Club, which he owned and operated just outside the city limits in Sandusky with Sam Spina, or like the Jungle Novelty Inn, run with the Farah brothers in Youngstown. These and many clubs like them across the country were the biggest rage, with the new sound of swing music hitting the country like a hurricane. Everyone wanted to be a part of this new sound.

In his gambling clubs, Brancato insisted that there should always be a guard at the front door, and when possible, even on the roof of the buildings, to ensure that only the right people got into the building. Several men were stationed throughout the club to ensure that anyone who lost all their money would not go crazy and try to steal or make trouble for the other men and women in the club.

Frank insisted that not one of his customers would leave the joints broke. He told his men working on the casino floor that they were to give the big losers at least $20 in their pocket when they left the club, no matter how much they lost.

There were always very young and attractive cocktail waitresses, normally dressed in soft, sexy attire. There were separate rooms for big-stakes poker games, but slot machines, blackjack and craps tables were all in the same room, so when someone would win; the sounds of happiness by excited men and women would give excitement to the other one hundred to two hundred guests in the club, encouraging them to think that they could be the next big winner in the club that night.

In one corner of the dance floor was a sparkling new box that called to everyone who came into the joint, "Come over and see me; see what I have." As new patrons walked past the dance floor, they stood and stared at the brightly colored box with lights flashing. It was known as a jukebox, and would play music for the crowd whenever the band was not playing.

In the back of the gambling joints, away from the normal crowd, they would have a room for the horse racing wire service. By now, Tony Accardo from Chicago was trying to move in and take over the action in the Cleveland area.

During an interview in 1941, Brancato reported to the FBI that he was still working at the Jungle Novelty Inn on Applegate Road in Youngstown, where he said he had been a manager for six years, making only $60 a week and selling sweaters in downtown Cleveland during the day, trying to make a living to feed his family. He also reported he was in business with two other men, Sam Spera and Tony Anastasia, in another club called the Terrace Club, located outside the city limits in Sandusky.

Frank filled out a questionnaire with fifty questions for the Selective Service local board dated February 16, 1942, filed at the Shaker Heights City Hall. It listed him as living at 3689 Chelton Road in Shaker Heights and claimed that his income came from working as a sweater salesman in Cleveland and Akron. It also said he was employed at the Jungle Inn club on Applegate Road in Youngstown. Frank Brancato was assigned order number T10644 and serial number T1560 on his citizenship papers.

This investigation dealt with insuring the government had current and correct information on Frank Brancato's home address, correct job and who would know where he would be. It did not deal with his current immigration status, since it was already removed.

The *Cleveland Plain Dealer* on April 23, 1942, had a small article about the Dead End Club in the city of Lindale, on Cleveland's west side:

John Blank was arrested as the operator of the notorious gambling club located on West 117th St. with two other unnamed *men. Blank has been reported to be working with the "Mayfield Road Gang" and under Brancato's supervision. Blank was fined $100 and was given a six-month suspended sentence by Judge Samuel Silbert.*

The FBI file report from February 4, 1943, said Frank Brancato was known to drive a 1941 Cadillac sedan, was living at 3689 Chelton Road, and was a friend of John Scalish and John DeMarco.

On July 20, an FBI file stated while they were investigating DeMarco, who was now living in Shaker Heights, the Cleveland Police Department had advised the FBI that Brancato was a known policy operator in the city of Cleveland and a key member of the Mayfield Road Gang, in business with others who did hijackings and dealt in stolen goods. Brancato was also speculated to be behind a major hijacking that took place on July 19 in Cleveland, Ohio, along with Jesse Logatto. Logatto had made several phone calls from his home phone to actively dispose of the stolen items from the hijacking on July 19. The same memo says the police knew that Brancato was a smart man and a known hijacker in the city and a racketeer, but as of yet they had not been able to prove any hijacking case against him.

Later, during one of Frank Brancato's many deportation hearings, the *Cleveland Plain Dealer* reported in an article in 1954 that Frank's attorney, Henry C. Levine, had informed the police that Frank was selling sweaters in the Cleveland area from 1943 until 1946 to businesses that were looking to advertise their company on these sweaters. Brancato's income was minimal, but he could not recall the company who had hired him as a salesman.

In 1944, the *Cleveland Plain Dealer* reported that Frank Brancato helped to illegally bring back a friend who had been deported to Italy. The man was Rocco Russo, a well-known criminal to the local police. The police speculated that Frank somehow had brought Russo back to Cleveland to help him with the gambling joints that he was operating, and to help as a strong-arm when needed. Also coming with Rocco were two other men the FBI would not identify for several years: forty-three-year-old Salvatore Brancato, Frank's brother, and another unknown man.

On August 27, the *Plain Dealer* reported that, "With only one slight and logical reservation, Mayor Frank Lausche last night gave his blessing to a *Who's Who* of Cleveland racketeers, gamblers, policy operators and other public enemies compiled by Detective Inspector Frank Story and Detective Martin Cooney."

70

Mayor Lausche proclaimed, "I fully subscribe to what has been done... providing everyone in the category of being a known underworld figure is paraded before the view of the public. The greater the light is shone on what these men are doing, the more possible it will be to drive them out of the community."

To date, eighty-five names and photographs have been identified, along with descriptions listing their known habits, with their activities listed in this book. Among the elite members are Frank Brancato, once allied with the Mayfield Road Gang and described as a gambler, along with Frank Hoge, onetime king of the numbers racket, Dominic Sospirato, policy operator and racketeer, George Angersola and Milton Rockman, convicted a few years ago of policy blackmail, along with Angelo Sciria, policy muscleman, and so the list goes on...

On September 13, the *Cleveland News* reported, two men held up a truck at gunpoint and picked up approximately $15,000 in a fur hijacking. The driver was John Kilbane, a retired fireman who was now working for a company named Euro-Cleaners. He was delivering the furs to Up to Date Laundry Service on East 20th Street. Kilbane told the police that two men got into his truck while his assistant was delivering a fur to a customer. The two men instantly blindfolded him and tied him up before he could get a good look at them. They drove around the city for almost an hour, then stopped and disposed of the furs. Kilbane was found unhurt, but bound and gagged in the back of the truck. The police investigation took several weeks, as they brought in several of their highly suspicious persons of interest from around the city for interviews. Their main focus at this time was on Frank Brancato. Kilbane was not able to identify any of the men, let alone Brancato, in the cab with him, and with no other information to go on, the police could not hold or charge Brancato for this robbery.

In October of 1944 Frank and Virginia's young red-headed daughter, Ninfa, traveled to New York without her family's or her father's permission to marry the man that she had fallen in love with— her first cousin, John Brancato, the son of Frank's brother John, who had died years earlier. Frank was terribly disturbed and condemned their marriage from the start. The couple would return to Cleveland, and it took several years for Frank to forgive them both. The couple would have six children.

On October 14, the Cleveland FBI office reported that Brancato still resided at 3689 Chelton Road and was a known card dealer and gambler and who did not work at a steady job, but he continued to operate a 1941 Cadillac sedan.

Another FBI file said it was mentioned in the *Cleveland Press* on September 4, 1945, that Cleveland's biggest and fastest dice game was at 2647 East 40th Street, where Angelo Amato (born in Licata, Sicily, in 1910) and Frank Brancato were the two front men for the syndicate and put up the money for this operation in a "sky's the limit" game. It was noted that Amato was a cousin to Brancato, and the game was being held at The Producers Athletic and Social Club on East 40th Street. The report listed charter members of the club as Angelo Amato, Joe Ortega and Tom Lehotsky. The club was very busy from 2 p.m. until 7 p.m. daily and could take in between $20,000 and $25,000 per day, with anywhere from fifty to seventy-five people in the club gambling at one time. The club was located in the heart of downtown Cleveland.

An FBI document showed the records of the U.S. District Court in Cleveland, Ohio, reflected that on April 26, 1946, Angelo Alfred Amato was sentenced to six months for receiving a quantity of stolen coffee hijacked from an interstate shipment in Cleveland in July 1943. At the time, a witness stated the possible buyers of the coffee were told to call a phone number listed to a house then occupied by Brancato.

According to Rick Porrello's book, *To Kill the Irishman*, Jack Licavoli, along with his cousin Leo Moceri, kept busy with the infamous Jungle Novelty Inn. It was originally a famous brothel that was now operating as a gambling joint managed by Frank Brancato, John Farah, and Tony Delsanter. Over its many years in business, numerous murders and disappearances had been traced to this casino, its operation and its associates. Several years ago Jack Licavoli was suspected of the brutal murder of slot machine czar Nate Weisenberg, who was shot in the face by a shotgun blast. Licavoli was arrested and then released for insufficient evidence. Mike Farah, John's twin brother, was another partner in the Jungle Inn and was reportedly killed by Tony Delsanter for giving Jack Licavoli problems.

By the mid-1940s, adult entertainment was becoming very popular in the major towns across the country. Strip clubs typically adopted a nightclub or bar-style atmosphere, but could also adopt a theater or cabaret style.

Frank Brancato was always seen in these downtown clubs and was believed to have been a major part in the Cleveland operation, who helped to put together many of these hot nightclubs in the downtown area to help bring additional income and profits for the Family.

On May 28, Frank Brancato was picked up as a suspicious person in an ongoing investigation in the Pittsburg area. He was questioned for several hours, then held overnight and was released the next day.

On July 18, Frank was issued a charter membership to the Producers Athletic and Social Club, located at 2648 East 40th Street.

The following story was told to me by a friend whose mother lived on Murray Hill:

By the fall of 1945, the Cleveland area was having a rash of small-time robberies and break-ins in the many neighborhoods around the city. Little Italy was getting hit the hardest, for some unknown reason. While investigating one of these break-ins, an older Italian woman who was upset over what was happening in her community began to tell a young police officer that many of the young girls in the normally quiet neighborhood had been getting beat up by their mean husbands over the past year, just because their dinner was not ready or the children were crying for some reason. All the women were too scared to tell anyone, including the police, about the beatings. If they did, their husbands would be mad at them and would beat them even more. Many of the women had bruised jaws and black eyes, and one woman even had a broken arm. The old woman could not understand why these Italian men were so mean and cruel to their own wives. Some of these men even hit their children for no reason at all.

Concerned, the young officer asked, "Has anything been done to stop these men?"

Now gleaming and smiling, the old lady said, "Oh, yes, I went to see Tony Milano myself. My cousin's sister-in-law is his cousin, so he was the one I wanted to talk with. So when he was in town one day at the IAB club, I asked him for his help. He was very upset that Italian men would treat their wives in this fashion, and he assured me he would have someone come and look into the matter and that the beating of women would not be tolerated in his city."

"So then what did he do?" the young officer asked, now very interested in the old lady's story.

"I was not surprised, but Tony kept his word and sent over Frank

Brancato and another man. Over a one-week period, every evening the two men went to each of the houses that the beatings were taking place. Speaking in Italian, Brancato and his friend asked the men to come outside and talk in private. The men did as they were told, since no one could refuse a request from Frank Brancato. In a very short meeting and speaking in Italian; Brancato warned each man if he had heard that they continued to beat up on their wives or their children, that these actions would not be tolerated in his neighborhood. Their wives and children were to be taken care of by their husbands and not abused physically or sexually, and if they did not stop these beatings, they would have to answer to him. Of course, all of the men denied this allegation made by Brancato. Then, without any warning, the man with Brancato punched them in the face several times as a reminder of what their wives had looked like so many times before."

"Did the beatings stop?" the excited young officer asked.

"Yes they did, for the most part, except for two men who did not care one way or another or were not scared of Frank Brancato."

"What happened to them?" the young officer now asked

"One man who continued to beat his wife started on his children for no reason at all. He was found lying half dead on the west side of town with two broken ribs, two broken hands, a broken jaw and nose; he will never eat solid food again."

"What about the other man?" the officer asked.

Now smiling more than she did before, she said; "One night the doorbell rang on one of these homes, and when the man came to the door, he received a small wooden box on his front steps. It was shaped like a child's coffin, and when the man opened it up; he found a dead fish, wrapped up in an Italian newspaper."

The young Polish police officer looked puzzled. He did not understand what this meant and proceeded to ask the old woman.

Smiling, she calmly explained, "It is an old Sicilian warning. If he did not stop what he was doing, he would be sleeping with the fishes the next day."

Interested once again, "What did the man do?" the officer responded.

"The man left his family and went back to the old country. He did not want to die, and he knew he could not stop hitting his wife."

CHAPTER NINE

1946-1949

"When you look at your life, the greatest happinesses are family happinesses."

~ Dr. Joyce Brothers

On July 6, 1946, Frank and Virginia's oldest son Joe married the woman of his dreams, Josephine (Dolly) Licata, whom he had met in Brooklyn a few years earlier while visiting his aunts and uncles. Joe and Dolly were married at the Holy Family Church on East 131st and Chapelside Avenue in Cleveland, and would later have three children together.

On the advice of his attorney, Frank Brancato worked very hard toward trying to regain his American citizenship. He sold his shares in the gambling den known as the Terrace Club in Sandusky.

In 1947, an FBI special agent assigned to follow and report on Frank Brancato's activities reported that Thomas LaPuma had asked Frank to help him in his failing business, so he had become a partner in the LaPuma Spumoni Company in 1946. Frank was interested in gaining legitimate opportunities at this time .One day he brought in his investment—$7,000 in cash in $100 bills. Today, that amount would be equal to $70,996. LaPuma claims he repaid Frank in an attempt to buy him out, but he could not produce any documentation to prove that he had done this. LaPuma testified that he had paid him back in cash.

In 1947, Frank told the FBI he was a partner in the LaPuma Spumoni Company with Thomas LaPuma. They sold fresh bakery products, Italian ice, and spumoni on Murray Hill, but he "did not receive any large amounts of money from his investment and the business was not doing so well at this time."

On November 22, 1947, young Isabella, (Bella) Brancato would marry the love of her life, the handsome and charming John Bisco. The beautiful ceremony was held at the local Catholic Church. Bella had her younger sister Jennie, who was only sixteen years old, as her Maid of Honor. Jennie's partner as a groomsman was her eighteen-year-old boyfriend of only six months, James Monastra, who was studying to become a barber. Their lavish wedding cost Frank an estimated $10,000. The happy couple had three boys.

By the end of 1947, Frank Brancato was now a capo for his friend John Scalish, who was by now the boss in Cleveland, along with their friend John DeMarco. They were starting to build ties with other organized crime families around the country.

According to a July 15, 1948, *Plain Dealer* article written by Robert Drake and Bill Todd,

> *Sandusky tavern permit holders told liquor agents how they have been approached by men who claim they represented Jack Morris, offering protection by Sandusky area state liquor inspectors, "If the proper kind of gambling equipment was installed." Thirty different tavern owners have come forward and discussed how they have been approached as well. Jack Morris is a known lottery agent in the area and the main letter to the courts dealt with the Terrace Club, a known gambling spot outside Sandusky, which has flourished for several years, making enormous amounts of money. Terrace Club has attracted gamblers from Cleveland, Toledo, Detroit and Chicago and was once owned by Frank Brancato and who is the person who is speculated to have the muscle to protect the tavern owners from the liquor inspectors.*

On December 30, the *Cleveland Plain Dealer* announced that the city of Cleveland had been probing into the top men involved with the policy game operating in many locations throughout the city. The main men listed in the probe and under their immediate investigation were Frank Brancato, Angelo Sciria, Angelo Lonardo, and George Angersola.

Reported by the *Cleveland Press* in 1949, Frank Brancato had been a partner in another well-known club known as the Jungle Novelty Inn Club in Youngstown, Ohio.

> *In a spectacular raid by the local police and federal officers; the club was closed down (when) they found gambling equipment including dice tables, slot machines and several tables for playing blackjack and other card games. Brancato had reported to the Cleveland Retail Credit Bureau how he was the manager and reported to no one. The Cleveland Press also learned that Brancato told the Bureau from 1945 until 1947 he was earning*

only $900 a month from the Terrace Club cafe when he was operating it in the Sandusky area. The club had opened in late 1944 or early 1945 and ... he was only getting about 25 percent of the profits from the operation.

One report given later in the Kefauver committee hearings in the 1950s stated that ... Brancato earned or received $100,000 during 1945-1947 while the club was open for business.

In 1949 Jennie Brancato's close friend Helen Sciria had an older brother Paul, who had developed a crush on her. Paul had asked Jennie out for a date several times, but she was not interested.

Frank was watching over Helen and Paul and their mother, since their father was away "at college." He told Paul that Jennie liked someone else and dating her would not be good for him or her.

Paul was heartbroken, but he moved on to find that special person he was meant to be with. Paul found her and they married a few years later. They had two children, and Paul went on to have a wonderful and successful career as a popular Cleveland television and newspaper reporter. He started the Italian American *LaGezzetta* newspaper sold in Cleveland.

In June of 1949, when Paul was graduating from John Adams High School, Frank went to visit his home as he often did, to give them some money to help pay the rent or to buy food or clothes. Frank asked Paul what he wanted for a graduation present. "I know your father would like to you have something nice," he said.

Angelo Sciria was now away "at college" at the Ohio State Penitentiary, where he was incarcerated for an attempted murder conviction. Angelo Sciria was released from prison several years later. Now in bad health he opened up what became a popular restaurant on East 131st and Miles Avenue, named SOS Hickory BBQ. Mr. Sciria pasted away from a long illness on April 16th, 1977 at Hillcrest Hospital.

Paul, being a young smart-ass (his own words to me, not mine) and knowing "Mr. B." was always around looking after him and his sister, said, "Mr. B., I would really like a car—a new Studebaker for my present."

"A Studebaker! That is a very expensive car, Paul," Frank exclaimed.

"I know; I thought I would just ask."

"I'll see what I can do," Frank said, shaking his head.

A few weeks later Frank brought over a brand-new blue-on-blue Studebaker Champion coupe for Paul, at a cost of approximately $2,400—the equivalent of about $22,800 in today's dollars. "Paul, here is your graduation present. I know your father would want you to have it."

Paul hugged him and thanked him for his kindness and for the generous gift that he never really expected to get.

Before the year ended, Frank received word that his sister Elena who lived in Rome had died suddenly.

～

BRANCATO WEDDING

Helen and Jennie continued with their lifelong friendship. Jennie asked Helen to be in her wedding party to James Monastra, and Jennie was in Helen's wedding to "Buzzy" LaMarca. Buzzy was a barber and a good friend of Jim Monastra as well. Jennie went on to become the godmother of one of Helen's daughters, Sally. Jennie, along with her sisters Bella and Ninfa were also good friends with Helen and her sister-in-law Mary LaMarca. They continued to stay close until the loss of Jennie and then her sister Ninfa. Several years later, they lost Mary.

When Jim and Jennie would go out on dates, Mr. B always insisted that his young daughter be accompanied by his wife or his son Nasher, since both of his daughters were already married. Jennie enjoyed Jim's company. The two would often go to the movie theater. Mrs. Brancato was always seated behind them, acting like she was watching the movie, but in reality she did not fully understand most of the words, since she did not speak much English. Instead, she watched every move the young couple made. If they then decided to get a soda or a bite to eat after the movie, V accompanied them and sat with them. Jim would then take Jennie and her mother home. Mrs. B. would go into the house while Jim and Jennie sat on the porch, if it was a warm summer evening, and talked until it was late and Jim left for the night. If the weather was bad, or if it was winter, or if Mrs. B. did not feel well and could not accompany the young lovers, Nasher would often drop them off at a local dance or movie and pick them up at a designated time. Then he would take Jennie home without his parents knowing the truth.

The planning of the wedding between James Monastra and Jennie Brancato was a major event that summer for Mrs. Brancato, who cherished and enjoyed the upcoming celebration. V had been sick and almost bedridden for several months when her pain was unbearable. She took great pride in planning this event with Jennie by her side, doing everything from the invitations to the cake, the flowers, her dress, and the bridesmaids' dresses. The big day was on Monday, September 4, 1950, a Labor Day weekend. She found a local photographer to take their cherished wedding pictures.

Mrs. Brancato had suffered for several years from complications related to her diabetes. The weakness in her heart and legs began to show more and more as the days and months went along. This was probably the main reason why Jennie's wedding needed to be so special for Mrs. Brancato. Yes, their other children had very nice weddings and were given a nice wedding gift, but Jennie's wedding was different to Mrs. Brancato. She knew in her heart she did not have much time left on earth, and she believed she would not be alive long enough to meet or be with all of her future grandchildren.

Frank Brancato was able to book the very elegant and exclusive Hotel Statler in Downtown Cleveland for his daughter's marriage. Jim and Jennie had spoken with the priest at Saint Dominic Church on Van Aken Boulevard and saved the date.

As the date of their marriage drew closer, James was sure that Jennie and he were both getting the nervous jitters that all married couples do the few months before. Jim and Jennie were both taken aback and surprised by the number of people who responded that they would be happy to attend their wedding. There were only one hundred people or so from Jim's side, but Jennie had invited all her friends and many of her friends' parents. They both thought that her mother and father had only about two hundred fifty or so guests coming to their wedding, which would make a total of about three hundred fifty people. Little did they know that there would be a few more people attending and sharing their special day than they expected.

The wedding day was a beautiful late summer day. The temperatures ranged from sixty-four degrees in the morning to seventy-four degrees by the late afternoon. It was a picture-perfect day with no rain in sight. The wedding ceremony at St Dominic's was amazing, and the church was full with family and friends from the Brancato side as well as the Monastra side to witness their ceremony.

Isabella Brancato wedding to John Bisco

*Mr. and Mrs. James Monastra at the bridal table for their
wedding dinner*

Jim's mother Angela and his father James on the left

Mrs. Virginia Brancato with her husband Frank on the right

The bride and groom both had a room at the hotel to freshen up from their earlier wedding and to get ready to meet and greet their guests at their lavish reception. Jennie's beautiful wedding dress would be worn for the reception, and Jim wore his handsome white tuxedo. Both looked like royalty, at least for the day.

Jennie with her mother, Mrs. Virginia Brancato in their home

After posing for what seemed to be hundreds of pictures they arrived into the main hall. As they set up the reception line, both were taken aback at the number of people who had taken the time to attend their wedding and to bring their generous gifts. To the amazement of the newlyweds, there were hundreds—no, the count was closer to between 1,500 and 2,000 people at their wedding reception.

Mr. Brancato had invited all of his friends and family from New York, his brother Joseph, his sister Antoinette with her family, and friends from other cities to come to his daughter's wedding. Mr. and Mrs. Brancato were surely proud to have his youngest daughter marry Jim.

One of Frank's friends was the manager of the famous Italian big-band leader known as Louie Prima. Frank asked him as a personal favor to have his band play for the special couple and their guests for the evening. The guests of the wedding were thrilled to hear the live music played by the Italian band they had listened to and enjoyed so many times in their homes.

The crowd truly enjoyed their evening of great food and wonderful entertainment till almost 1 a.m., when Jim and Jennie finally departed for the night and their honeymoon suite.

Some of Jim & Jennies wedding guests enjoying the wonderful live music

Courtesy of: James P Monastra

*Mr. Louie Prima, Frank Brancato, Unknown man, and
John Bisco*

***Mr. Louis Prima and the newlyweds Jim and Jennie
Monastra***

Mr. and Mrs. Frank Brancato at their daughter Jennie's wedding in 1950, along with brother-in-law John, with Bella on the right, and Jennie's sister Ninfa directly to the left of Mrs. Brancato, toward the back.

For their wedding gift, the Brancatos gave Jim and Jennie a two-week honeymoon vacation in Hollywood, Florida, along with a brand new car.

"The great gift of family life is to be intimately acquainted with people you might never even introduce yourself to, had life not done it for you."

~ Kendall Hailey

86

CHAPTER TEN

Kefauker Hearings

The United States Senate Special Committee to Investigate Crime in Interstate Commerce was a special committee of the U.S. Senate which existed from 1950 to 1951 which investigated organized crime that crossed state borders in the United States. The committee became popularly known as the Kefauver Committee because of its chairman, Senator Estes Kefauver.

Organized crime was the subject of a large number of widely-read articles in several major newspapers and magazines in 1949. Several local crime commissions in major cities and states also had uncovered extensive corruption of the political process by organized crime. Many cities and states called for federal help in dealing with organized crime, yet federal law provided few tools for the U.S. government to do so.

In particular, many cities and states were concerned with the way organized crime had infiltrated interstate commerce, and how it threatened to hold the American economy hostage through labor racketeering.

On January 5, 1950, Senator Estes Kefauver introduced a resolution that would allow the Senate Committee on the Judiciary to investigate organized crime's role in interstate commerce. However, the Senate Committee on Interstate and Foreign Commerce already claimed jurisdiction over this issue. A compromise resolution was substituted which established a special committee of five senators, whose membership would be drawn from both the judiciary and commerce committees.

The Kefauver Committee held hearings in fourteen major cities across the United States. More than six hundred witnesses testified in the proceedings. Many of the committee's hearings were televised live on national television to large audiences, providing many Americans with their first glimpse of organized crime's figures and their influence in the United States. Kefauver became a nationally recognized figure, which enabled him to run for president of the United States in 1952, and then in 1956 (his runs failed, but he became his party's vice presidential nominee in 1956).

A *Cleveland News* article written in October 13 by Drew Pearson was headlined, "Mafia Uses its Friends, Protectors in High Places."

In Washington, Senator Kefauver's determination to investigate the Mafia requires a lot more courage than what appears on the surface. Not only is it dangerous from the point of personal safety, but it is dangerous politically. The Mafia has many friends and protectors in very high places. President Truman had no idea what was happening and probably his naïve military aide Major General Harry Vaughan did not suspect it, but the Mafia was making a play for the White House and pulled through the late William Helis, a close friend and partner of Frank Costello. The Senate Expenditures Committee was in the middle of unearthing real dynamite in regards to this during the Maragon-Vaughan investigation, when the hearings were hushed up. How the Mafia pulls wires in high places is illustrated by Sylvestro Carolla, New Orleans hatchet man for Louisiana Mafia Chief Marcello, who helps operate Costello's gambling joints in and around New Orleans.

Here is an authorized roll call on some of the top Mafia leaders and the most powerful rulers of crime in the United States...

Mentioned in the article was Frank Cappola, a.k.a. "Three-Fingered Frank," who was prominent in the New Orleans Mafia, then showed up in Kansas City.

Then there was Sam Maceo of Galveston, Texas, who was first a humble barber. Then he broke into the bootlegging rackets, and owned several Galveston night clubs, bars and two hotels. Maceo was also a powerhouse in Texas politics. Biaggio Angelica of Huston, Texas, was Maceo's subordinate in the Mafia. Next was Joe Di Giovanni, a.k.a. Joe Church of Kansas City. Joe was the Mafia chief in the Kansas City area, coming from Brooklyn, New York.

Next in this article was Tony Lopiparo, chief of the Mafia in St. Louis, but tied in closely with Kansas City Family; he would later be sent to Mexico by Lucky Luciano.

Next mentioned in the article was Frank Milano from Akron, Ohio. Milano was known as a top power of Ohio Mafia leaders and closely connected to Mafia leaders in Chicago and Michigan. He was also the boss of the old Mayfield Gang. Milano was connected with West Coast Mafia Boss Jack Dragna and his brother Antony, who lived in Hollywood, California, and owned interest in a food company and an Italian newspaper in Cleveland.

Mentioned next in the article was Big Al Polizzi of Coral Gables, Florida, who was considered to be second to Frank Milano in the Ohio Mafia. Al was said to have had his fingers into many legitimate enterprises, including olive oil, food importing and beer distribution and real estate in Coral Gables.

Many of the Kefauver Committee's hearings were aimed at proving that an Italian–Sicilian organization based on strong family ties centrally controlled a vast organized crime conspiracy in the United States, but during all the interrogations and meetings, the committee never came close to justifying such a claim. Rather, the committee uncovered extensive evidence that people of all nationalities, ethnicities, and even religions operated locally controlled, loosely organized crime syndicates at the local level.

The committee's final report, issued on April 17, 1951, included twenty-two recommendations for the federal government and seven recommendations for state and local authorities. Among its recommendations were: The creation of a "racket squad" within the United States Department of Justice; the establishment of a permanent crime commission at the federal level; and the expansion of the jurisdiction of the Judiciary Committee to include interstate organized crime.

The report also called for federal studies into the sociology of crime; a ban on betting via radio, television, telegraph, and telephone; the establishment of state and local crime commissions; and a request that the Justice Department investigate and prosecute thirty-three named individuals as suspected leaders of organized crime in the United States.

However, the committee's work led to several significant outcomes. Among the most notable was an admission by J. Edgar Hoover, Director of the Federal Bureau of Investigation, that a national organized crime syndicate did exist, and that the FBI had done little about it at the time.

The Kefauver Committee was the first to suggest that civil law be expanded, and then used to combat organized crime. Congress responded to the call, but it would not be for another nineteen years, until 1970, that they would pass the Racketeer Influenced and Corrupt Organizations Act (RICO) as a direct response to the committee's recommendation. This Senate hearing was responsible for the deportation of over one hundred known criminals in the United States.

An FBI file in Cleveland reported that a confidential and somewhat reliable informant in November of 1950 informed them the city of Cleveland had been very quiet since the Kefauver Senate Committee hearings had started.

Frank Brancato was subpoenaed, like many others in the city were, and was scheduled to testify at the hearings on two different days, but for some unknown reason, he was never called to testify in the proceedings.

In November 1950 the FBI did a credit check of Frank Brancato's involvements with banks. Agents checked the Shaker Savings Association, the GMAC Banking for a car loan, and National City Bank in Cleveland. The files reflected no additional information or changes in Brancato's financial situation.

On November 8, the FBI received information from a confidential informant that had furnished reliable information in the past that Brancato had advised many of his close friends not to worry about his deportation hearings that were pending against him. He said the red tape would take years to clear up before the government could do anything to harm him.

It was believed by our family that by the end of 1950, our grandfather designed his very elaborate plan to deceive the Cleveland police, FBI, and other agents in the Immigration and Naturalization Service (INS), as well as the Internal Revenue Service (IRS). The master plan had to ensure that the government agencies all believed that he was not a wealthy man, and as a matter of fact, was on the poorer side and living day-to-day. He pretended he no longer had any interest in any gambling operation or other illegal activities in Cleveland or in Ohio that could give the government any reason to investigate or try to deport him.

Frank's well-conceived plan was to ensure he did not have his name on any home, automobile, or business, nor would he be named as the owner or partner of any business venture. He would have others named as the owner, manager or operator. Frank even went so far as to have his trusted friends, Frank Visconti, his partner in Captain Frank's Seafood Restaurant, John Scalish, and John DeMarco play a major role in his plans to fool the government agencies and the Cleveland Police

Department.

Together, these men would tell others that Brancato was broke and always asking them for money to pay his bills. When he would come around to see them, they were even seen by others giving him money. They told others it was because of the old days, and they explained that Brancato was down on his luck.

John Scalish never disclosed who his actual underboss was to anyone, to help both his friends, DeMarco and Brancato. All the men under Scalish knew that they took orders from Brancato and DeMarco without question, just as if they came from Scalish himself.

The Cleveland police, the FBI, and the INS agents would often get reports from their informants that Brancato was the number-two or number-three man in the city, when in fact other men considered Brancato to be the street boss for Scalish.

Some very reliable sources even informed the FBI director that Brancato was considered by some people to be the head of the organization in Cleveland, but the FBI never believed this statement. They knew very well John Scalish was the boss, and would be until he died.

DeMarco had always had a weak heart, and the police knew he could never take on the actual day-to-day pressures. DeMarco was happy to help his good friend Frank Brancato against the government. All of these different accounts of who was the actual underboss in Cleveland and how much money Frank Brancato did or did not actually have helped him with his many court battles against the FBI and INS agencies. This would cause the government a difficult time in getting Frank into the courts and in front of a grand jury to deport him back to his native Italy.

Brancato knew very well that if he was caught in an unlawful act of any kind and sentenced to a prison term of any length; it could cost him his family, his life, and freedom in America.

This would become the first time the FBI would be confused by the actions of an organized crime figure. The next occasion would be much later, with the late Vincent "The Chin" Gigante in 1997, who became the head of the Genovese crime family in New York in 1987. He acted up in public with loud rants and rages; he even walked the streets of New York in a bathrobe and talked to trees and birds. Gigante portrayed himself to be a very sick man who was mentally disturbed, and doing crazy and unheard of things that caused the FBI and other federal agents to investigate him even more. It was just a ploy by Gigante to keep himself out of jail.

CHAPTER ELEVEN

Deportation Hearings

1950-1954

Starting in the 1950s, the FBI in Cleveland had Frank Brancato, along with John Scalish, John DeMarco, and other top hoodlums in cities across the country put under daily surveillance by special agents. There were hundreds of these reports filed by the FBI. Some of the information is also confirmed by newspaper articles written in Cleveland and in Washington, D.C., about Frank and his activities.

On June 25, the *Cleveland News* ran a story by Webb Seely, who wrote:

> *Gambling was going full blast once again at the Pettibone Club only thirty minutes later in a known Brancato operated gambling club after Geauga County Sheriff Stuart Harland failed to dampen for the refined group of patrons who watched the Cleveland Indians play the Philadelphia Phillies on TV at 4:30 in the afternoon. By 6 p.m., the same patrons told reporters there were over four hundred people in the club gambling, drinking, and playing slot machines, keno and craps.*

According to an FBI file concerning the theft and disposition of several stolen automobiles, the records of the national Automobile Theft Bureau at Pittsburg, Pennsylvania, reflected that one of the vehicles transferred was a 1950 Cadillac sedan to the new owner Frank Brancato, who lived on Moreland Avenue in Shaker Heights, Ohio. It further reflects that this automobile was transferred to Frank on November 15, 1950, and then to the Hersch Auto Sales in Cleveland, Ohio. This car was subsequently recovered a year later at Milton, Massachusetts, bearing a changed motor number.

According to the FBI files in November, an informant advised the Cleveland FBI office that criminal activity by Brancato and his hoodlum element friends had been rather quiet during the past two months, due to the fact that the Kefauver Investigation Committee was due to arrive in

Cleveland within a few months.

1951

The *Chronicle Telegram* from Elyria, Ohio, had an article on January 3, which said Cleveland Safety Director Alvin Sutton put out an order to locate six present or former Clevelanders as he prepared for the Kefauver Crime Investigation Committee's first meeting later that month. The first interview would be a secret session, although the public hearing would be held in late March or early April. Subpoenas had been sought for Morris "Mushy" Wexler, who headed up the Empire News Service, Moe Dalitz, attorney Samuel Haas, gambler Morris Klienman and his aide Louis Rothkoph, gambler Frank Brancato and Harry Brook.

Three men from the Miami area were wanted as witnesses as well; John Angersola, a.k.a. John King, and his brother George, along with Al Polizzi. Klienman and Brancato were both believed to be vacationing at the Desert Inn hotel in Las Vegas.

According to a *Plain Dealer* article on January 13, several records from the Colony Club were now in the possession of the Kefauver interstate crime investigation, as they showed a three-state tie-up of gambling elite. The gambling clubs mentioned were The Colony Club in Chesapeake, Ohio, The Huntington Athletic Club across the river in West Virginia, and the Beverly Hills Country Club outside Newport, Kentucky. Included in the records was the Terrace Club in Sandusky, Ohio, once owned by Frank Brancato and Detroit partner Peter Licavoli, brother of James Licavoli, a known Cleveland racketeer who later worked in the Youngstown area.

In the sheriff's report, he mentioned others who were included as big men in the operation: Charles Fischetti and Frank Costello, the alleged "Mr. Big" of the national rackets. The sheriff's investigation believed that eight states were involved with this gambling operation: Ohio, Kentucky, West Virginia, Nevada, Michigan, Illinois, New York and Florida, and possibly California. Crime boss Mickey Cohen would figure into the hearings held in Ohio.

The *Coshocton Tribune* in Ohio reported on January 13, the first witness to appear before the Kefauver Crime Committee session next week was to be Governor Frank Laushe and Cleveland Mayor Thomas Burke. Governor Laushe was believed to tell the commission of his efforts to get rid of the sheriff's officers in the counties where rackets flourished. The mayor was expected to speak about the rackets in Cuyahoga County, as records had been brought in for review by local government officials during closed-door meetings. Identified to bring in their records were Shonder Birns, Frank Brancato, Harry Brook, West Coast gambler Mickey Cohen, Anthony Milano, James Licavoli and John T. Fleming, a reputed city police captain.

A January 15 article from a Sandusky, Ohio, newspaper article said that Frank Brancato was a known gunman and had been identified by the Associated Press dispatches as the owner of the Terrace Club, formerly operated just beyond the Sandusky city limits. Brancato continued to be the subject of searching examination by the Kefauver Crime Investigating Committee, according to reports.

The Sunday *Plain Dealer* described the developments of hearings in Cleveland in connection with the crime probe as "Brancato Day." *Plain Dealer* stories reported:

> *Brancato, reputed Prohibition-era gunman, ex-convict, gambling club operator and now a spumoni king, trudged down the long corridor to the closed-door hearing room in early afternoon for the second time in three days. Under his arm he carried a bundle of personal records, apparently missing from the batch he had delivered on Thursday. Brancato spent a few minutes and then left the room without a comment to newsmen. Earlier records of Brancato's spumoni firm had been delivered by Pat Romeo.*

> *Brancato, a partner in the Lupuma & Brancato Spumoni Company, formerly (drew) a $3,100-a-month salary from the hot spot known as the Jungle Inn, where he was a dealer. Brancato was a known partner in the Terrace Club. Freed in the murder of Raymond and Rosario Porrello, Brancato was convicted only of perjury. The deportation action against him has never gelled in his case.*

> *On February 11, the Plain Dealer revealed the Terrace gambling club owned by Frank Brancato, located in Sandusky, was offered up for sale ... Terrace Club has been closed since Plain Dealer reporters visited the gambling club. Along with the club is five acres of land.*

The FBI file dated August 15 mentioned that Brancato had a crew of men doing large-scale hijackings and robberies around the city. They would steal whiskey, jewelry, and furs, and commit other crimes of violence. This informant advised agents further that Brancato was subpoenaed to appear as a witness before the Kefauver Senate Committee, but did not testify. The same informant advised them that Rocco Russo, a known associate of Brancato's, admitted on the witness stand that he was a longtime friend of Brancato. The informant told them that the name of Brancato came up frequently during Russo trial. Russo was tried and convicted in Sandusky court for the dynamiting of the home of an Italian barber. He was sentenced to a term in the Ohio State Penitentiary for this crime.

The FBI reported on August 28, the U.S. Immigration and Naturalization Services filed its first paper to deport Francesco Brancato in case # 0707-K-2129 for violation of the United States immigration laws.

In 1951, Brancato reported to the FBI that he was now a partner in the Fulton Fish Company, located in downtown Cleveland, and before that he was selling used cars. After about eight months of doing this, he got a different job as a tire salesman with Cardinal Tire Company. Mr. and Mrs. Frank Brancato were now living in their new home at 16301 Westview Avenue in Cleveland, Ohio.

On November 8, a confidential informant told FBI agents once again that Brancato had confidentially advised close friends and associates he was not concerned about the deportation proceedings against him. The informant told agents that Brancato claimed the red tape would take years before the government could do him any harm.

By this time, the FBI was watching Frank Brancato weekly and filing a report to the Director of the FBI. Agents would continue to make semiannual inquiries into his financial assets in all the banks in Ohio every year until he died in 1973.

1952

A *Plain Dealer* reporter wrote an article dated July 14 stating that he had interviewed a man who claimed he had lost $500 within one hour in a dice game at the well-known Pettibone Club (known as the former Arrow Club). The club boasts about having clientele from as far away as Geauga County to Youngstown, as well from the greater Cleveland area. The managers in charge of the games were brothers Scotty and George Goltsman, who were part owners in the club along with Morris Kleinmen and Tommy McGinty. The Goltsman brothers never disclosed their other partners, but these were the same men who worked in the Martinique or the Chagrin Valley Social Club, and in the Pettibone. The Chagrin Valley Social Club in Willoughby is where Brancato was thought to have a piece of the operation.

Frank Brancato was brought into the Cleveland FBI office on November 26 and was questioned in connection with what agents called a basic criminal-type investigation. At this interview, Brancato denied having any knowledge whatsoever concerning gambling operations in Cleveland or other activities that were currently under investigation. He adopted a closed-mouth attitude; an endeavor that agents believed was to convince them that he was either illiterate or not interested in what they wanted to accuse him of.

Brancato advised the agents that he was under a deportation proceeding which was being appealed, and said he would not jeopardize his freedom. He advised them that his only financial interest at the present time was in the operation of the Captain Frank's Shrimp Cocktail Company, in which he was a partner. Brancato resided in his home on Westview Avenue and he told agents he currently drove a 1951 Oldsmobile. Brancato denied being associated with any underworld persons or organization. Brancato did, however, admit he regularly plays pinochle with many of his friends.

1953

A confidential FBI informant advised them on October 6 that the boss of the Cleveland mafia was John Scalish. Scalish made all the final decisions for the Syndicate and then gave the orders to his capos, John DeMarco and their street boss, Frank Brancato, who carried them out.

On December 23, Chief of Police Frank Story and Deputy Inspector of detectives had raided The King Fin Club on Euclid Avenue and arrested Leonard Adelman, who was a known associate of Frank Brancato.

1954

According to an FBI report, an informant advised them on February 9 that the Cleveland Syndicate was under the control of John Scalish. The informant stated he had heard that Scalish received a portion of all dues and assessments from certain unions in the Cleveland area from those in control of these unions, and then a portion of the money was then "kicked up" to the East Coast, and believed to be given to Vito Genovese.

The *Cleveland Press* reported on March 20, 1954, that

(A) mystery bullet mailed to an immigration service investigator at his Parma Heights home was shown to Congressman Charles Vanick during a conference with General Joseph Swing of the U.S. Immigration Commissioners. Swing has been the lead investigator in the investigation into the Frank Brancato deportation fiasco. ... (A) bullet was wrapped in an Italian newspaper and was then mailed to the home of Agent Arthur Laverdier, who lives in Parma Heights; it was received by his wife Verna.

The bullet came in a brown manila envelope, which was in a small brown box. In the box was the bullet, wrapped with Brancato newspaper clippings. Glued to the bullet was a piece of tape with only the initials "A L" on it.

Swing did not get into the details of his investigation, but believed the bullet was not fired from any weapon, and there was no link to Brancato case at this time except that it was the same type of .32 caliber bullet that was successfully removed from his body in the 1930's by Dr. Romano.

An FBI informant told them in June (that) there is still in existence an organized group of Italian hoodlums who committed burglaries and stick-ups in the Cleveland area. He stated their headquarters was the Young Lounge Bar on East 9th Street. Members in the club included Brancato, Frank Visconti and Angelo Amato.

On July 31, a confidential informant living in the Detroit area informed the Detroit FBI office that "Frank Brancato is the head of the Cleveland Syndicate," that he might be in possession of jewelry and furs taken in a robbery on June 21, 1954, worth over $90,000. The informant told Detroit police that a fence might make contact with Brancato in order to secure information in regard to the current location of the jewels.

By August the FBI was contacted by another confidential informant, who stated Brancato had a front man, and that he had not been able to find out who this man was, but believed he was Sam Borsellino. Their headquarters was reportedly Young's Lounge Bar on East 9th Street. Members included Brancato, Visconti, Sam Perry, Tony Lombaro, John Izzy Oddo, Angelo Lonardo, and Angelo Amato. Agents noted that Oddo, who was born in Palermo, was considered to have always been a combination man for one of the biggest men in gambling in the "bath beach section" of Brooklyn, New York.

A "combination man" is one who organizes and sets up the illegal games, and then he operates or works the games and takes most of the profit.

On August 10, an informant told FBI agents Brancato was unfriendly with the leader of the Youngstown Italian hoodlum element, Joe DiCarlo. The informant said Brancato had been getting a rake off from the narcotic business paid by Sam Papalardo and John Montano.

On August 24, a confidential and reliable informant told them that Frank Brancato was known as a capo and street boss to many men and he was definitely considered an enemy of Leo Moceri, the Youngstown Italian hoodlum leader.

A document dated September 21, was filed into the Federal Court records regarding the deportation hearing on behalf of Frank Brancato by his defense attorney, Henry Levine. This was an investigation on the criminal activities and arrest records of Francesco Brancato, his birth name, from 1914 until the date of the report, which was completed by the City of Cleveland police department and signed by the Chief of Police Frank W. Story.

It goes on to state that a careful search had been made through the files of the City of Cleveland police department and that NO records were found on Francesco Brancato, age of fifty-seven.

In the affidavit below you can clearly read from the office of the Chief of Police; Frank Story and the City of Cleveland Dated September 21, 1954

To whom it may concern;

This is to certify that a careful search has been made through the files of this department and no records (were) found on Francesco Brancato, fifty-seven years of age and residing at 16301 Westview Ave. in Cleveland, Ohio, who was born on September 7, 1897, ever having been arrested by this department for any crime or offense; neither is he wanted at this time in connection with any pending investigation.

According to the statement of Francesco Brancato, he has been a resident of this city since 1914 to the present time.

Signed;

Respectfully yours, Chief of Police Frank W. Story.

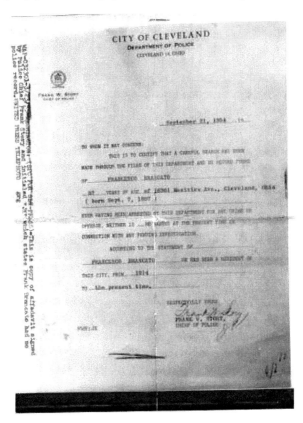

The Plain Dealer reported the mystery bullet linked to Frank Brancato's smoldering deportation case turned out to be a dud. The bullet bearing all of the marks of an ugly threat fizzled away. In Washington, Congressman Charles Vanik of Cleveland admitted that he was told the threat was not believed to be connected with the Brancato case in any way, and that the FBI in fact had three other suspects currently in mind for the mailing of the bullet, but Vanik did not disclose who these men were or where they stood in their investigation.

On September 24, the FBI was advised by a confidential informant that Brancato was considered by many men as the number one big time hoodlum in Cleveland. The informant stated Brancato knew everything illegal that was going on in the city and regarded John DeMarco as the number two big-time hoodlum in the city of Cleveland.

The same informant told the FBI that when the race wire service was eliminated and the gambling rackets curtailed, the narcotics racket became the biggest source of illegal income in the country, and that most of the top hoodlums now had some connection with the narcotics racket. He said Brancato had succeeded in muscling into the narcotics racket in Cleveland through his European connections in Italy, who, at his request would threaten to stop their source of supply to established narcotics dealers in the Cleveland area unless they did business with Brancato.

The informant told agents that he heard Brancato had been getting a rake off the top of the narcotics rackets in Cleveland for the past few years.

This is the only reference to narcotics in Frank Brancato's twenty-five-plus-year history. The FBI believed that he and his friends John Scalish and John DeMarco worked very hard keeping the narcotics traffic out of Cleveland.

On October 30, a Cleveland hoodlum told the FBI that Brancato was involved in gambling in Cleveland as well as in Kentucky. Brancato was also contacted by Joseph Costello, a known racket figure in St. Louis, Missouri, who was suspected of holding some hot big money. He had asked Brancato if he was interested in some cheap money at a cheap price. Brancato told Costello that he knew of no Italian who would want the money, since it was possibly very hot and not worth the risk. Brancato felt the only person who might take a change on the money would be Jewish fences. The FBI checked the bank accounts of Brancato and his children to see if any large amounts of cash had been deposited or withdrawals made; none were found.

On November 15, a different source told FBI agents that Brancato told people that there was a very large sum of money involved, and that he could buy it at a cheap price from his connection, and that it was not counterfeit. Brancato spoke the name of his friend, but the informant could not pronounce the name properly, since Brancato had a very heavy Italian accent. The FBI was not sure whether this was the money from a St. Louis kidnapping of a young boy named Bobby Greenlease that they were currently investigating, but the possibility was there and worth their time to investigate.

Robert C. "Bobby" Greenlease was the son of multimillionaire automobile dealer Robert Cosgrove Greenlease, Sr., of Kansas City, Missouri. Bobby was the victim of a kidnapping in September 1953 that led to the largest ransom ever payout in U.S. history at the time.

Carl Austin Hall and Bonnie Emily Brown Heady had kidnapped six-year-old Bobby from Notre Dame de Sion, an exclusive Kansas City Catholic school.

The kidnappers were drug-addicted alcoholics then living together in Saint Joseph, Missouri. In the early 1930s, Hall had attended Kemper Military School in Boonville, Missouri, with Paul Robert Greenlease, Bobby's adopted older brother.

Hall and Heady sent Bobby's father a message demanding a ransom of $600,000. Greenlease, desperately hoping to save his young son, held off the police and FBI and paid up.

However, the pair had no intention of returning him to his family. Before the ransom demand was even issued, the young boy had been murdered by his abductors.

Hall and Heady collected the ransom and got away for a short period of time.

CHAPTER TWELVE

Immigration Battle

Early - 1955

On January 4, 1955, the *Cleveland Press* reported, Louis Carriere, with his brother Mike, had reopened a gambling joint located at Som Center Road and Euclid Avenue.

The Lake County Sheriff Paul Cage is ready to help Willoughby Police Chief James Billson if and when it is needed. The Carriere brothers have operated other gambling clubs around the city, one being the well-known Martinique Room. The police speculated that the Carriere brother were in a partnership with Frank Brancato, since they have done business together in the past years and Brancato has been seen inside the building many times, looking around and not gambling.

On January 20 an informant told the FBI he had heard a considerable amount of stolen jewelry had come into Cleveland from an out-of-town theft. Brancato had helped to get the unset stones to a jeweler that would be very hard to identify in Cleveland, and would receive a large payoff once they were set and sold.

According to the FBI file on Frank Brancato on February 10, a confidential informant advised them Brancato owns a major interest in a restaurant called Captain Frank's Seafood house, often referred to by others as Captains Frank's Restaurant, which is located on the East Ninth street pier.

On February 23, a confidential informant told the Cleveland FBI office that Brancato was the head man in the Cleveland Syndicate, and nothing could get done in the city without his permission first. The informant said many of the younger boys come to him first for his advice or his permission to do a job, first out of respect, then out of fear of his possible retaliation.

An FBI file dated March 10 says both the *Cleveland News* and the

Cleveland Press carried similar page-one stories about Brancato's deportation order being voided by the Board of Immigration Appeals Court in Cleveland. The story said the board had compassion and felt sorry for him, and that a deportation would be a hardship on Brancato and his family, since his invalid wife was dying.

On March 11, the *Cleveland Press* reported that the U. S. Immigration Bureau offices in four cities were unable to locate or produce the files in the deportation hearing case against Frank Brancato. Earlier, the article said, Brancato had beaten an order that he be deported to Italy by a favorable ruling of the U. S. Board of Immigration Appeals in Washington, D.C. "Affidavits from numerous people attested to Brancato's good character," said the board in announcing their decision, adding that it would be a hardship on his wife, who has been sick for over nineteen years.

The names of the people who testified on Brancato's behalf were not mentioned in this article, but the *Cleveland Press* reporter was told to speak to the immigration examiner in Buffalo.

Anthony L Montaquila, executive assistant of the Board of Appeals, said, "You will have to get the names from the record of the hearing before the immigration examiner in Buffalo.

John Murphy, the INS agent in charge in Buffalo, stated to the reporter, "All of Brancato's files were sent back to Cleveland."

J. S. Kershner, in charge of the Cleveland office, announced, "We have only a small file on Brancato; his main file is in Detroit."

James Butterfield, the agent in charge of the Detroit office, said, "The usual procedure is for the file to come to my office first, but after checking on it, I think it is still in Washington. I am also not familiar with this case."

Henry Levine, Brancato's attorney, said he could not remember the names of the witnesses as well. "But if I did, I would not tell you. They were store owners and shopkeepers, and people like that."

In Washington, immigration officer Montaquila of the board of appeals claimed, "There is no file here. The only person to appear to argue was Brancato's own attorney, Levine. No one appeared from the Immigration Bureau."

At the bureau, Sidney Rawitz, assistant examiner, explained, "We didn't appear because we thought the case was good enough not to need argument from us." Raymond Farrell, Assistant Immigration Commissioner, disclosed, "We checked Brancato's record from the time he came here from Licata, Sicily, to the day of the hearing in Buffalo before the special investigation. We even went as far as to dig into the Kefauver records out of the basement, and checked every detail from the police records. We thought we had an iron-clad case for the deportation order against him. There is nothing in the records to show that Brancato has been a person of good moral character since his release from prison in 1936."

On March 11, The *News* reported, "Ex-Bootlegger Convinces U.S. He Has Reformed":

Frank Brancato has become the second survivor of Cleveland's bootleg wars to stave off deportation to Sicily for his racketeering past.

Brancato has convinced a Washington Appeals Court Board that he has been a respectable man in recent years. The first man was his boss, Frank Milano, another bootlegger and head of the organized crime family in Cleveland.

Both of the cases were complicated by the fact that the men had become naturalized citizens many years ago.

In suspending a 1953 deportation order against Brancato, the United States Board of Immigration appeals cited his latter-day respectability, and released that it would be an undue hardship on his wife and family to deport him.

The *Cleveland Press* on March 12 stated:

The evidence that Brancato was a big-time gambler was withheld from the Board of Immigration Appeals in the original hearing that resulted in the suspension of the order to deport the racketeer.

Thomas G. Finucane, Chairman of the Board in Washington, told a Press reporter, "The board heard nothing about Brancato being a gambler and we never saw the Kefauver Committee records about his gambling activities. This would have struck me right between the eyes if I'd seen anything like that. It was also never brought up during his deportation hearings that Brancato was a partner in the well-known classy gambling joint call the Terrace Club in Sandusky, Ohio."

Evidence gained by the Cleveland Press showed the committee that Brancato had earned $25,150 in 1945, in 1946 he earned $57,360 and in 1947 he earned $16,370. In all, for three years the club was in business, it took in a total gross income of $729,281. It was also learned how the club paid off several local police and other officials in the city with kickbacks to the claim of over $40,000 in those three years.

"This missing evidence is the second mystery in deportation victory for Brancato, a bootleg war gunman and gambler. The other mystery is the location of the Immigration Service files and records in this case, that cannot be found anywhere."

The *Cleveland Press* ran an article on March 12:

A new racket charge was leveled today against Frank Brancato in the fight to upset the racketeer's current victory in a deportation case.

The new charge is that Brancato was a known partner in the Youngstown Jungle Inn, located in Trumble County. This information was found in the files of Kefauver crime committee. Vanik is conducting a personal investigation into how Brancato, a known racket gangster, won a surprise order from the Board of Immigration Appeals suspending the deportation order against him.

Testimony putting Brancato in the Jungle Inn was given in Cleveland in 1951 by Edward Allen then the Youngstown Chief of Police, and now the Chief of State Liquor Enforcement for the Ohio Liquor Department.

Allen testified Brancato was a known partner in the Jungle Inn, along with the Farah brothers and several other men. Undercover officers confirmed Brancato was in regular contact with Farah brothers and Joe DeCarlo, the racket boss operating in the Youngstown and Buffalo areas.

On March 13, the *Cleveland Plain Dealer* had an article indicating that Frank Brancato's attorney felt gambling is not grounds for deportation.

Defense attorney Henry Levine discussed his client's interest and partnership in the Sandusky Terrace Club. His interest is in operating the restaurant area and consisted of checking over the dinner orders and soda drink concessions for the three-year period that he worked in the club. The plush club was closed by the Erie County authorities after the Plain Dealer reporters publicized the place in 1947.

Levine went on to say that it was not brought up before "because gambling is not grounds for deportation and that Mr. Brancato has never been convicted of it. All we had to do was prove, which we did, that he had been in continuous residence here for ten years without a court conviction of any kind, and that he had a dependent, native-born wife. Frank's Terrace Club income was disclosed in his yearly income tax returns, proving once again that he is a good citizen."

Levine added that the decision of Arthur Loveland, the immigration inquiry officer, proclaimed, "There is no evidence on record that Brancato has been other than a person of good moral character for the past ten years."

On March 14, the *Cleveland Press* ran a story saying:

The Kefauver file on Franck Brancato included the Terrace Club gambling joint in Sandusky, Ohio, but for some unknown reason it was not discussed or explained in today's public committee meeting. Congressman Charles Vanik was told that the Brancato deportation hearing would possibly be reopened in the introducing of the next Kefauver hearings.

In Cleveland, it was first learned that the Kefauver reports did not include any information about Brancato, since he was never confronted publicly with the Terrace Club evidence. The article stated Brancato was a bootlegger and known gunman here, and was not called to testify in these hearings. The Kefauver probers never called Brancato to testify, even though he was subpoenaed along with several other men in Cleveland's crime family.

Other FBI documents stated the *News* carried a story March 14 with the names and addresses of the persons who had given testimony of "good moral character" in affidavits which were produced in the Board of Immigration Appeals court by his attorney Henry Levine, on behalf of Brancato.

An FBI document mentioned this article that appeared in the *Cleveland Press* on March 14, headlined "Brancato: 'Good Citizen' Wields Mysterious Power:"

Fortune has smiled twice on Frank Brancato, and each time he has been saved by mysterious circumstances, and has been supported by good citizens. Last week in Washington, good citizens of Cleveland were cited as authors of affidavits which saved Brancato from being deported back to Italy.

Eighteen years ago, other good citizens of Cleveland were responsible for a hidden communication of Brancato's release from Federal Prison by Governor Martin Davey.

In early December 1936, Brancato walked out of the state prison a free man, freed by only Governor Davey's order. Outside the Governor's office, no one knew of his secret release.

Practically no one in the Ohio Parole Board knew of the gunman's release. The Cleveland police first learned from the Cleveland underworld grapevine in January 1937 how Brancato was secretly released and in the city. His secretly-won freedom became the crime sensation of the day.

It was noted that after the newspapers laid down a barrage of questions to Governor Davey and his office, and that of the Ohio Parole Board, no one was able to give the citizens of Ohio a good and satisfactory reason on why or how Brancato was released from prison in 1936, or how it was kept quiet for over two months.

Some of the character witnesses for Brancato were Larry Simon, Joe Miceli, John Russo, Dominic Biondo, Frank Zummo, Sam Cardinal and Steve Volpe.

According to an FBI file on March 15, the *Cleveland Press* had an article that said:

Joseph Nellis, formerly an assistant to Kefauver and now practicing law in Washington, D.C., told Ohio Congressman Charles Vanik that Frank Brancato's involvement was as a partner in the notorious Jungle Inn, which was characterized as one Ohio's biggest and toughest gambling joints.

Congressman Vanik is conducting a personal investigation of how Brancato, a known racket figure, won a surprise order from the board of Immigration Appeals suspending a deportation order against him. Vanik immediately asked for full details.

Other evidence before the Kefauver hearings showed Brancato earned almost $100,000 in the three years the Terrace Club in Sandusky was open.

Testimony putting him at the Jungle Inn setup was given by Edward J. Allen, then a Youngstown Police Chief and now the chief of Ohio State liquor enforcement for the Liquor Department. Allen showed the court a chart which became an exhibit in the Kefauver committee hearings that indicated Brancato and James Licavoli were sharing the rackets profits, along with Mike and John Farah of Trumbull County.

Brancato was a well–known figure at the Jungle Inn, according to Mr. Allen...

The notorious and high-scale gambling joint was raided in August 1949 by state liquor agents under Anthony Ruthowski, then State Enforcement Chief. The search warrants were signed by Common Pleas Judge Lynn Griffith. There were over seven hundred guests in the club gambling that evening, and the club has been closed since that raid. Allen has additional files on phone conversations which Brancato has had with Joe Aiello, the well-known racket boss in Youngstown, Ohio, and Joe DiCarlo from Buffalo, New York.

On March 16, the *Cleveland Press* carried a story subtitled, "Here is another chapter of the Frank Brancato story as found in the files of the Kefauver senate crime investigation hearings."

The story concerns the alleged smuggling by Brancato of Rocco Russo back into the United States, and his subsequent placement of Russo as an employee at the Terrace Club in Sandusky. The story points out that on January 25, 1951, Russo was convicted of the bombing of a barber's home and was sentenced to the Ohio Penitentiary.

According to the FBI file on Frank Brancato, the *Cleveland Press* ran another article stating Brancato had been under surveillance by the Immigration Service Agents and had been seen in the company of racketeers and criminals, including Louis Finkelstein, a known pickpocket; Tony "Pee Wee" DeAngelo, a known racketeer; Angelo Sciria, who was in prison and having his own deportation troubles; John DeMarco, a known racketeer; Angelo Lonardo, described as the younger member of the old Mayfield Road Gang, in which Brancato was a gunman during the bootleg wars; Dominic Sospirato; and Sam LaMarca, a.k.a. "Sam the Barber."

While Frank Brancatio was testifying before a House committee, according to Allan may, Crime Town USA, Brancato told the committee that back in 1948 Joe DiCarlo from Youngstown contacted him to place a bet with a well-known Cleveland bookie for $16,000. The bookie then went to see Brancato for a recommendation. Brancato stated "I told the bookie that Joe was alright, so the bookmaker extended him the $16,000 credit to bet on the Braves to win. The 1948 World Series matched the Cleveland Indians against the Boston Braves. The Indians spoiled a chance for the only all-Boston World Series by winning a one-game playoff against Boston. Though superstar pitcher Bob Feller failed to win either of his two starts, the Indians won the Series in six games to capture their second championship.

The bookie then went to see Brancato later after the game and told Brancato; Joe hasn't paid it yet? Brancato claimed DiCarlo welshed on the bet and told the bookie in his broken English, "Soma times you win, and soma times you lose!"

CHAPTER THIRTEEN

Police Shakeup

The FBI file said the *Cleveland Press* on March 23 carried the first of a series of stories involving the failure of the Cleveland Police Department to produce criminal records of Brancato. It attributed the administrative lack of action taken by the Cleveland Safety Director to either carelessness or willful failure to produce his complete records.

The FBI reported on March 23, the *Cleveland Press* ran another article on the Kefauver hearings in Washington. It stated:

> *Senator E. Kefauver today asked Immigration Commissioner Joseph Swing for a complete report on Brancato activities since last July. Swing gave Kefauver a list of five racketeers who have been deported, and twelve others where cases were pending. Brancato's name was not on this list. "I want to know why," Kefauver demanded.*

In the FBI files, it states that on March 24, the *Cleveland Plain Dealer* carried a long front-page story about the failure of the record bureau in the Cleveland Police Department. This story was entitled "Police Shakeup Ordered in Wake of Brancato Lapse."

Officer Burnett was shifted as boss of the record room, along with two other clerks who were fired after reporting that no records were found on the racketeer.

Safety Director John McCormick ordered both of these investigations, along with a shakeup in the office of records and the revamping of authority. He was quoted as saying, "We have too much repetition of negligence of duty in the records room." The article says that even though Police Chief Story was on vacation in Florida at the time, he would still be called in to testify.

According to the FBI file on Frank Brancato, the *Cleveland Press* carried a front-page article on March 24 entitled, "U.S. Aide Knew Brancato Facts." The article contained statements that Immigration

Service investigator Robert A. Earl wrote a report dated October 29, 1954, in which he stated that he found that Brancato "has been of good moral character while a resident of the United States for the past ten years to this present time."

The story said Earl and Edwin Topmiller knew more about the criminal past of Brancato and his present associates and habits than other agents in the service, that they were completely familiar with the gambling evidence against Brancato, that they were given all the information gathered by the local Cleveland police on Brancato, including the information concerning his links to the Terrace Club.

The article said that an investigation was being conducted to determine who might have been responsible for the failure of this information to reach the Immigration Board of Appeals.

The FBI file cited a March 25 story in the *Cleveland Plain Dealer* which pointed out that Samuel J. Cardinal, who was alleged to be Brancato's employer, and who was running the Cardinal Tire Company on Woodland Avenue, had served three federal penitentiary terms. The story noted that Cardinal was one of the people who gave "good moral character" affidavits on behalf of Brancato.

The FBI file says on March 28, the *Cleveland Press* had a front-page article that stated the files of the Cleveland Retail Credit Bureau reflected that for six years Brancato was the manager of the Jungle Novelty Club in Youngstown, and that he admitted in 1946 that he had been paid $900 a month by the Terrace Club in Sandusky, which was actually a notorious gambling joint.

An article in the *Cleveland Plain Dealer* on March 29, 1955, said:

Congressman Robert Mollahan in Washington last night declared he would ask his subcommittee staff to look into the muddled Brancato deportation case. "If the facts warrant it, I will then order a congressional investigation."

Mollahan is the chairman of the subcommittee on legal and monetary affairs of the House Government Operations Committee.

Cleveland Congressman William Minshall said he would like to see a congressional inquiry to determine whether the gambling evidence against Brancato was deliberately withheld, or simply lost or overlooked."

Congressman Minshall admitted, "A house probe of Brancato's past could definitely be in the best interest of the public."

A *Plain Dealer* article on March 31, written by Phil Goulding, was headlined, "Inquiry Officer Gives Board Facts on Clevelander":

The Board of Immigration Appeals today received credible information of Brancato gambling activities which it did not have when it previously suspended its order to deport the Cleveland alien.

The Chief Special Inquiry Office of the Immigration and Naturalization Service's reported he could not offer up any reasonable explanation of why the data was not included in the Brancato file when it went to the board of inquiry for the deportation hearing.

The board was given signed affidavits by Brancato that he was in fact a dealer at the famed Jungle Inn in Youngstown, a known gambling place, along with being the manager at the Terrace Club in Sandusky, Ohio.

Henry Levine, Brancato's attorney, argued that the case against Brancato not be reopened. Levine insisted, "It is unfair that the Immigration Commission was submitting confidential information which could not be divulged."

Chief Inquiry Officer Sidney Rawitz stressed inconsistencies in Brancato's occupation between 1943 and 1946.

Defense attorney Levine denied that Brancato had ever testified or had been questioned by Senator Kefauver's crime committee.

"No court would allow such evidence to get into this case without a formal questioning of the man in question, and obtaining his affirmation or denial of the so-called claims."

The *Cleveland Press* had a story on April 4 reporting that Chief of Police Frank Story alleged "That someone may have perpetrated a fraud on the police department" in obtaining a whitewash of Frank Brancato's extensive police records.

Mayor of Cleveland Celebrezze discussed with Safety Director John McCormick and with Chief of Police Frank Story at City Hall for hours and wanted a full and complete investigation on how the report on Brancato dated September 21, 1954, could show that he had no criminal record.

Mayor Celebrezze told Chief Story he wanted a full investigation and report on the Brancato muddle, along with an answer to his question "Was it intentional or otherwise?"

Agent Loveland did include in his file a special report on Brancato that Robert A. Earl, Immigration Service investigator and considered to be "a Brancato expert" to Loveland, that Brancato was of good moral character for the last ten years.

Chief Story contended, "I cannot conceive that anybody who has been in the police department for any length of time would not know about Brancato's police record."

It was reported how Patrolman Kieran was deceived, as he thought that the original request was for a passport and for nothing else. Patrolman Kieran is Chief Story's secretary, and handled the Brancato request. Safety Director McCormick wanted answers to this "whitewashing report on Brancato."

The *News* reported on April 5 that:

Chief Story has drafted new procedures on how a passport is to be processed in the city of Cleveland moving forward to insure the same concerns that took place in the Brancato case do not happen again.

A request for a passport will now be reviewed by a detective. The person must come into the station in person and their fingerprints will be taken to insure the proper identity of the applicant...

Henry Levine, Brancato's attorney, brought in the request for Francesco Brancato, Frank's birth name. The two clerks who performed the background check for the police could not find any file for a Francesco Brancato, a notorious hoodlum in the Prohibition days. The clerks were later fired.

Miss Rita McCridden, who was a typist in the records room, and who had handled the original request for information made by Brancato's lawyer, Henry Levine, under his birth certificate and passport name of Francesco Brancato.

Chief Story's secretary, Patrolmen Kieran, who handled the request after Miss McCridden was later transferred to another division in the Cleveland police force, while clerk Miss McCridden, lost her job, along with one other clerk, Ms. Margret Leypoldt from Lakewood. Ms. Leyoldt was a stenographer in the identifications room. Both women ... made between $4,000 and

$9,496 a year.

Brigadier General Joseph M. Swing of the U.S. Immigration Committee reported to the press he "placed the whole blame for the Brancato situation on Immigration Officer... Arthur Loveland." Loveland did recommend to the board not suspending the deportation order against Brancato. Loveland was however, charged with failing to include derogatory information in the files that was sent to the Board of Immigration appeals court.

Loveland was relieved of his duties by General Swing within days of the incident. A Washington spokesmen confirmed that "all proceedings in the Loveland case will be in private hearing and nothing further will be disclosed to the press. But if criminal action would be filed against Loveland, that would become a different case."

Miss McCridden filed an appeal with the Cleveland Police Department to the Civil Service Commission on her unjust firing. She was fired for "not finding Brancato's police record, with the results that the racketeer got a whitewash report" from the police.

Her boss, Deputy Inspector Chester Burnett, was removed from his job because of the Brancato report. Safety Director John McCormick proclaimed that Miss McCridden's principal error was that she did not check her findings with her superiors before she filed the report with the court, (and) that she should have asked someone when she did not find any information on his arrest record.

This caused the major shakeup in the police department. McCormick removed Inspector Burnett, who headed up the record bureau of the Cleveland Police Department, and gave his job to Deputy Inspector Ralph Schoenmaker, who was considered by many to be a very good organizer.

An article in the *Cleveland Press* on April 11 stated the Immigration Service had clamped secrecy on the Frank Brancato deportation case. It was now a confidential and purely administrative matter.

A spokesman for the service told reporters, "There will be nothing further made public by this government agency, except for announcement of disciplinary actions against Special Inquiry Officer Arthur Loveland."

Although Loveland recommended not suspending the deportation order against Brancato, he has been charged with failing to include derogatory information in the file sent to the Board of Immigration Appeals.

Loveland did include in the file a special report by the Cleveland office and Brancato expert Robert Earl, who is an Immigration Service investigator.

Earl reported to Loveland that Brancato was of "good moral character" for the past ten years.

General Swing relieved Loveland of his duties last week and filed dereliction of duty charges against him.

On Thursday April 14, the *Cleveland Plain Dealer* reported on a potential change of venue for further proceedings regarding Frank Brancato, with several choices of cities, including Seattle and Chicago.

Attorney for Brancato Henry Levine stated, "I have decided against holding the proceedings in Cleveland because of all of the newspaper publicity; Frank will not be able to get a fair trial here. But I have reserved the right to change my mind about where the hearings will be held."

In reopening the hearing, the U.S Board of Immigration Appeals court gave Levine the right to change cities for the hearings because of the prejudice brought on by all of the negative local newspaper articles in Cleveland.

Levine commented he is working diligently on his defense, and maintained Brancato has no arrest record in the last ten years and that he is entitled to a suspension of the initial deportation order from 1953.

Kefauver crime probers reported that Brancato is linked to the Terrace Gambling Club in Sandusky in 1947 and his old income tax records were expected to figure prominently in the renewed hearing.

On the next day, Friday, April 15, another article appeared that said Congressman Charles Vanik from Ohio, who obtained the transcript of the hearing held February 15 which said Defense Attorney Henry Levine was the only witness for Brancato in front of Chairman Thomas Finucane and other members Robert M. Charles and Miss Louise Wilson of the appeals board.

The Immigration Board still has not explained itself on why they have not opposed Levine's pleas, as he has showed the court the document that stated Brancato has been of good moral character for ten years. Mr. Levine's main argument articulated how the report that was filed in Cleveland court where it stated how Arthur Loveland found nothing wrong with Frank Brancato's criminal past. Loveland himself is quoted by saying "He (Loveland) says in plain English that the man (Brancato) is eligible for a suspension of deportation. Loveland goes on to denote that Brancato has established good moral charter and has not had a criminal record for the last ten years."

In the *Press* on April 22, a story said:

Senator Kefauver of the famed Senate crime probe of a few years ago, jumped into the Brancato deportation scandal. Kefauver, who had the Cleveland racketeer before him in the 1951 crime hearings here in Cleveland, sought a public airing of the Brancato case by the Senate Judiciary Committee. Congressman Charles Vanick from Cleveland said, "Conditions surrounding the Brancato case call for a wide-scale investigation in public view."

Kefauver affirmed, "The Judiciary Committee might find the muddle over the Cleveland alien symptomatic to the need for a more effective approach in the handling of all deportation criminal cases."

The *Cleveland Press* carried a front-page story entitled, "US Aide knew Brancato Facts" and they also carried statements from the Immigration Service investigator Robert A. Earl, who wrote a report dated October 29, 1954, in which he declared that, after a complete and thorough investigation, he found Brancato "Has been of good moral character while residing in the United States for the past ten years to the present time."

The story went on to say that Robert Earl and Edwin Topmiller knew more about the criminal past of Brancato, as well as his present associates and habits, than other agents in the service. It said both men were completely familiar with gambling evidence against Brancato and they were given all the information gathered by the Cleveland police, including information concerning his tie up with the Terrace Club near Sandusky, Ohio. The article says an investigation was in place to determine who might have been responsible for the failure of this information to reach the Immigration Board of Appeals.

According to an FBI file, an informant advised the Cleveland FBI

117

office that Brancato was like a friend and father figure to many of the young Italians in the Cleveland area and he especially tried to help those men who came into trouble or difficulty with the police. Brancato would often help these men by asking his close friends who owed him favors to bail out the individual from jail and help them by giving them a job. Even if they did not agree, many of these men could not refuse the request from Brancato to help other Italians.

On April 21, the *Cleveland Press* reported:

Congressman Robert Mollohan from West Virginia, who is the chairman of a subcommittee of the House Committee on Government operations, sent an ultimatum to Brigadier General Joseph Swing, the U.S. Immigration Commissioner.

The letter demanded a complete and accurate report on the deportation hearings involving Frank Brancato and the full information, including pertinent documentation on all parts played by Arthur Loveland, Robert Earl and John Underwood.

Senator Mollohan from Tennessee stated two main reasons for this hearing: first was exceptional congressional interest in the way this case reflects negatively on the Immigration Service, and the second was the widespread interest across America in the Brancato case itself.

Congressman from Cleveland Charles Vanik was a major supporter of these hearings, and had several behind-closed-door meetings with Senator Kefauver, who is insisting that the government take future action against what he called these embarrassing proceedings by the agencies involved with Brancato's deportation case.

On April 22, the *Cleveland Press* reported:

Senator Kefauver of the famed Senate crime probe of a few years ago jumped into the Brancato deportation scandal. A few years ago U.S. Senator Mollohan from Tennessee, who held the Cleveland rackets hearing in 1951, sought a public hearing case in the Senate Judiciary Committee.

Senator Kefauver backed up the suggestion of Congressman Charles Vanik. "Conditions surrounding the Brancato case called for quick action and a wide scale investigation."

The Senator from Tennessee went on to say, "The Judiciary

Committee might find the muddle over the Cleveland alien to be sympathetic of the need for a more effective approach in handling the deportation hearings." Brancato's record also was referred to in the report of the Senate Committee Investigation Organized Crime in the Kefauver Committee of 1950-1951.

An article in the *Cleveland Press* on April 25 said:

The House Government Operations Subcommittee having jurisdiction over the Immigration Services today voted for a full-scale staff investigation of the service handling of the Frank Brancato deportation fiasco. This will be the first step as they prepare for a public hearing committee on the fiasco.

"The fact that neither General Swing nor any representative of the Immigration Service appeared here today is an insult to this committee and to the Congress," acknowledged Chairman Robert Mollohan.

Mollohan went on to say General Swing failed to give the committee pertinent information and documentation on this case. He did not disclose the neglect of duty charges against three service employees. Charges were filed against Arthur Loveland, Special Inquiry Officer; Robert Earl, the Cleveland agent who reported Brancato was of "good moral character" for the past ten years, and Earl's supervisor, John G. Underwood.

"It appears there is no question but there are some unusual circumstances which make fully justified this query by our committee," declared Congressman Mollohan.

A *Cleveland Press* article dated April 26 said:

Investigators for a congressional committee will be given a censored Immigration Service file in the Brancato deportation fiasco. The file will be given to the staff of Congressman Robert Mollohan's government operation subcommittee, according to Robert Seltz, Immigration Service publicist.

Brancato's file will be screened by the service to remove all confidential information covered by a presidential order protecting government files. This will eliminate income tax information, hearsay reports and unsubstantiated information.

Robert Mollohan's committee asked General Joseph Swing of the U.S. Immigration Commissioner to provide his complete file to the committee, including any documents he may have on Brancato's case. The committee quickly voted to have a full-scale investigation on how the Cleveland racketeer was able to get a deportation order suspended.

Another article revealed that an order had been given to reopen the Brancato deportation case, with hearings to be held in Cleveland by the Board of Immigration Appeals, which had formed what they called a secret file on the Cleveland racketeer Frank Brancato that would show how he had been heavily involved with the gambling across the state of Ohio for over ten years. In the hearing in Washington D.C. board Chairman Thomas Finucane mentioned that the *Cleveland Press* and the *Cleveland News* had been pressuring him to reopen the case. Finucane went on to say, "We are concerned only with the facts and merits of this case, and not with any innuendoes."

Defense Attorney Henry Levine argued that the government case against Brancato was being reopened merely "To gratify the desires of the *Cleveland Press* and *News*." He waved copies of the papers as he argued this point in front of the board.

CHAPTER FOURTEEN

Stormy Battle

According to an article written by Ted Prinsiotto in the *Cleveland Plain Dealer* on May 1:

The real battle against the federal government and Brancato deportation hearings will possibly be the stormiest in Cleveland history, and will be played out in a Chicago courtroom.

Brancato's attorney, Henry Levine, explained to reporters that "no matter what happens in Chicago, or anywhere else in the country, we will fight this battle; I will take this case to the Federal Supreme Court, if necessary."

Two men have earlier testified how Brancato is a man of good moral character; one man is Angelo Sciria and other is Mr. Mangione.

Three immigration officers have been blamed for neglect… They are special inquiry officer Arthur Loveland of Buffalo, investigator Robert Earl of Cleveland and supervisor John Underwood of Cleveland.

The *Cleveland Plain Dealer* reported on May 3:

A secret FBI probe completed some weeks ago has reports that Brancato's underworld pals have raised a secret $30,000 slush fund to beat his deportation case.

The report, first heard by federal immigration agents last January, had been linked in news stories yesterday to a sudden transfer of Cleveland immigration Chief John Lehmann.

"The FBI probe has been finished, and the report has been turned over to the Immigration Service, but the results cannot be divulged at this time," released Robert Seitz, who is an officer with the Naturalization and Immigration Services.

From other sources it has been learned the FBI had found no basis in the rumor warranting further action or investigation of Brancato. The money reportedly had been raised to help stop the deportation of Brancato, and other alien racketeers...

On May 4, the *Cleveland Press* reported that city officials in the immigration department in Cleveland would be interviewed and questions asked about how the mishap could have occurred in the Brancato case.

Questioned were Curtis Johnson, staff director, and J. Plaphnger, counsel for the Legal and Monetary subcommittee.

Both men refused to discuss their plans, saying they had been instructed by Mollohan to make a confidential report.

It was learned by a source that Robert A. Earl, the man who signed the mysterious "good moral" character report that enable Brancato to upset his deportation hearing, will be questioned at great length. Earl is facing trial for neglect of duty charges against him for the Brancato deportation mess-up.

New immigration agent in charge is John Lehmann, who verified, "The hearing for Brancato in the government attempt to deport him will be held in Chicago on May 17 in the Immigration Services office."

On May 5, the *Cleveland Press* ran an article headlined, "Brancato Mess Gets Smellier Daily":

The sum of $30,000 has been raised by his underworld pals to help him "beat his deportation rap." The Cleveland paper wants to know how it was spent and who contributed to the fund.

The disclosure of the fund was made to the paper at the same time that Jacob S. Kershner suddenly was removed as the agent in charge of Brancato's case in Cleveland. Kershner has been transferred to St Albans, VT.

The Press asked what backed this move. "The public cannot have confidence in the Congressional Committee hearings conducted by the Immigration Services which concluded its investigation, and then cancelled the deportation order against Brancato, with the suspension of a Buffalo official. We are still a long way from the bottom of this corrupt affair."

On May 11, the *Cleveland Plain Dealer* ran an article by Ted Princiotto that revealed IRS agents found in a twenty-month period from 1948-1949 that the Jungle Novelty Inn was estimated to have between four hundred to eight hundred players a night, where some nights went as high as one thousand or more players as the club grossed over $1,310,000. All the while, Frank Brancato was believed to be a silent partner,... paid under the table by the Farah twins,... who failed to pay his share of the estimated $343,000 in taxes. It was one of the most notorious gambling clubs in Ohio until Governor Frank J. Lausche ordered a crackdown on these types of operations in 1949.

One of Frank Brancato's deportation hearings was held in Chicago, Illinois, on May 17.

According to the FBI files, the deportation hearing against him reflected testimony by Frank Brancato himself that in 1937 he applied for a job at the Jungle Inn nightclub. It was known as a gambling joint in Youngstown, where he was a dealer until 1939 or early 1940.

While still in Chicago, Brancato testified that in 1944 and in 1945 he started the well-known Terrace Club in Sandusky. Brancato had owned 25 percent interest, which he paid no money for the shares he owned.

Brancato later testified that his attorney suggested that he give up his shares in the club and the proceeds and give them to his sons, Joe and Nasher Brancato, but three to four months later, the club was closed down. Brancato testified that the largest one-year profit earnings were $20,000 to $25,000.

In another FBI file, the testimony at the Immigration and Naturalization Service Chicago hearings on May 17 noted that nine witnesses testified for Brancato on his personal history and background. At this hearing, all testified in part as to their personal knowledge that Brancato has had legitimate employment that was earlier claimed by Brancato himself.

In a *Cleveland Press* article dated May 19:

Mr. Brancato has lost the first and possibly the major round on his newest fight against deportation to his native Italy.

The immigration officer Aaron Maltin in his Newark office revealed, "It would take up to two weeks to review all the evidence brought out in the two-day hearing in Chicago."

The court had hundreds of pages of documentation linking Brancato to gambling with men with criminal records. At the conclusion of the hearing, Matlin called Brancato in front of him and asked, "If you are deported from the United States, what country do you wish to be deported to?"

In his broken, heavy Italy accent, Brancato simply replied, "to the old country, to Italy, and if not there, to Mexico."

Maltin went on to tell Brancato that he only had one choice, and that Mexico could not be one of them.

The claim was demolished in a daylong cross-examination of Brancato by Prosecutor Dominick Rinaldi, who brought the racketeer's commercial gambling operation down in 1947.

The record going to the board this time, however, contains hundreds of pages of testimony linking Brancato to gambling and with men who have a criminal record.

Evidence not refuted from 1937 to 1947, his principal livelihood was from gambling enterprises in Youngstown and Sandusky.

Another article in the *Cleveland Press* dated May 19, reported from a Chicago press bulletin, "Charges Brancato Muscle—U.S. Examiner says gambler forced his way into partnership":

A surprise witness for the government, Jack C. Stewart, told the committee how Brancato testified to him in May of 1947 that he had interest in the Sandusky Terrace Club, which was a known gambling joint, and that Brancato made his living by gambling, but he in fact gave his interests away when he first learned that gambling was illegal in Ohio.

In the same article, reporter Forrest Allen states:

Brancato, a known racketeer, was nervous and sweating on the witness stand today as the Immigration Services prosecutor charged that he muscled his way into a partnership in the Sandusky club."

Brancato testified, "My brother-in-law Charley (Chito) Balsamo and a friend of mine, Angelo Laurie, were looking at several buildings in the area to open up a club, then the owner of the Terrace Club wanted to bring me in as a partner to open up his club.

The owner of the Terrace Club wanted to bring me in as a partner for 25 percent of the profit after he had heard that I was looking to open one or two other gambling joints in the area in the near future."

Brancato admitted in court how the Terrace Club on Route 13 near Sandusky was a good moneymaker for a few years, and the best year, it paid him $57,000 with no money up front from him, and his partner in the club was Sam Spina.

A witness told the court that Brancato gave his 25 percent share of the club to a friend, Dominic Sospirato, for no money in 1946.

Mr. Brancato also testified, "I could not make any money in the fruit and vegetable business in 1937, and I went looking for a job—any job—I needed to feed my family. There weren't any jobs available. So I ended up at the Jungle Novelty Inn that was located in Youngstown. It was a gambling club with dice, cards, roulette, horses and bingo games. I dealt cards, blackjack and was strictly a salaried man. Work all day and draw your pay, that is all it was. Then the war broke out and the Jungle Inn closed for the duration. Well, instead of looking for another job, I started to sell sweaters again."

An article in the May 23 *Cleveland Press* said the House Subcommittee, headed by Congressman Francis Walter, had voted to hold a public hearing on the Brancato fiasco. "We will go into all phases of the Immigration Services handling of the Brancato deportation hearings," he said.

On May 24 the *Cleveland Press* ran an article, "The Brancato Mess, Compassion, or Fix?" stating that the integrity of the U.S. Immigration and Naturalization Service was now called into question.

It is time for some responsible government official, the president if nobody else is interested enough, to act, and to clear up the Brancato scandal. If Brancato can detour around laws and get exactly what he wants, how many others can do—and have done—the same thing?

The issue is much more than the special kid-glove treatment of the racketeer. Currently the INS is looking to place Brancato's case into what they call "The Compassionate Category," with his wife being seriously ill and believed to be dying. Brancato isn't deported in either case, because the United States government feels sorry for him.

Is the bowing and scraping to Brancato mere compassion, or is this compassion for Brancato on the part of the INS, or is it a fix developed by his attorney? The public have a right to know the truth.

Another article written by Ted Princiotto in the May 25 *Cleveland Plain Dealer* said slot machines brought in an estimated $373,000 in profits in 1948 alone for the club (the equivalent of $3,509,389 in today's money). Another moneymaker for the club, bingo was just a (come on) for our customers and became a moneymaker for the owners of the Jungle Novelty Inn in Trumbull County, where gambling was wide open, with dice along with poker tables, as these games turned more profits for the club. Games like bingo and chuck-a-luck were known as games for women only. The club was fined $343,000 and $60,000 in penalties assessed against them since 1949. Named in the suit were John Farah, Ralph Colletto, Edward Tobin and Anthony "Tony Dope" Delsanter.

On May 26, a *Plain Dealer* article written by Ted Princiotto said it was disclosed in a federal court in downtown Cleveland that slot machine profits were set to have the house getting a 79 percent payout of all the games played.

Revenue Agent John A. Varley of Youngstown testified that on the basis he concluded the club made $638,000 from its battery of one hundred slot machines. Horse books standards call for a 12 percent profit margin on all bets made. Dice tables are set at a 10 percent profit and the club's profits on that game alone is estimated to be $252,000 in 1948 and $179,000 in 1949. The Treasury Department estimates that the club made 12 percent profit on $810,000 bet in 1948 and $576,000 in 1949.

The Jungle Inn was raided on August 12, 1949, by Ohio state liquor agents, who were acting on the direct orders of Governor Frank Lausche. The Jungle Inn had a staff of sixty-five people nightly and would have between five hundred and eight hundred customers or players a night. There were three dice tables, two poker tables, one hundred slot machines, one roulette wheel, a chuck-a-luck game, and bookies willing to take any horse bets from any racetracks around the country. Like most of the other gambling hot spots, these clubs had four to six small lookout turrets placed between four and six feet off the ground that allowed men to oversee the gambling action around the complete floor of the casino. There were men armed with shotguns to deter robberies and also to give protection to their clients.

When Brancato's name was mentioned, defense attorney Levine, who was in the courtroom, objected at once. Presiding Judge Bruce told them their motion was sustained. A partner in the club, Ralph Coletto, related that, "Brancato was there most of the nights and we paid him to watch over the roulette wheel." Coletto said Brancato was not a partner in the Jungle Inn. The only four partners listed were John and Mike Farah who had 40 percent shares (the FBI strongly believed that Brancato had up to 20 percent of their share, but this could never be proven in court), Edwin Tobin had 25 percent, Ralph Colletto had 25 percent, and Anthony Delsanter had 10 percent.

The *Cleveland Press* ran a story on May 26 written by *Press* Washington writers Dick Preston and Bob Crater which said Chairman Francis E. Walter of the House Immigration Subcommittee had ordered field investigators into Cleveland, stating that, "A person would have to be gullible or naive to believe that the Brancato fumbling was 'due to stupidity.' The article goes on to say:

U.S. Immigration Commissioner Joseph M. Swing announced that special inquiry officer Arthur Loveland was being suspended for twenty days without pay. Last September, Loveland held a hearing where he ordered a stay of deportation for Brancato, but he failed to develop any of the gambling records on Brancato, who was a known Cleveland racketeer. Loveland admitted he knew nothing of Brancato's gambling past and that he never read the file, which contained numerous reports written by Robert Earl concerning it.

Cleveland Immigration Investigator John Underwood and Robert Earl were given a seven-day suspension each without pay.

It was earlier that Earl reported Brancato "was of good moral character for the past ten years" and Underwood approved the report written by Earl.

Walter told the reporters "If these men were as stupid as to do what they did, they should not be allowed to be in the position to do it again." Walters also is interested to know if the FBI was actually called in on the report of a $30,000 slush fund for Brancato defense that was being raised in the Cleveland area.

Congressman Charles Vanik proclaimed, "The American people are certainly entitled to know if the full Brancato file was not presented to the Appeals Board, and if not, why not. Was it a total disregard of the law, or just gross negligence of these few men?"

The *Cleveland Press* ran an article on May 29 which said evidence that Brancato had received substantial income from the Terrace Club could be found in the files of the Cleveland Retail Credit Bureau.

This same file links Brancato to the Jungle Inn, where he remarked he was the manager of the club and had "no supervisors."

This is the same notorious Jungle Inn... near Youngstown, which was closed down in 1949.

Immigration Service Investigator Robert Earl, in an official report last October 18, reported to his supervisors how the Cleveland Credit Bureau has been checked on Brancato and "No derogatory records were found."

At this same time of Earl's report, the true nature of the Terrace Club was well-known to Immigration Service men working on the Brancato case. A bombing trial in 1950 had definitely established its business and shown Brancato's connection with the club.

The *Cleveland Plain Dealer* reported on May 29:

Congressman Robert Mollahan in Washington last night asked his subcommittee staff to look into the muddled Brancato deportation case. "If the facts warrant it, I will then order a congressional investigation" Congressman Minshall proclaimed "A house probe could definitely be in the public's best interest in view of the newspaper stories about this case."

Chapter Fifteen

Congressional Hearings

On June 2, 1955, *Cleveland Press* writers Dick Preston and Bob Crater reported from Washington:

Former Cleveland Immigration Chief Jacob Kershner withheld reports of a $30,000 slush fund for (Frank) Brancato for ten weeks before sending the information to his superiors.

Kershner did not tell the Washington immigration headquarters about the rumors until after the Brancato case had been exposed by the Cleveland Press in March.

The Washington office, in turn, did not ask the Cleveland FBI to investigate until after a congressional committee had questioned Immigration Commissioner Joseph Swing about the fund last week.

The timetable of delays was revealed by General Swing as he explained that an earlier FBI checkup was based on the report from Kershner which neither mentioned Brancato nor the alleged amount of funds.

This was nearly ten weeks after January 13, when immigration agent Arthur Laverdier told Chief Keshner that the $30,000 defense fund reportedly was being raised to help Brancato and Bruno Corasanitti.

An FBI file stated on June 1955 that a special inquiry from the immigration investigation was conducted by the Cleveland office concerning an allegation that Brancato was able to raise $30,000 to "beat the deportation rap against him." A source told the FBI a collection was started by some of his "boys," meaning the criminal element in Ohio, to collect money for his defense fund. Another newspaper report was headlined "FBI nips report that pals raised fund to aid Brancato."

While Frank Brancato was testifying before the House Committee, according to Allan May *"Crime Town USA."* when asked about Joe DiCarlo from Youngstown, Brancato testified that back in 1948 before the Cleveland Indians played the Boston Braves in the World Series Games. Joe DiCarlo wanted to bet $16,000 on the Braves to win. The bookie contacted Brancato and he vouched for DiCarlo. "I told the bookie that Joe was all right," so the bookie extended him the credit and took his bet. After the game, the bookie went to see Frank and told him "Joe hasn't paid it yet." Brancato claimed DiCarlo welshed on the bet and told the bookie, in his broken English, "Soma times you win, and soma times you lose."

On June 7, the *Cleveland Press* ran an article by Dick Preston and Bob Crater:

Amendments to the Walter-McCarran Immigration Act will be sought to plug loopholes found by such criminal aliens as Brancato, one of the authors of the act said today.

The subcommittee listened to several hours of testimony showing how Brancato and sixteen other criminals around the country had avoided deportation for many years.

"It is evident that if an alien has a good lawyer and plenty of money, it is difficult to get rid of him," acknowledged Congressmen Francis Walter.

On June 10, the *Cleveland Plain Dealer* ran an article which reported:

Today Robert Earl testified to the committee that no one asked him to go easy on Brancato on his deportation case. "That never entered our heads at all," declared Robert Earl.

The Plain Dealer office in Washington reported that immigration investigator Robert Earl, during his interrogation that lasted several hours, swore he had never received any kind of presents or money from Brancato or anyone else connected with him.

He went on to declare he had never talked with anyone he suspected of being an in-between agent for the Italian alien.

Earl went on to emphasize, he had no occasion or reason to lie. Brancato had never threatened him or anyone in his family, that there have been no offers of bribery or pressure of any kind by Brancato or by people within his service or by members of the House or Senate.

Earl told the committee that he, in fact, had made a mistake in signing a ten-year good character record on Brancato's behalf.

On June 12, the *Cleveland Press* reported:

Police Chief Frank Story proposed that a Cleveland Detective Sergeant testify in front of the congressional committee which last week heard an Immigration Service agent... cast doubt on the trustworthiness of the Cleveland police in the Brancato case.

Before the House Committee on Government Affairs, Robert Earl testified that he concealed from the Cleveland police how he had been keeping an eye and watching Brancato's activities closely.

"Our records and reports of the time referred to by Robert Earl show his testimony to be false," Chief Story told the reporter. "Earl testified that when he and other INS agents rode with Cleveland police at night, he didn't tell the police he was watching Brancato because he did not want the word to get out onto the streets or back to Brancato."

Detective James McArthur told Chief Story that Earl told McArthur they were trying to have Brancato's bond lifted because he was associating with known criminals.

Robert Earl has been suspected of lying to the committee in Brancato's hearing and Chief Story told the reporter that Detective Harold Lockwood could be called to testify and answer Earl's earlier testimony.

Chief McArthur has over eighty-eight police reports dated between May 18, 1952, and March 26, 1954, on Brancato's activities in Cleveland.

On June 24, The Corpus Christi *Times* ran an Associated Press news service article from Washington that the house investigators quizzed ex-racketeer Frank Brancato of Cleveland on the hope of "clearing up rumors" about the possible bribery and political influences that may have been helping him evade deportation. Chairman Mollohan announced that his purpose in calling the onetime professional gambler from Ohio, was to testify and to help clear up the many rumors and hearsay that keeps creeping up in their investigation of why his deportation did not move forward. He said they needed to determine whether Brancato had threatened, bribed or intimidated officers to enable him to stay in the country.

On June 25, the *Cleveland Press* ran an article written by their

Washington writer, Robert Crater, who reported:

Brancato testified he was broke and that he had spent over $11,000 in 1950 for his daughter's extravagant wedding, where there were two thousand people who attended the affair. (Editor's note: the modern equivalent to $11,000 spent in 1950 is $103,504.)

Brancato also testified that he received $38,000 in 1947 as a cut of his profits from the closing of his gambling joints.

Brancato drives a new car every year, mainly a Cadillac, and has expensive imported tailor-made suits made out of the best fabric available, and wears a diamond ring on his left pinky finger with the initials "FB."

Brancato tried in vain for several days to give a hard-luck story to the Senate House Subcommittee on Government Affairs headed by Congressmen Robert H. Mollohan and Congressman William E. Minshall, but neither man believed a word Brancato told them about his financial situation. Minshall did most of the questioning as he asked Brancato,

"Do you have any money in a safe deposit box or buried anywhere?"

Brancato answered, "No, but if I had, I dig it up; I could use it," trying to confuse the congressman.

Minshall then inquired, "Where did you get the $11,000 for your daughter's wedding?" Brancato answered, "From my friends; it is customary for friends to give money for a wedding,"

Minshall then asked Brancato, "Where did you get the $4,600 to pay your defense attorney fees to Henry Levine?" Brancato's simple answer once again, "Only from my family and relatives; I had to borrow it all."

Brancato went on to testify his only income is the $65-a-week job where he is paid as a salesman for Cardinal Tire Company.

The next question came from Cleveland Congressman Charles Vanik to Brancato. "Are you the owner in the Captain Frank's Seafood House?"

Frank just looked at him and in a calm voice answered, "No, Frank Visconti and I are very good friends. I was only in partnership with him in a shrimp business that went out of business several years ago." Brancato went on to say "Everybody thinks I have money, but I am broke, dead broke."

Vanick then inquired "How high can you count?" Brancato smiled at him and answered, "$100,000." Brancato's Attorney Levine pointed out, "Put some money in front of Frank and you will see how well he can count."

On June 25 the Bridgeport *Telegram* in Connecticut ran an Associated Press article from Washington:

Frank Brancato told the house investigator yesterday that he is a kind of man who can get a new car every year, buy two to three suits a year at a cost of $80-$100 and take care of his invalid wife on only $105 a week.

Brancato explained to the committee that he has been retired for several years from his position of prominence as an Ohio gambler.

He explained to a government operations subcommittee, that he is able to do all of this buying because "I do not have any expenses."

The subcommittee is trying to find out how he has been able to avoid deportation since 1951, despite his checkered past, which includes a spell as a bootlegger, a perjury conviction, and a murder charge that he has been cleared of.

The handsome, balding 58-year-old told the amazed investigators, he did not know that he was doing anything wrong or illegal when he was a partner of an Ohio gambling casino in the mid-1940s.

"I am telling you the truth," he told Chairman Mollohan, "I did not know that I was breaking the law; the clubs in Cleveland were wide open."

Brancato told the investigators he gave away his interest in the casino in 1947 when he was advised by the immigration authorities that gambling was illegal, and that he would be jeopardizing his citizenship.

Asked whether he did any payoffs to the local police, he responded "I only went there to get my paycheck. These monthly checks were sometimes $9,000 and sometimes nothing at all." Since then I have worked as a contact man for the Cardinal Tire Company for $65 a week and his son Nasher gives him $40 a week to live above his garage. He still testified that he only has pennies in a savings account but he buys a new car every year.

June 30, a *Cleveland Plain Dealer* story headlined "Lawyer to Appear before Appeals Board today" reported:

> *Another plea to cancel deportation proceedings against (Frank) Brancato, who is fifty-eight years old, will be in Washington today. Henry Levine will appear once again before the Immigration Board of Appeals ... which once granted and then revoked an order suspending the bootleg-era racketeer's 1953 deportation order.*
>
> *In his brief, Levine charges that the "pressure of the newspapers" had forced the appeals board to reopen the case and "has governed and directed the activities of this case." Levine will also argue how seriously ill Brancato's wife is, and (that she is) not expected to last much longer, and deporting him will be a hardship on the family and his wife, who is a native-born American.*

On July 1, a *Cleveland Plain Dealer* article by Phil Goulding said:

> *...On June 30, the lawyer for Brancato, Henry Levine, told the board how "Brancato is a reformed character and has fulfilled the intent of the law and is thereby entitled to be suspended of the latest deportation order against him."*
>
> *Levine went on to testify that "Of course he belonged to the criminal element in the past and he knows that his background was bad, or he never would have been ordered deported."*

The article says Levine fought to show how his client was charged with illegal activities in the mid-1940s, when he was a partner in the Jungle Novelty Inn and the Terrace Club, where the government claims he earned over $8,000 from 1943 to mid-1947.

Defense Attorney Levine told the court,

> *"I should not think it would not disqualify a man if the income was over only two and a half years out of the ten-year period that the court normally looks at when reviewing a deportation hearing."*
>
> *Attorney Levine also submitted a nine-page brief in which he noted that Brancato's hearing was conducted by a hearing officer appointed by the Immigration Service, and such an appointment was not in accordance with the Administrative Procedure Act prior to repeal of the three sections by congress.*

The *Cleveland Press* reported on July 8:

Frank Brancato, notorious racketeer and gambler, has been ordered deported.

The Board of Immigration Appeals has turned down his plea for a stay of execution reversing the ruling back on March 8, which granted Brancato's plea for a stay of deportation to his native Italy.

In that decision, the board disclosed that it would be a hardship, but today's ruling came after the disclosure in the Cleveland Press of Brancato's extensive gambling activities in the ten-year period in question.

The Press campaign also brought up disciplinary action against three employees of the Immigration Service, and the transfer of Jacob Kerschner, formerly the agent in charge in Cleveland.

The Justice Department in Washington refused to comment on today's development, saying, "It had no such announcement at this time."

On July 8, a *Cleveland Press* article by its Washington correspondent, Dick Preston, said the Immigration Service was seeking an official agreement that Italy would accept Brancato for deportation. A spokesman said he took the oath of citizenship back in 1929, and it was revoked several years later, in 1939, but officials would be asking for a travel document that would send him back to his native country.

Brancato is out on a $5,000 bail until they can secure an Italian visa, but there have been many reports that Italy may refuse to accept him back into their country.

Chairman Francis Walter of the House Immigration Subcommittee believes that the U.S. can halt all future immigration from Italy into the United States if the Italian government refuses to accept Brancato back.

On July 9, the *Cleveland Plain Dealer* ran an article written by Ted Princiotto which stated defense attorney Henry Levine planned to file an appeal and a writ of habeas corpus challenging the legality of his deportation with the federal courts once again on behalf of his client.

The article said the appeals court might rejected it based on claims that Brancato had reformed, and Italy might refuse to accept to take Brancato back.

A *Cleveland Press* report on July 27, written by *Press* Washington writers Dick Preston and Bob Crater said "shocking inefficiency and unskilled performance in the Immigration Service" had caused the Brancato mess. It said the hearing was unable to prove this mess resulted from improper influence from the immigration personnel. The investigating committee also stated that there were at least eight points at which the U.S. Immigration Service bungled. Listed were a half dozen reforms that were needed to keep it from happening again. The article credited the *Cleveland Press* with prodding the service into reopening the case, and as a result, the deportation order against Brancato was restored.

Today's report wound up a congressional investigation of the Brancato fiasco—for the present time.

Another subcommittee (which) held a few hearings on this case is not expected to take any further action against Brancato. It goes on to blame a service speed up for starting the "unnerving confidence in which official after official failed to do their duty."

The U.S. government is now in negotiation with Italy to persuade them that the country accepts Frank Brancato. Congressman William Minshall and Charles Vanik have been playing major roles in bringing this case to the attention of Congress. The eight errors that were mentioned in the article are:

Delays from 1939 to 1951 before taking action to deport Brancato, who had lost his citizenship in 1939. No explanation was ever furnished, the report stated.

Giving Brancato a "good character" report written by the immigration agent Robert A. Earl. The committee goes on to say Earl failed to follow instructions in the investigation handbook.

Faulty instructions in the book itself, which did not require that "The complete file be forwarded as a matter of course to the investigator."

Handling of the Brancato case, listed by the Attorney General as "top priority," in a routine manner.

Lack of "proper supervision" by Robert Earl's Cleveland superiors, John Underwood and Jacob Kershner, to catch his mistakes.

Failure of the top Washington officials to assign an examining officer to present the government case last September before special inquiry officer Arthur Loveland.

Failure of Arthur Loveland to read the file.

Failure of the service to send a representative to the Board of Immigration Appeals when Brancato's case went before it in February.

Service officials testified they thought they could correct any miscarriages by asking for re-hearings. This was the official excuse for not being represented at the hearings where Brancato beat the deportation rap against him.

On July 28, the *Cleveland Plain Dealer* reported:

Representative William Minshall summed up the feeling of the House investigation in the mishandling of the Brancato deportation case.

"The Immigration and Naturalization Service repeatedly fumbled the ball, producing a shocking inefficiency and a historic comedy of errors to deport a top priority racketeer.

"Those agents showed a shocking inefficiency and unskilled performance in the service of judicial procedures as are unable to find proof of improper influence or a congressional fix.

"Ample evidence exists that the Immigration and Naturalization Service for some time has been unable to remove from our midst aliens of Brancato's character, due to their lack of prompt and forceful action, and in other cases due to the recourse if judicial remedies (are) available to aliens."

Minshall concurred. "I am pleased with the results of the Brancato hearings; our careful investigation disclosed no criminality. The subcommittee's investigation indicated an acute need for service wide training programs."

Throughout the months of July through early September, many of the newspapers in Cleveland continued to report several other stories on how the fight to deport Brancato by the U.S. government was a fiasco or a cover-up or even possibly involved a payoff to higher government officials to help the racketeer and gangster to stay in the country. To stop the deportation and a big waste of the taxpayer's money if they decided not to deport him back to his native Italy based on all the records of his misconduct and racketeering charges over the years.

On September 7, the *Cleveland Plain Dealer* announced the death of Virginia Brancato, the wife of racketeer Frank Brancato, at the age of fifty-two at Marymount Hospital in Garfield Heights. They reported that Mrs. Brancato had been suffering with diabetes, and had been semi-invalid for the past nineteen years. She succumbed of a heart attack. Mrs. Brancato had been suffering with coronary artery disease for many years as her body became weaker and weaker.

The article said in March of 1953, Brancato's defense attorney Henry Levine was able to use documentation obtained from his wife's doctor, Vincent Ippolito, that stated her heart condition was terminal, and that she could die at any time, and that deporting her husband Frank back to Italy would be an undue hardship and stress on the dying woman and her family, which included five children and several grandchildren.

Doctor Ippolito's affidavits were offered to the court to show her condition; they were never challenged in the deportation controversy. The article continued by saying that "his deportation hearing is at a standstill, with no immigration agency seeking to obtain travel documents from Italy to accept him as a deportee."

Causing more pain and suffering to the Brancato children, less than two weeks after burying their mother, Mrs. Virginia Brancato, on September 19, their loving father Frank was taken from them without any warning.

CHAPTER SIXTEEN

Kidnapping of Mr. B.

The *Cleveland Press* reported Frank Brancato was:
"Kidnapped from the Cleveland Federal Building by immigration agents today, and was started on his way from Cleveland to Boston, and then on to Rome for his 3:30 pm deportation flight."

But while on the mid-air flight from Cleveland to Boston Attorney Henry Levine won a legal battle with the federal courts in Cleveland that grounded the group of men at least temporarily, when they landed in Boston.

Federal Judge Charles McNamee cited the unusual procedure had ordered the immigration service to return Brancato to his Cleveland courtroom for a proper hearing.

In Washington, General Joseph Swing, U.S. Commissioner of Immigration, announced he would order Brancato detained at Boston until the legal issues could be battled and settled. Federal Judge McNammee's last-minute decision halted the execution of a carefully laid plan by General Swing which would have placed Brancato on a flight for Rome at 3:30 p.m. that same day.

This has become the climax of Brancato's sixteen-year-old fight to escape deportation that found him pinning his final hope of success.

In the morning, before leaving his home on Westview Avenue, where he was currently living with his daughter Bella and her family, Frank told her, "I will be back in a few hours," as he kissed his daughter on the cheek goodbye.

Brancato was waiting outside the downtown office of his attorney, Henry Levine, in the Williamson Building, when Levine arrived there shortly after nine. Together, the men walked into the Federal Building, which was located across the street, and then went to the fourth-floor headquarters of the immigration service.

Brancato freely surrendered to John M. Lehmann, Cleveland's Chief of the Immigration Service. Levine left the room and walked down to the third floor office to file a writ of habeas corpus with the federal courts on Brancato's behalf.

As Levine disappeared down the staircase; Brancato was quickly hustled out of the office by several INS agents to a waiting elevator, and whisked to the basement, then into a waiting car. By the time his attorney Levine was able to file his writ for Brancato, the agents were already speeding toward Cleveland Hopkins Airport in Brookpark.

After filing the writ and heading back upstairs to see his client, Levine heard what had just happened to his client. Levine got angered and shouted, "They shanghaied him! This is jungle law, not American justice."

Horrified, Levine rushed to see Federal Judge James C. Connell, but Connell refused to handle his complaint and case, saying he was currently trying a patent lawsuit, and could not be involved with his case.

After hearing this, Levine actually ran to see Judge Charles McNamee, who agreed to look into this matter. He quickly summoned Lehmann and U.S. Attorney Summer Canary into his chambers. Lehmann proceeded to tell the judge he was under direct order by the Detroit office to take Brancato as soon as Levine left the office and before the writ could be filed in federal court.

Judge McNamee asked, "Is it true that the man was spirited away and kidnapped?"

Lehmann simply replied, "The writ had not been filed at the time we took him, and Brancato was in our custody, so we took him to the airport."

Judge McNamee ordered Lehmann "to return Brancato to this courtroom, no matter where he currently is, and he is entitled to a hearing."

Lehmann then asked, "Are you ordering me, sir?"

"Yes, I definitely am," was the judge's simple reply.

During their conversation, defense attorney Levine threatened to obtain contempt citations against Lehmann and his immigration service superiors if they failed to comply with the judge's order.

140

Before the legal argument raged on in downtown Cleveland with defense attorney Levine, Brancato was now sitting comfortably in the Cleveland Hopkins Airport waiting room, flanked by the two immigration agents. They would not permit him to speak to anyone or to use the phone to call his attorney or his family. Without handcuffs or luggage, Brancato and the agents boarded Flight 614 for Boston at 11:11 a.m.

Originally the immigration office had planned to use its own plane to rush Brancato from Cleveland to Boston, but their DC-3 developed engine trouble the day before, and was still being repaired at Washington this morning.

Replying to the judge's order, General Swing said, after Brancato arrived in Boston, it would be decided whether to detain him there until after a hearing is held in Cleveland Federal Court in his absence, or to arrange to hold the hearings in Boston. If not, Brancato and the two agents who accompanied him would be on the next Pan Am flight headed for Rome that afternoon.

Earlier that morning at the Federal Building in downtown Cleveland, Brancato had joked with the reporters and photographers covering his story, telling the cameraman, "Go on, take a couple more; you only have thousands pictures of me already."

In the Federal Building, waiting to post a bond for Brancato if he was permitted to remain at liberty on bail, was his bondsman, Dominic C. Lonardo.

Later in 1963, Dominic would be charged with impersonating an FBI agent, and sent to jail. Years later, Dominic's brother, Angelo A. Lonardo, would become a made member of the Buffalo Family. Dominic was the son of Brancato's good friend and former associate, Big Joe Lonardo; who was murdered years ago during the corn sugar wars.

On September 20, a *Plain Dealer* article written by Ted Princiotto was headlined, "One-Way Ride to Rome for Brancato Foiled."

Frank Brancato was taken on a two-way ride yesterday. The bold U.S. immigration agents attempted to fly the prize deportee out of the country secretly, before they brought him back on the next plane.

The trip was planned in advance by the INS as a one-way ride to Rome, Italy, but ended last night when the fifty-eight year old Cleveland racket figure was flown back to Cleveland on a United

Airlines flight at 7:30 p.m. from Boston, at a Federal Judge's order.

Stepping jauntily from the airliner, Brancato was observed smiling and in almost a gleaming spirit as he set foot on the Cleveland runway.

U.S. District Judge Charles J. McNamee put a dramatic end to the spectacular attempt to get rid of Brancato in a swift, surprising coup that almost caught Brancato's lawyer flat-footed.

The *Cleveland Press* reported:

American law—which (Frank) Brancato flouted for decades—today gave Brancato yet another break.

The fifty-eight year-old gunman-gambler and racketeer was released on a $5,000 bail, pending the outcome of a new legal battle over his secret deportation.

The article dealt with his return flight to Cleveland from Boston that arrived back in town at 7:30 p.m. that night of September 19, where he was placed into a holding cell overnight until a hearing would be held the next morning.

The U.S immigration agents made a sad attempt to fly Brancato out of the country secretively, before it was foiled by the quick actions of his attorney.

After his arrival at the airport in Cleveland, Brancato was seen walking in front of the two INS agents, who accompanied him to Boston. Brancato was walking straight and tall as he was seen smiling at the reporters and photographers in the area and was in very good spirits as he set foot onto the runway. When asked how he was feeling, Brancato simply responded, "Pretty good."

The U.S. Immigration Service will be compelled to prove—as it has been trying to do with off-and-on energy for the past sixteen years—that Brancato's long, lawless career merits booting him out of the country, and all technical requirements for deportation have been complied with. Brancato told reporters that he was happy to wake up in a county jail instead of a jail in Rome.

Several months earlier, a rush deportation order was given by the same immigration commissioner to get New Jersey racketeer Joe Bacardi out of the country. The Italian agreed, and accepted his deportation.

Several years later, the FBI, led by J. Edgar Hoover, on the orders of Robert Kennedy, once again tried to do what they had failed to do with Brancato: To kidnap another gangster from the south and deport him to his homeland before his lawyers could get involved and save the man, as they did with Brancato.

This time the man was Carlos Marcello, the boss of Louisiana. After becoming president, John Kennedy appointed his brother Robert as U.S Attorney General. The two men worked closely together on a wide variety of issues, including the attempt to tackle their largest opponent, organized crime.

In March 1961 Attorney General Robert Kennedy, acting on requests which had been first made to President Eisenhower's administration and by former Louisiana State Police superintendent Francis Grevemnerg, took steps to deport Marcello to Guatemala (the country Marcello had falsely listed as his birthplace). On April 4, 1961, Marcello was arrested by the authorities and taken forcibly to Guatemala. Just as in Brancato's case; Marcello was quickly returned to the United States by a federal court order within a week's time.

Brancato's attorney, Henry Levine, has agreed to surrender Brancato's U.S. citizenship on the basis that his original naturalization petition lacked the signatures of credible witness. The two men who had originally signed his petition in April 1929 were later identified to be gangsters.

The next morning, Judge Charles McNamee ruled that Brancato would be released on a $5,000 bond, which was gladly paid by Dominic Lonardo. The judge also ordered that the hearing in regard to the writ of habeas corpus entered by his attorney Henry Levine calling that Brancato was still a naturalized American citizen since 1932, when he was convicted of perjury. The hearing would be held the next Tuesday, preventing his exile from the United States.

Judge McNamee will be called upon to decide the validity of the deportation proceedings conducted by the U.S Immigration and Naturalization Service, which was climaxed when the efforts to get rid of Brancato by trying to fly him secretly out of the country. Levine was quoted, "We will take this case to the Supreme Court if necessary to get Frank released"

An article in the *Cleveland Press* on September 20 reported:

Yesterday the U.S. Immigration Service agents pulled a fast one on

Brancato. Federal agents were all set to get him out of the country secretly, before he could protest.

At first glance, this would sound like justice at last. But is it really justice, is this what decent citizens want? Is this the American tradition of fairness and liberty? Of course the answer is NO. Evil as Brancato is, he is still entitled to every single protection of the Constitution. Even if he has himself violated its lofty principles, he still enjoys the rights it offers to all men. Justice may be slow this way, but it is still justice.

An article in the *Cleveland Plain Dealer* on September 21 said:

Brancato, the elusive deportee, was a freer man yesterday than at any time since his deportation arrest in 1951 as an undesirable alien. His old immigration bond, which strictly curbed his travels, associates and hangouts, was lifted when the racket figure's case reached U.S. District Court.

After narrowly escaping a sudden expulsion to Italy, Brancato was brought before Judge Charles McNamee. Brancato, meanwhile, will be freer to do as he wishes under the court's $5,000 bail than under his former deportation order.

Brancato is retraced to this area and is prohibited to be around criminals and ex-criminals, and is required to report twice a month on his activities.

Judge McNamee will decide the validity of the unorthodox deportation attempt by the U.S. Immigration and Naturalization Service, which climaxed their efforts to get rid of Brancato by trying to fly him secretly out of the country. Levine explained "We will take this case to the U.S. Supreme Court if necessary and... this case could easily go on through 1956."

In an article written on September 24 by *Plain Dealer* Washington reporter Phil Goulding wrote:

Immigration Commissioner Joseph Swing declared at the hearing today "That the United States would have been rid of Frank Brancato had it not been for these Simon-pure judges."

The article goes on to say that Swing told reporters,

"We gave it the old college try." He added later to reporters that "he'll probably be here for another two and half years now."

Swing was referring to the service's attempt earlier this week to whisk the Cleveland alien and racketeer to Boston and then to Italy before Brancato's attorney, Henry Levine, could secure a writ of habeas corpus.

Stopping the process was Federal Judge Charles J. McNamee. Judge McNamee ordered that Brancato be brought back to Cleveland until a hearing could be held on the writ filed by Levine that morning.

Defense attorney Levine explained, "The trouble with General Swing is that he was a longtime Army man. We cannot use Army tactics instead of the laws and procedures of our courts. The courts are our last resort when we seek justice. People have been saying the government should not have tried to kidnap Brancato. But it was not the government, it was only Swing."

Congressman William Minshall said, "If General Swing is indicating that our legal processes should be bypassed, I think he is in error. I am anxious to see Brancato deported in accordance to the law and the findings of the Justice Department, but he should not be deprived of his legal rights."

General Swing later testified how Brancato was the first denaturalized Italian citizen that the Italian government was willing to agree to accept, and they are being very cooperative with his deportation.

An informant in Cleveland notified the FBI that he had heard from several sources that John Scalish was the "number one big-time hoodlum in Cleveland" and he knew everything that was going on in the city, and that Brancato was "the number two big-time hoodlum in Cleveland."

The same informant told agents Brancato had succeeded in muscling into the narcotics rackets in Cleveland by getting a kickback from the dealers operating in Cleveland if they wish to stay in business, or he would cut off their supply.

On October 5, defense attorney Henry Levine filed a thirteen-page brief in federal court in Cleveland on the facts of law, and asked that the Brancato deportation case be dismissed. Judge Charles J. McNamee told the court that he would be reviewing these documents very closely and would examine the declaration very carefully, and only then would he determine if the government had enough evidence to proceed with the deportation case against Brancato. U.S. Attorney

Summer Canary said that he would ask the Court of Appeals if the case could be placed at the head of docket.

An article in the *Cleveland Press* on October 11 said:

Federal Judge Charles McNamee today denied racketeer Brancato's request for a court order to prevent his deportation to Italy. After reading the thirteen-page document, Judge McNamee reported he has examined the deportation records and found ample evidence to sustain the findings of the Immigration Service. Brancato was not a person of good moral character, and therefore not entitled to discretionary relief.

Brancato has been fighting deportation since he lost his citizenship in 1939. The Press showed that Brancato, in fact, had been a partner in a big-time gambling operation for part of the period involved in his case.

Henry Levine, Brancato's attorney, replied, Brancato would appeal Judge McNamee ruling.

An FBI file stated on December 24 that the *Cleveland Press*, as well as the *Plain Dealer* reported Brancato pinned his hopes to remain in the United States on an appeal in his deportation case filed yesterday with the U.S. Court of Appeals in Cincinnati.

It goes on to describe how his attorney, Henry Levine, filed papers challenging the ruling last October 11 by U.S District Judge Charles McNamee, who had upheld the deportation proceedings against his client.

The appeal involved legal questions never raised before in the courts. The chief legal question in this case involved interpretation of the laws as to whether Brancato was an Italian alien in the eyes of the law when he returned to the country in 1930 from a visit to Italy.

The report pointed out that Brancato had been found guilty of perjury, a deportable crime, two years later. Levine had always argued in the court proceedings unsuccessfully that Brancato was a naturalized American citizen when he returned from Italy. The government in 1939 denaturalized Brancato, charging he failed to produce credible character witnesses when he received his citizenship papers in 1929.

Chapter Seventeen

1956

O n February 15, the *Cleveland Press* ran an article that said: *The Immigration Service ... has tightened its nationwide rules as a direct result (of) the Brancato deportation disaster. Hereafter there will be a special agent examining officer assigned to all disputed cases. The Board of Immigration Appeals will require that they be provided with "all his records and information" and district directors and local agents in charge are to give close supervision to aliens subject to deportation.*

These new rules will be helpful, no doubt, in all future cases. The Brancato case mess-up would have never developed in the first place if all the Immigration Service employees involved had been on their toes.

This new set of rules and guidelines will entirely correct "The shocking inefficiency and unskilled performance by agents."

A congressional committee which investigated the Brancato case reported these mistakes it found in the Immigration Service. Meanwhile, Brancato is still in this country and fighting to stay here.

On February 26, all the Cleveland newspapers, as well as the FBI, documented a fire that took place at Captain Frank's Restaurant on East Ninth Street. The fire completely gutted the restaurant.

Frank Visconti said he planned to rebuild the restaurant. The restaurant would reopen one year later.

The *Cleveland News* ran an article about how the U.S. dealt with Salvatore Brancato, the younger brother of Frank, who came into America illegally several years ago after having spent fourteen years in prison in Sicily for a murder. He had been successfully deported the previous year.

This year the government dealt with the nephew of Frank

Brancato, Giuseppe Brancato, who is thirty-three years old. The lesser-known Brancato came into America illegally and entered into the country from Philadelphia in August of 1948 with his father from their hometown of Licata, Sicily. He was found working for a construction company in Parma and living in a rooming house on Kinsman Road and East 137th Street.

FBI files documented other legitimate businesses claimed by Brancato that were set forth in his testimony at the Immigration and Naturalization Service hearings in Chicago May 17.

The FBI files reported that on October 5, Brancato reported to the Los Angeles Police Department to register that he was in town visiting some friends. Los Angeles police files indicated that he was an ex-con. Brancato was photographed and fingerprinted before he left the police station.

On October 11, the FBI reported Brancato and Frank Visconti were observed by intelligence division officers, and were seen in the company of Nick Licata and Tom Dragna, who, according to the police, both ranked high up in the Los Angles Sicilian crime family and were on the list of the Who's Who among top Sicilian mobsters in America.

Visconti and Brancato were later brought in for questioning and denied any interest in organized crime. Frank Brancato told officers he was just in Los Angeles visiting friends.

When asked by FBI agents why they were in Los Angeles, Visconti said, "Frank (Brancato) and I came out because I wanted to get some fresh ideas on how to update and redecorate my new seafood house. I wanted to invest $100,000 in the near future, and do it in a new, unique motif." Visconti later admitted to agents he had once been arrested about twenty years earlier, and served time for a narcotics violation and for counterfeiting. Visconti told officers, however, "The counterfeiting connection was a fluke." He explained that he was paid off in counterfeit money that was in his possession and hence, the arrest and conviction was for counterfeiting.

Visconti complained mildly regarding the lack of entertainment and courtesies shown to him and Brancato by Nick Licata. "If Licata would have come to Cleveland, he and his guest would be treated like kings, and we would have even met them at the airport when they arrived."

According to an FBI source, the next day Brancato and Visconti visited the Casa Blanca Hotel in Hollywood on North Rossmore Street in Los Angeles. The hotel manager promptly called the police, who again made contact with both men. Brancato had $1,700 in his pocket, while Visconti had $800.

The manager and the police told both men that they were not welcome guests. The manager cautiously told them that the hotel had been taken over by a large hotel chain from New York, and they did not want and would not tolerate hoodlums as guests any longer.

FBI agents stated this lavish hotel had changed hands many times over the past few years and was always known as a mob hangout, and would be used for many meetings by nationally-known underworld figures.

While being detained in Los Angeles, the police had asked Brancato whether he knew of Anthony Brancato in Kansas City.

Brancato replied, "No, I do not know him… he is no relation to me."

NOTE: Anthony Brancato was killed in the well-known "two Tonys murder" several years earlier. Mobster Jimmy Fratianno had contacted Tony Brancato and Tony Trombino and asked to meet them about a proposed bank robbery in Hollywood. However, the real purpose of the meeting was to kill both men. On August 6, 1951, Brancato and Trombino were found shot to death in the front seat of a car near Hollywood Boulevard. Fratianno, Nick Licata, Charles "Charley Bats" Battagila, Angelo Polizzi, and Leo "Lips" Moceri were arrested for the crime. However, since Licata set up a phony alibi for everyone involved, no one was charged with the murder. The two Tonys murder would remain unsolved until Fratianno entered the federal Witness Protection Program over 25 years later and admitted to murdering the duo.

The *Cleveland Press* on November 27 reported:

The Justice Department will be asking to take the Brancato case to the U.S. Supreme Court for a decision by the U.S. Court of Appeals, which had earlier released Brancato from deportation.

Assistant U.S. Attorney Eben H. Cockley reported today he was requesting the appeal because "The Brancato decision has important implications of the deportation laws in our country, as was well as some constitutional issues that seriously need to be addressed."

Last week the U.S. Court of Appeals in Cincinnati, Ohio, reversed Judge McNamee in a 2-1 decision, arguing that the deportation of Brancato would be "a punishment falling into the criminal law category."

The Cleveland Plain Dealer on November 28 stated:

Frank Brancato, the sixty-year-old, was back to peddling tires at Cardinal Tire Company with a bounce in his step yesterday for the first time in five years, as the threat of deportation was lifted from his bald head.

Brancato was the winner in a very important court round last week when the U.S. Court of Appeals in Cincinnati rejected the legal theory behind several deportation actions against him.

When his defense attorney Henry Levine was asked "What is Brancato doing now?" his simple reply was, "He is selling tires, just as he has been for the last several years."

Government lawyers were debating whether to appeal the case in the U.S. Supreme Court, and whether they should challenge Judge Cockley's ruling to allow Brancato to go free.

1957

An FBI file dated February 26, 1957, stated that, according to an informant, Frank Brancato was a partner in the Fulton Fish Company in Cleveland. This company delivered fresh fish to grocery stores, bars and restaurants in the Cleveland area. The report also said that he was connected to Captain Frank's Seafood House, which had burned down the previous year, and they were planning to remodel. They believed that Brancato was the majority owner, along with his close friend Frank Visconti, who was a front man for Brancato. The Seafood House Restaurant was located behind the current Rock 'N' Roll Hall of Fame, where Voinovich Park is located.

The FBI file noted that on July 29, Brancato was picked up by the Cleveland Police Department for questioning in connection with a robbery that had taken place at East 157th and Kinsman. After a few hours of questioning Brancato was released, but before he left the precinct he was fingerprinted once again and they reshot his arrest photo and he was given a new Cleveland Police Department identification number of 90341.

150

The police also informed the FBI that records reflected Brancato was also arrested in July and that he was issued license plates for a 1957 Lincoln four-door sedan. They said the plates, LP 962, were not transferable to another vehicle in Ohio.

It was noted in the FBI file that Brancato was also known as "The Boss, Mr. B., or The Duke."

Early in November of 1957, Brancato advised the Cleveland FBI office that he was going to visit New York later in the month.

On November 14, 1957, expensive cars with license plates from around the country started rolling into the small town of Apalachin, New York.

The Apalachin Meeting was to have been a historic summit of the American Mafia at the home of mobster Joseph "Joe the Barber" Barbara.

The meeting was to have been attended by roughly one hundred Mafiosi from the United States, Canada, and Italy.

Local and state law enforcement officials, curious about the sudden influx of luxury cars, raided the meeting, causing Mafiosi to flee into the woods and the area surrounding the Barbara estate. More than sixty underworld bosses were detained and indicted, including Scalish and DeMarco.

Scalish had attended the meeting with his chief lieutenant, John DeMarco.

Weeks later, after the now-famous Apalachin meeting, a detailed investigation was conducted. The Albany, New York, FBI office reported that they were not able to locate Brancato at any hotel in the area or on the estate of Joseph Barbara, where the conference was to have taken place.

Scalish and DeMarco were convicted of refusing to testify to the Senate Rackets Committee about the conference. All the men stuck to the same story—that they were going to New York to see a sick friend. Joe Barbara Sr. Scalish had invoked his Fifth Amendment rights some thirty-five times before the hearing closed.

For a short while, Brancato took over the day-to-day operation of the Cleveland Mafia while Scalish and DeMarco were away in prison.

New York Judge Irving Kaufman's original decision had been hailed as a milestone in the war on organized crime. On November 29,

1960, the higher courts not only reversed the convictions but ordered that the charges against all the men be dismissed.

An FBI document in Brancato's file referenced a memo, dated November 27, to the New York Bureau and all field offices, with instructions concerning administration of the "Top Hoodlum Program." All federal offices across the country were instructed to forward photographs of the top hoodlums to the New York office. Since that time, the New York office had been forwarding information of these men. The purpose of this memo was to channelize photographs of the top hoodlums submitted by the New York Office into the individual case files. The photographs will be attached ... and filed in the individual case files. A copy of this memorandum will be filed as well, without indexing it. It was recommended that approval be granted for the preparation of two hundred fifty copies of this memo to be used in filing photographs of all top hoodlums.

At one of the many interviews the FBI had with Frank in downtown Cleveland during their own investigation into the famous Apalachin Meeting, Brancato was asked once again about why he did not attend the elite meeting in upper New York State.

Frank reached into his suit pocket and produced a memorial card in honor of his late brother-in-law, Batistsa Cracchhiolo, ths husband of his departed sister, Elena who had died in Rome. Soon after her death, Batista relocated to New York, but saddenly he abandoned his two children, leaving them in Rome. He died on November 16, 1957, at the age of fifty-eight, and the funeral services were held at the Andrew Torregrasso Funeral home in Brooklyn, New York. The Cleveland police did not know what to do. The story the FBI told them seemed to have been the truth. Brancato was not there to attend the Mafia meeting... or was he?

On December 6, the Cleveland FBI was notified by Frank Brancato that he was going to Florida for several weeks, and was planning on staying at least four weeks to avoid the cold winter weather in Ohio.

The FBI believed that he was going to Miami to visit his close friend Al Polizzi and would have the Miami FBI attach a detail to watch him closely.

The file also reported that Frank owned a two-story house on

Westview Avenue in Cleveland that had a full two-car garage and what looked like an apartment above the garage. The report stated he took possession of this house on November 10, 1950, after his daughter's wedding in September, when he claimed to have been broke.

The FBI report said Frank's son Nasher was still living above the garage in a completely furnished one-bedroom apartment. He was seen coming into the apartment after three in the morning and going out by seven in the evening over several months.

According to FBI files dated December 9, Assistant United States Attorney Russell E. Ake advised that no action was taken on the Court of Appeals decision and that the deportation case against Brancato was in a closed status.

On December 12, an INS agent informed the FBI in Cleveland, and made available the report with the interest to reopening the hearing in the matter of deportation proceedings against Brancato.

On December 19, FBI documents noted an Allegheny County detective and a detective from the Pittsburgh, Pennsylvania, made available to agents their records reflecting that Brancato had been picked up on May 28, 1945, with an unnamed man by one detective from Pittsburgh. Both men had large sums of money in their possession. Teletype messages sent to Akron and Cleveland disclosed that neither man had an outstanding warrant for their arrest. Both men had been released the next day with no charges being filed against them.

In an FBI file dated December 27, the Director of the FBI wrote a memo to all field offices asking for their personal attention to a four-page brief about Frank Brancato.

Your attention is directed to this letter to the Cleveland, New York, and Miami offices and a copy that is being furnished to your division. Brancato is the object of the Top Hoodlum Program that has been clearly outlined. It was emphatically stated that immediate and continuous investigative attention should be given to this matter looking toward establishing, through active investigation, the current activities of the Top Hoodlum Program in your division.

It is noted from the period the investigation commenced on December 5 and cut off on December 12, only six days were actually devoted to Brancato's case. From a review of the contents of this report, it would appear that most of the time spent was consumed by file reviews. It is not obvious, that this investigation was not immediately instituted after receipt of the above letter, nor was it continuous. This situation must be immediately corrected, and he is considered to be armed and dangerous.

An analysis of this report reflects it contains primarily information from your files and from information secured from the local police. It was particularly stressed in the above letters about the Top Hoodlum Program that these investigations should be designed to find out the business activities, both legal and illegal, of the top hoodlums in your area and to establish who were connected with them in those endeavors. You were also advised that a primary purpose of the Top Hoodlum Program is to develop any violations within the Bureau's jurisdiction, and to obtain complete and current intelligence information regarding the person under investigation. You should make sure that all agents in your office working the top hoodlum cases do not lose sight of the aims and purpose of this program.

In addition to the leads set out in the report, there are set forth hereafter some specific matters which should be resolved during the investigation of this subject.

The report reflects Brancato, of Italian birth, was naturalized on November 15, 1929; however, he was denaturalized on April 12, 1939. It is indicated that Brancato apparently filed an application for a writ of habeas corpus which was dismissed, resulting in an appeal to the U.S Circuit Court of Appeals. It appears that the appellate court ordered the case remanded, with instructions to enter a judgment sustain. The application for the writ and advised, no action has been taken by The Court of Appeals decision (is) that Brancato's case is closed. In view of this information, it cannot be determined whether Brancato is now a naturalized citizen or an alien. You should contact the U.S. Immigration and Naturalization Service or the U.S. Attorney and resolve this point.

His report contains an alphabetical list of past associates of Brancato, consisting of eleven pages. There is an additional two and a half-page list of recent associates.

As pointed out in the bulletin to New York dated November 27, 1957, every top hoodlum undoubtedly has subordinates who carry on legal and illegal operations under his direction. It is therefore necessary to fully identify and describe the activities of these persons. It was also pointed out that one top hoodlum will no doubt associate with other top hoodlums, both within your divisions and in other sections of the United States. It was stressed that the nature and extent of this association be fully investigated and reported.

In view of the above information, you should re-evaluate the list of associates set forth in the report, and establish which of those appearing on the list are actually connected with Brancato in his activities, and (learn) the nature and extent of their association. Full and complete identifying information must then be developed on all of the individuals. It is reflected in the report that Mr. and Mrs. Brancato rented an apartment at the Hotel Sovereign in Cleveland on April 4, 1957, for one month. Since the subject's wife is known to have died in September 1955, you should attempt to identify this woman.

Additional information appears in the report indicating controversy. An informant in 1953 stated the "boss of the Mafia in the Cleveland area is Scalish." This informant revealed, Scalish gives all the orders and makes all the final decisions for the syndicate operations in Cleveland. The report also stated that two other informants in 1954 and 1955 stated that Brancato was the "head of the Cleveland syndicate." Still another informant in 1954 described Brancato as the "number-one big time hoodlum" in Cleveland and DeMarco the "number-two big-time hoodlum."

As indicated above, Scalish was considered by many informants and the FBI in 1953, 1954, and 1955 as being the head of the Syndicate in the Ohio area.

It is obvious that ingenuity, initiative, good judgment and alertness will be necessary by all field agents in order to develop the information being sought by the Bureau in these investigations. For this reason, it is expected that you will continue to give this program your personal attention in order to assure that it is effectively administrated by all.

By the years end, Frank received notice once again that a younger sister Carmela died in Rome.

CHAPTER EIGHTEEN

1958

According to an FBI document dated January 1958, information was received from an agent that Brancato and two other Italian men made a trip to the state of New York the week of Thanksgiving 1957. The Albany field office was unable to verify Brancato's presence in Apalachin, New York, or surrounding areas on or about November 14, 1957. Brancato was now driving a 1958 red-and-white Lincoln Club Coupe which he purchased in Wheeling, West Virginia. Brancato appeared to have a financial interest in the Rivera Supper Club, located in Cleveland, Ohio and was reported to have interests in several other legitimate businesses in Cleveland.

In an FBI file dated January 3, a confidential informant advised that Brancato, Scalish, DeMarco, and others regularly met to play cards and gamble in a back room at LaMarca's barbershop on Kinsman, but the police had not been able to catch the men gambling. The informant also told them that he could not be sure, but in his opinion, these were local high-level meetings of the Italian hoodlum element.

The Michigan State Police reported on January 3 that Sam Finazzo had been arrested several times by Michigan State police for conspiracy to violate gambling laws. Sources said Finazzo had a long history and association with Italians in Detroit and other major cities, and was allegedly a member of a numbers gang. Finazzo had eighteen different arrests from 1934 until 1950. When asked by the police, he confirmed that he knew Frank Brancato.

According to an FBI file dated January 10, a reliable informant told them that he was not aware of any criminal activities that Brancato was engaged in at the present time. Brancato in the past had become wealthy through his gambling interests in Cleveland and in Akron, but there was currently no organized gambling going on, and in his opinion, Brancato was not active in Cleveland. The detective stated that he was not in a position to know whether Brancato had gambling interests outside the Cleveland area. To his knowledge, the only gambling that was going on in Cleveland was the numbers racket that organized by Shonder Birns, one of the top hoodlums in Cleveland, and a few black men within the black community, one man being Donald King, who was confirmed to be a major figure in the numbers racket. King stayed confined to the color element in the city, and he was not aware of Brancato being connected to or receiving any proceeds of these operations.

On January 22, the Cleveland FBI office contacted the Albany, New York office once again to see if they could determine whether Scalish, DeMarco, and Brancato stayed at a hotel in the area at the time of the Apalachin Summit around the time of November 14. After several interviews at several different hotels and motels in the area, they were able to find that Scalish was listed and identified as having stayed at the Parkway Motel in Vestal, New York, where he had made reservations for six people who occupied the other rooms, but none of the occupants in other rooms could positively identify Brancato. DeMarco was never identified as being at this motel, either. Brancato's 1957 auto was never found in the area.

On January 30, an informant told the Cleveland Third District Vice Squad and the FBI that Brancato had been seen with a well-known pimp and hoodlum. Brancato was the man in charge of the Cleveland prostitution ring, and that is why he had been seen at all the top strip clubs in downtown nightly, including Frolics Bar on Short Vincent Street, which he was believed to own with his good friend Angelo A. Lonardo, along with the Gay Nineties bar on Walnut Street.

Both of these joints had been known to use what is called "B-girls," better known as bottle girls or gold diggers. These were very attractive young women, dressed in very little clothing, who would entice men to buy them a drink. Unknown to the men, the drinks were at an inflated priced over what a regular bar would sell to a normal customer. The higher cost was just for their companionship and to enhance the bar's profits, and naturally, the girl's income. These women were also referred to as being "champagne hustlers."

Normally the women would only stay and talk to a man or a group of men as long as they would keep buying her a drink. Once he stopped or refused, she would get up from the table and thank the man for his company and move on to another man in the club who looked to be alone. One woman told the police it was not uncommon for her to have twenty-five to thirty shots of whiskey per night, and she went as high as fifty shots on one occasion. This same informant went on to tell the FBI that he had heard a rumor that Brancato had been thinking about investing large sums of money in the Seaway Bar on East 9th Street and St. Clair, and had been seen there quite often and late in the evenings.

In early February an unidentified female told the FBI Brancato frequented the nightclub scene in downtown area, where he was often seen with young women in their early twenties to their thirties. Brancato had been considered to be a so-called playboy by many of the girls. The informant said that he normally just sat at the bar, and drank his Scotch. He watched what was going on in the clubs at all times, and was a good tipper, and seemed to always have money in his pockets. For a man of his age he was good looking, only about five feet six inches tall, and in good physical shape. She said his light blue-grey eyes sparkle through his glasses and he had a real quality about him. She said he had a very nice smile that made the girls all feel very comfortable around him. The girls all seemed to enjoy being with Frank. She also observed him to be a fun-loving man and to be an immaculate dresser, with well-tailored, expensive-looking suits, and a beautiful large diamond pinky ring on his left hand. He enjoyed being seen with many of the young girls and often would take them to Captain Frank's Seafood House after the clubs closed down at two in the morning, for something to eat and drink, and he always paid the bill for them.

On February 17, the Cleveland FBI office requested a registration search from the Pennsylvania office for the license plate C 8939. The auto was seen in the vicinity of LaPuma Spumoni House while Brancato was inside the building.

The FBI in Pennsylvania reviewed the motor vehicle registration bulletin 14, which reflected that a 1957 Pennsylvania registration was issued to Joe Corbo, who was born in Italy in 1904 and was living in Allentown, PA. Joe operated the Corbo Fur Shop. FBI stated that further research was needed on Joseph Corbo, and his partner, listed as Sam Kaplan, to determine whether Brancato had connections with either man.

In February the FBI installed a two-way radio system to communicate with their home office. They also learned that it was very likely that Brancato was a major partner in a new gambling joint called the Riviera Supper Club on East 12th and Chester in downtown Cleveland. Brancato had been seen by FBI agents inside the club, where he was seating guests, answering the phone, and issuing orders to bartenders and waitresses. He also was seen going into the kitchen several times and seemed to be the man in charge, according to the FBI agents.

Captain Frank's restaurant on the north side of East 9th Street was still being remodeled after the fire. An FBI report said Frank Visconti was only a front man for the restaurant, and Brancato actually owned it. The restaurant was scheduled to reopen on February 21.

According to the FBI files dated February 12, records from their Detroit office were reviewed by agents regarding Samuel Salvatore Finazzo, born on November 14, 1907, in Partinico, Sicily. On June 20,1935, The Detroit *Daily News* reported that the Detroit Police Department conducted a raid on June 20 and found a blind pig operation, also called a speakeasy or an unlicensed saloon—an establishment that illegally sells alcoholic beverages. Police arrested Sam Finazzo. In the raid they seized whiskey, gin, and wine. Finazzo was also listed in the Federal Bureau book of narcotics.

FBI investigation into Finazzo's activities in Detroit showed he was arrested for narcotics and violation of gambling laws. He had a long police record dating from 1934-1950 and was a known associate of the Italian numbers gang and possibly with Pete Licavoli.

Agents also reported that Brancato had a major financial interest in the Riviera Restaurant on East 12th Street and he and Visconti were trying to sell it, since it was struggling.

During an interview with Sam Cardinal, the owner of Cardinal Tire on March 24, the FBI asked to see his accounting books regarding employee Frank Brancato. Sam got the books and showed him Brancato's Social Security Number and his pay, reflecting $65.63 per week gross. His take-home pay was $54.63. Cardinal told agents that Brancato was allowed $67.50 per month for car expenses. He said Brancato worked every day and spent most of his time making contacts and collections from company accounts that were delinquent in their payments.

Cardinal told agents that, to his knowledge, Brancato had no other income and no interest in the Rivera Restaurant, Captain Frank's Restaurant or in the Fulton Fish Market. Cardinal related that he has known Brancato all of his life and he was fifty-two. He suggested to Brancato to purchase the 1958 Lincoln he was currently driving to help promote tires for his business and that a big car would impress potential new clients. Cardinal was empathic in stating that Brancato had no financial interest in the Cardinal Tire Company, and he had not put up any money in the past or present with this business or to support it in any way.

~

On April 3, an FBI file reported, at approximately one in the afternoon, two agents went to Brancato's home on Westview Avenue and knocked on the door. His daughter Bella answered and let the agents into the house after they showed her their ID and had given her their names. She asked if they would mind sitting down in the living room while she went to get her father, who was taking a shower. Bella returned a few minutes later and told the men, "My father will be out shortly; can I get you a cup of coffee?"

Both agents accepted the offer and waited about fifteen minutes, until Frank showed up dressed in a nice navy blue suit and tie.

As both agents stood up, Brancato extended his hand and shook hands with both men. One of the unnamed agents in the report mentioned to Frank that they had to discuss a few items with him. Frank replied that he was about to go out for lunch, and how about they go out together? Both agents looked at one another and accepted his offer, and the three men were soon on their way to Captain Frank's (where Frank Brancato normally ate his lunch) on East Ninth Street in Brancato's new 1958 Cadillac.

During the luncheon, the agents made no attempt to question Brancato in public in any manner. Both men stated in their report that Brancato was very friendly and cordial to them. He showed them respect and spent a great deal of time telling them about his health, and in particular an eye condition in his left eye that was giving him considerable difficultly and that he has been taking treatments for it. Frank told them he had had a terrible trouble with gout lately, and was on a rigid diet and a few pills to help ease his pain. Brancato said his attorney, Henry Levine, informed him that he was only allowed to speak to a judge or the commissioners of a hearing, and no one else.

Brancato also said he would like his comments put out on television or radio at this time, if it was possible, because he wanted to declare to everyone that if he had muscled anybody and they had evidence to support such a contention, then they could hang him in

Public Square.

Brancato told the agents he had helped a lot of people, but mainly young men who had come out of prison who were referred to him by a mutual friend. He said he had helped these men secure jobs and had not had any of them turn bad. If they did, he would not hesitate to tell the employer to let the men go immediately.

After their luncheon, Brancato brought the agents back to his home on Westview. He casually mentioned that he had been given a few bottles of whiskey from friends and he could not drink it, since it was not Scotch, so it would destroy his stomach. He said he had no use for it, and offered the whiskey to the agents. Both agents looked at one another with a smile and graciously declined the offer, and then Brancato told them if they ever needed tires for their personal cars, to come and see him at Cardinal Tire Company, where he worked every day. Both agents shook hands with Brancato and left his home in their car.

On April 10, special agents from the FBI invited Brancato to meet with them at their office in downtown Cleveland. Brancato showed up as promised and stated that he would be perfectly willing to answer all questions. The FBI mentioned that he was there for an exploratory interview, and that other subsequent interviews were planned for later in the year, and that he was present that day to answer questions in regard to his income.

The agents asked about Captain Frank's Seafood Restaurant on East 9th Street. Brancato declared that he had no interest in that restaurant, and that he was only good friends with the owner, Frank Visconti. He said he had been offered an opportunity to invest a little bit of money in the first restaurant many years ago, and now with the new restaurant after the fire, but declined both offers.

FBI agents then asked about his partnership in the Captain Frank's shrimp business. Brancato told the men that this business was concerned with freezing fresh shrimp, then they would package it, and sell it around town to the bars, taverns and restaurants. He said the process was done at the Fulton Fish Market on Woodland Avenue. The partnership was later dissolved when the men found out there was not enough profit for all the partners.

Next the agents asked about the Fulton Fish Market on Woodland Avenue. Brancato's response was simply that the shrimp business was run out of the market, but he claimed he had no financial interest in the company.

Agents asked about the Riviera Restaurant on East 12th Street. Brancato told them that it was operated by Frank Visconti and his son-in-law, Frank Ferrara. He said the restaurant had been sold by Visconti and that Visconti had lost close to $60,000.

Regarding the LaPuma Spumoni Company, Frank told the agents that at that time he did not have any interest in the company. He said he had sold his shares in the business back to Mr. LaPuma several years earlier, when it was apparent that the business was not making a profit and "LaPuma needed the money more than I did."

Next was the Gay Nineties Club on Walnut Street in downtown, known as a hot club, where many men and women in high society would hang out late in the evenings and have some drinks. Many of the girls who danced and waitressed at the club were known to be prostitutes by the Cleveland Police Department. The FBI felt Frank was the head of the prostitution ring in Cleveland and they were trying to get enough evidence against him before they could arrest him. Frank's simple answer was that he had no current financial interest in any of the clubs.

Next he was questioned in regard to the Frolics Club. Frolics was just like the Gay Nineties Club, considered to be a hot spot in the Cleveland entertainment district as well. The FBI assumed Frank organized the girls from this club, as well as having a financial interest in the club business. Just as before, Frank declined having any financial interest in this club.

The FBI next asked about LaMarca Barber Shop on Kinsman. Brancato answer was he had no financial interest in the shop, but he did go there daily for a shave. He said he was not able to shave himself properly with either a straight or electric razor, and preferred to get his shave at the LaMarca brothers' shop.

Next he was questioned about the meeting in Apalachin, New York. Brancato answered that he had heard that such a meeting had taken place but he was unaware of the location of this town, and he absolutely did not attend the gathering. He recalled that he went to the home of his friend John DeMarco about the time of the alleged meeting had taken place, and when he asked his wife where John was she said she did not know. Brancato said he had been in Brooklyn, New York, attending the funeral of his brother-in-law, Batista Cracchioli, who had owned a fish store and lived on Union Avenue in downtown Brooklyn. He said this was the first time in many years that he had gone to see his sister Anntonetta and her family in New York.

Unkown to Frank, in Rome Angelina's husband Attilio Terraneo was a nasty and greedy man and would beat his wife quite often while their mother Ninfa was living with them. Frank continued to send plenty of money overseas to help support them and was so generous he specifically asked that the money was to buy an apartment for each and every one of his sibling; within the same block, so that they could all be together and near one another. The greedy Attilio demanded that Ninfa give him all the money attended for her children. Ninfa who was scared for the life and of her daughter Angelina, finaly gave in to keep the mean greedy man quite; and to keep him away from beating her young daughter. But when the money ran out he killed Angelina on June 13, 1959.

The FBI agents asked about John DeMarco and his relationship with him. Brancato mentioned that they were close. Frank told the agents he had asked DeMarco to go on a vacation with him several times and try to relax and get over his heart problems. DeMarco told Brancato that on the advice of his doctors, he was too sick to travel or take any type of vacation.

Agents then asked Frank if he had any hobbies. Frank replied he liked to play cards, particularity pinochle, and occasionally to shoot craps. He used to enjoy playing the horses, but he had run into some bad luck awhile back, and now he only went occasionally. When asked why, Brancato replied that he would bet big on long shots, hoping for a big payday that never happened. On one day he lost $8,500, and was in debt for a total of $10,000 to the track now. If he went to the track at all, he said, "Now I only stay at the $2 window."

At the conclusion of the meeting, Brancato declared that he would be happy to speak to agents at any time, and said if they ever had any questions on anything, that he would come in and talk to them directly and he would be happy to answer any and all questions.

According to the FBI, in the early morning of June 17, the New York police raided "Club 23," a well-known restaurant and bar in Brooklyn, New York. They had received information that a major mob meeting was being held at the club. They arrested eighteen men and women and found that they had one individual in custody who was listed on the Top Hoodlum list in Cleveland, that being Frank Brancato.

The New York police notified the local FBI agents in Cleveland of his arrest. Brancato stated his age as sixty and gave his address as 3320 Woodland Avenue in Cleveland. When asked by the police why he was in Brooklyn, Frank replied, "I have been up here visiting relatives and one evening my brother-in-law offered me the use of an invitation to the opening of a tavern restaurant which was given to him by an Italian friend. Since I had nothing better to do, I decided to attend the opening and then about 11:30 pm or so, five squad cars of New York City Police raided the place and removed everyone except the bartender." Then everyone walked over to the police station that was right across the street, where he said he was questioned and after being fingerprinted and photographed, he was.

The FBI showed Brancato's photo to some of the men who were arrested in the Club 23 raid. Many of the men thought it was Frank Brancato and some did say it was him. Then, when asked by the FBI if they would testify that they knew Brancato, the men quickly disclaimed any information and knowledge about Brancato, other than that he was from Cleveland, and they would not be willing to furnish any information to a law enforcement agency.

The Cleveland FBI office informed their director that they were currently watching the top hoodlums in Cleveland.

John T. Scalish was considered to be the principal figure among the top Italian hoodlums and was tied in with a number of the Italian hoodlums in other field divisions across the country; several of these men were considered to be top hoodlum figures in the other offices.

Frank Brancato at the present time is the subject of the Cleveland office's penetrating program into the upper echelon of the top hoodlums. He is very close to John Scalish and John DeMarco and has an extensive acquaintance with other top hoodlums that are Italians throughout the country. Frank Brancato is considered to be the number-two man in Cleveland, and their street boss.

John DeMarco was arrested for being one of the men who murdered Dr. Romano back on June 11, 1936, and is an important figure in the Italian criminal element. The other man is considered to be Angelo Lonardo, a cousin to DeMarco. He has suffered two major heart attacks, one in 1950 and the other in 1958. It has been learned from his physician that because of his two heart attacks, the next one could kill him. His activity has been considered curbed, but (he) is being retained as a top hoodlum. John DeMarco is considered to be John Scalish's consigliere.

Louis (Babe) Triscaro at the present time is a top official in Teamsters Union local in Cleveland and is believed to have an interest in the vending machine business in Cleveland with John Scalish. He has connections with other Teamster Unions throughout the county. Triscaro is known to be a close friend and known supporter of Jimmy Hoffa of Detroit, who heads up the International Teamsters' Union. He has worked with Jackie and William Presser in the past as well.

The other cases will now be placed in a pending inactive status. Alex (Shonder) Birns is well acquainted with the top hoodlums in many cities across the country and is known to have been associated with them in various activities. He is primarily interested in the local numbers rackets in Cleveland only and... no top hoodlums in Cleveland have been actively involved with him at this time. There is no present likelihood of his being involved in any violence within Bureau jurisdiction.

William Presser is very active in the Teamsters Union and their affairs have not been in (the) active hoodlum element except for his contact with Louis (Babe) Triscaro, who is an official in the Teamsters in Cleveland. It is considered essential in the view of the national prominence of the Teamsters Union in racket activities that this case be coincided in a pending status pending any additional information.

Joseph Jasper Aiello; who mostly has operated in Youngstown, is much less active in his criminal activities at the present time, and is just doing some small-time robberies. Excellent information coverage in local burglary and crimes within local and state jurisdiction rather than being a contact man for top hoodlum element.

During an interview with the FBI, Frank Brancato was asked if he knew Samuel Salvatore Finazzo. Brancato stated that he did not know Finazzo that well, and Finazzo was connected in some way with the prizefighting game. Brancato revealed that Finazzo's wife would often come to Cleveland and spend time with V, his wife, until she died. Brancato stated he had not seen Finazzo lately but added, if there is a big fight in town, Finazzo would always look him up.

On June 26, the *Cleveland Press* reported:

Police Chief Frank Story related "The police department will continue to arrest bookies. What happens after that is up to the

165

judges and the prosecutors. Cleveland is pretty clean of bookmakers right now, and (I) intend to keep it that way. However, Judge John E. Sweeney never convicts a bookmaker unless he pleads guilty. A suspended sentence in my mind means nothing, unless there is a real effort to reinstate it when another violation occurs. I plan on keeping track of Brancato's gambling activities, and will do whatever I can to control his gambling rackets."

Each Sunday morning for years, Scalish would gather with such men as Lonardo, Brancato and DeMarco at a barbershop on Kinsman Road. When that area started to change, the weekly conferences were switched to a barbershop in Lyndhurst, or one on Chagrin Boulevard near Scalish's Gates Mills home. In Scalish's final days in the early 1970s, the Sunday discussions were held only at a local barbershop on Mayfield Road in Mayfield Heights.

Just how much money was there to be made on the streets? The answer is complicated. If the entire top loan sharking, bookmaking, narcotics, prostitution, gambling and labor racketeering were organized in Cleveland, the possibilities would be limitless. But times have changed. The leading Cleveland underworld figures years ago are believed to have put the money they have earned from gambling casinos in Las Vegas to other legitimate interests.

An FBI case file dated July 9 from Pittsburgh was titled, "Sebastian John La Rocca (Anti –Racketeering Top Hoodlum Investigation)":

The Pittsburgh Post-Gazette dated June 30 carried an article captioned, "Cop Found Bomb at Villa-Rosa Restaurant." This article describes how a small black powder bomb was found near the Villa-Rosa Restaurant and Cocktail Lounge located on Robinson Street, Pittsburgh, shortly after city detectives were notified by telephone that the establishment was to be blown up "in ten minutes."

Newspaper accounts stated the fuse had been apparently lit and somehow gone out.

It was reported a top hoodlum in Cleveland, possibly Brancato or Shonder Birns who (is) a known close associate of Sebastian John La Rocca, could be involved in the bombing. This restaurant is a known hangout for La Rocca when he visits the Pittsburgh vicinity.

The owner and several of his brothers were once prominent in the numbers racket on Pittsburgh north side, but recently claimed that they no longer are engaged in any criminal activity. Regarding La Rocca, it is pointed out that he has been subject of a pending top hoodlum investigation since he was registered in a hotel in the immediate vicinity of the Apalachin meeting in New York State. At this time La Rocca was considered to be the "boss" of the Pittsburgh LCN (La Cosa Nostra).

Another man mentioned is Michael Genovese; an investigated by this office is under way to add him to the top hoodlum program.

An informant advised the FBI on October 17 that he had heard, not only does Brancato receive a take from barbut games in the city of Cleveland, but he had also heard that Brancato received a take from barbut games in Wheeling, West Virginia. (Barbut is a popular dice game.) It is noted that Brancato purchased his current Lincoln from Wheeling, WV. The same informant told agents that it was his understanding that Brancato did not at that time participate in any jobs pulled. Brancato did furnish the money which might be needed to pull a job, but in turn; he would receive a big kickback after the score was made.

An FBI informant stated in October that Brancato had been talking about recently getting a new automobile, a 1958 Lincoln, and all his automobiles were on a dealer plan. They were sold as demonstrator models, and he paid only a few hundred dollars per year to maintain the car. The source told agents Brancato gets his automobiles serviced at Hub Ford Company on Kinsman Avenue. The source informed agents he has heard Brancato may have a piece of this company as well.

A document from the Internal Revenue Service dated November 19 advised FBI agents that their organization had not taken any official action against Brancato as of that date, and the agency continued to maintain official interest in him. If the IRS received any information of a pertinent nature concerning his activity, they would be notified.

In one of their meetings with Brancato, the FBI said he informed them that he received a severe whiplash the day after Thanksgiving in his 1958 Lincoln. He was hit from behind by a City of Cleveland work truck. The entire left front fender of his car was smashed flat into the left front wheel. Brancato was taken to St. Alexis Hospital for immediate treatment of whiplash and continued to get severe headaches. He was planning on suing the City of Cleveland for his suffering. His attorney would be Herman Pressman and Gerald Gold, whose law firm was in the Hipp Building.

The *Cleveland Press* on December 2 ran a column written by Milt Widder.

> *(Frank) Brancato, man about town, was hospitalized for a day last week in St. Alexis Hospital after the city Ford vehicle hit his auto at Kinsman and East 39th Street. Brancato was treated for contusions on his right wrist. Case number 26113 and it noted that the driver was hospitalized and the accident was noted as serious.*

Brancato was going to turn his damaged vehicle in for a new 1959 olive green Lincoln from Halken Shaker Motors. After taking the car out of the showroom and driving the car for only twenty-seven miles from the Shaker Heights auto dealership to Captain Frank's Restaurant and back, Brancato returned the car because it did not have full six-way power seats which he had ordered. It also did not have magic eye headlamps that he desired. He decided on a new 1958 Cadillac instead.

Frank told the special agents that, in his opinion what the city of Cleveland really needed was two well-operated gambling houses on the order of the old Mounds Club, which he helped to operate, and served excellent food, had a fine floor show, a good live orchestra for dancing, and had an assortment of gambling tables. The Mounds Club catered only to the nicer crowd, and the people who had the money to try their luck. It was not the type of club that catered to a working man's entire salary, so that he would have nothing left to feed or clothe his wife and children. "In my opinion if Cleveland had two such clubs, one on the east side of town and the other on the west side of town, they would attract convention business, which would help the city to grow and prosper. Then the city could build a larger new convention hall and new, large hotels in downtown Cleveland."

Just a side note; in the year 2010, the State of Ohio voted and passed a bill that would now allow legalized gambling in four locations. One location would be in the downtown Cleveland area, near where a new extensive state-of-the-art Medical Mark Convention Center was currently being built. The casino site was expected to help bring in additional new medical conventions to the city of Cleveland.

Cleveland's new Horseshoe Casino opened on May 20, 2012. The Rock Ohio Caesar's Company announced that the old downtown Higbee Building would be converted for a temporary location for the Cleveland Caesar's Horseshoe Casino. The Higbee Building was originally constructed back in 1931, and is located on Public Square. It was featured in the Santa scene in the movie *A Christmas Story*. Officials estimate that the makeover of the first four floors for the casino would cost $350 million and would create over 1,500 casino jobs for the city. Upon completion, the casino was projected to attract over five million annual visitors. On May 29, 2012, the second Ohio Casino opened in Toledo, named the Hollywood Casino, which is also owned by Rock Ohio Company.

In July 2012 the Horseshoe Casino in Cleveland announced that in the first eleven days in May they had $15 million in gross revenue, and for the month of June they had $26 million in gross revenue.

In April of 2012 the Hard Rock International Corporation; announced plans to remodel and build a combination racetrack and restaurant "racino" complex with slot machine on the site of Thistledown Racetrack in Northfield, Ohio.

As you can see, the big corporations of today and our current government have learned well from the "old timers."

CHAPTER NINETEEN

1959

On January 20, the *Cleveland Plain Dealer* reported in an article by labor editor Anthony Mazzolini that several racket figures had refused to answer questions before a special Federal Grand Jury. The grand jury was probing allegations regarding Cleveland-area industrialists who complained they were being threatened with labor difficulties unless they paid protection money.

The racket figures mentioned in the article were Frank Brancato, who was believed to be leading the plot against these companies, along with John Scalish, and his brother Sam, along with DeMarco. Frank Visconti from Captain Frank's Restaurant was also subpoenaed to testify in court.

Brancato was the first witness on the stand, but he refused to tell the Federal Jury anything but his name and address. Brancato also stated he was confused as to why he was called to testify. He said he was working as a tire salesman for the Cardinal Tire Company, owned by Sam Cardinal, and he no longer had any income tax problems, and was not connected with any union.

John Scalish was ordered to bring financial records of his cigarette vending business. Men from the Teamsters Union were summoned to appear, including William Presser, President of Teamsters joint council 41, Louis "Babe" Triscaro, president of Teamsters Local 436, and John "Skip" Felice, resident of Teamsters Local 293. The article said it was well-known that these men's income tax matters had been under government scrutiny for some time. Brancato retained Henry Levine to represent him in the matter.

Assistant Attorney General Max H. Goldschein had taken action against these four men before a special Federal Grand Jury, which was probing accusations by an unnamed Cleveland industrialist. The man said he had been threatened with labor difficulties by the four men unless he paid them protection money up front. The attorney for the four men was Henry Levine. Levine stated that his clients would not answer any of these "ridiculous questions," and they would use their constitutional right to plead the Fifth Amendment. There was no immediate indication what the reaction of the Justice Department would be to their refusals to testify.

The government was considering asking the U.S. District Judge James C. Connell to disqualify himself from the hearings, which were set to begin in his court on January 22. Connell was considered to be a top criminal lawyer in the past. The article related that several motions to quash subpoenas of witnesses who had been asked to produce all their records in court would be before the court at that time. It stated that many years ago, Judge James Connell successfully represented Brancato in a murder charge. Brancato was later acquitted of the murder and now might be under contempt of court for failure to talk to authorities.

On January 23 the Cleveland Police Department informed the FBI that there was very little information concerning Mike Sperrazzo in their file, only that he was picked up for questioning on Kinsman Road in 1945, and he was possibly working with Brancato. Agents noted they had no concrete information relating Sperrazzo running an illegal barbut joint on Bolivar Road. He was known as "Barbut Ralph."

A confidential source informed the FBI on January 27 that there was a new location of the barbut game, behind the Ohio Bell Telephone Company building on Huron Road. It was believed to be in an upstairs room. Brancato got a cut out of this game.

The source said Brancato drove a new 1959 green Lincoln sedan. Brancato had even tried to sell him tires and told him to come to the Cardinal Tire Company and he would get him a great deal on a set of tires. Brancato sounded to be very sincere in this sales pitch.

On February 26 a source informed the FBI that he had not seen or heard that much lately about Scalish, Brancato, DeMarco or Babe Triscaro. The informant believed the men were out of town at the wake for Joe Amato, who was eighty-three. The source also said he still had heard that Scalish was the top man among the Italian hoodlums, and Brancato still supplied the muscle whenever needed.

In February, Brancato informed the FBI that he and his good friend Sam Cardinal planned on leaving Cleveland once again, and would be going on a month-long vacation to Hot Springs, Arkansas.

On their way to Hot Springs, the men decided to drive to Mesa, Arizona, instead, and spent several days there in the baths that they had heard so much about. They then made their way up to Hot Springs before returning to Cleveland.

The file said the two men had enjoyed going there for the past several years, and that it was known to local police as a meeting place for several crime figures. Along with its famous Bathhouse Row, one of downtown Hot Springs' most noted landmarks was the Arlington Hotel, a known favored retreat for Al Capone.

Brancato told them that after he made his appearance before the grand jury, he and Cardinal should be back in town by March 1. They would be driving down in his 1958 cream-colored Cadillac and would be staying at a hotel on Prospect Street. Agents strongly believed Brancato wanted to see Owney Madden. Madden, who was originally from New York City, was a known criminal in Manhattan during prohibition, and also ran the famous Cotton Club in New York, and was a leading boxing promoter in the 1930s.

An FBI document from the Director of the FBI, J. Edgar Hoover, to the Little Rock, Arkansas, office, dated February 10, said:

Cardinal and Brancato (a top hoodlum of Cleveland) departed for Hot Springs on January 28. You should arrange thorough your informants and sources to establish coverage of Brancato's activities during his visits, particularly with reference to his contacts, who may be other hoodlums residing in or visiting Hot Springs. Keep Cleveland and the Bureau advised of any developments.

Years earlier Hot Springs had become a national gambling mecca, led by Owney Madden and his Hotel Arkansas casino. The period 1927-1947 was its wagering pinnacle, with no fewer than ten major casinos and numerous smaller houses running wide open, and known as the largest operation in the United States at the time. Hotels advertised the availability of prostitutes, and off-track booking was available for virtually any horse race in North America.

On April 3 FBI Agents stopped Brancato while he was at the Ascot Park Race Track and questioned him briefly concerning his recent trip to Hot Springs, Arkansas, with Sam Cardinal. Although obviously in a hurry, Brancato told agents that their trip and stay at Hot Springs was uneventful; in fact he said the weather was a little too cold. Brancato said he would be glad to discuss his trip in details with agents at a later date.

In June, while interviewing Brancato, FBI agents were discussing restaurants that have good food. Brancato told agents that when they are in Pittsburgh, Pennsylvania, they should eat at Villa-Rosa Restaurant on Robinson Street. Brancato even told agents to mention his name "and you will be taken care of very nicely." Also in the interview, Brancato mentioned that his sister in Italy had died some two or three weeks ago, and that he has not seen her since she was thirteen years old, and because of his alien status he was not able to go to her funeral.

The FBI received information once again concerning the alleged connection of Brancato with the operation of barbut games on the Bolivar Road area of Cleveland. It was suggested that Brancato received a weekly payment from the operators of these games. It was pointed out to agents that Barbut Ralph was in fact Michael Sperrazzo of Shaker Heights, who was the leading operator of barbut games in Cleveland.

On July 10, an informant told FBI agents Brancato had a "good thing" in connection with his dealings with Cardinal Tire Company. He told agents that as a result of Brancato's association with Babe and Joe Triscaro, the two men could send any amount of Teamster Union business to the tire company; Brancato would then always get his cut. The informant told agents that Brancato belonged to the Social Beneficial Lodge, a.k.a. St. Angelo of Licata. The source said all the members of this lodge originated from Licata, Sicily, and that DeMarco was also a member. Their meetings were the fourth Sunday of the month at Biondo's Funeral Home from 10:00 p.m. until 11:00 p.m.

According to the FBI file, Frank was interviewed on September 30, and was asked about Scalish and Visconti.

Brancato answered, "Frank V. built a lavish home in Pepper Pike and has received considerable unfavorable publicity, particularly in the local press. Because of this press, Scalsih was thinking of selling his lot, and not building a home at this time."

On October 2 the FBI received information from an IRS agent that they, along with other government organizations, were still interested in Brancato's activities, but at that time there was no positive action as to his actual financial status or his activities

On October 7 the FBI learned from an informant Brancato was still on the streets of Cleveland, even though he had no direct contact with him. He felt certain Brancato had a strong connection with the Italian hoodlum element in Cleveland, and he had always been a "power amongst the Italian boys" on Mayfield Road.

An informant told FBI agents on October 14 that Brancato and DeMarco were observed together on October 13 at the wake for Tommaso "Tom" Mangione at Biondo's Funeral Home. The informant told agents that, to his knowledge, Mangione had never been in the rackets, but was a member of the Society of Licata, the home town where Brancato and DeMarco were born in Sicily.

A *Plain Dealer* article on October 20 by J.C Dasohbach discussed the possibility that four witnesses would be called before the Federal Grand Jury and cited for contempt of court. Mentioned in the article were John and Sam Scalish, John DeMarco and Frank Brancato. All refused to answer questions put to them by Max H. Goldschein, attorney in the criminal division of the Department of Justice. Goldschein came to Washington to question these men in the grand jury investigation into labor union leaders and activities of vending machine operators.

The Scalish brothers are partners in the Buckeye Cigarette Service. Brancato is a known Prohibition gangster, and John DeMarco allegedly was at the Apalachin, N.Y., meeting in 1957. Attorney Henry Levine is representing DeMarco and Brancato and was informed that his clients would have to testify in front of Goldschein or they would be taken before the court. All four men have refused to answer all questions about their activities.

On October 26 the New York bureau of the FBI reported they had received information from a legal phone wiretap on Brancato's Ohio home phone number (WYoming1-9475) that Brancato was planning a trip to Las Vegas. The Salt Lake City FBI Bureau informed the Cleveland FBI office on December 27 that they would keep track of Brancato while he was in Las Vegas, and they would try to determine the length of stay at the Desert Inn, where he was registered.

On October 29 the Cleveland *News* reported DeMarco had suffered yet another heart attack in New York City. This was brought to the attention of the U.S District Judge. The conspiracy trial against the twenty-three Apalachin meeting attendees was about to start, so the judge shortly thereafter granted a separate trail for DeMarco, but the date had not been set.

An FBI file dated October 30· stated the *Cleveland Press* reported on the death of Frank Brancato's onetime gambling partner, Michael

174

Sperrazzo. Sperrazzo was killed in his own driveway at 5:20 that day. The local FBI office in Cleveland believed that the two men ran an illegal operation called barbut, a Greek dice game. Sperrazzo would often take bets on race horses as well.

The article said Sperrazzo was shot once in the stomach, and then apparently he was wrestled to the ground. The gunman then held down Sperrazzo with one foot on his chest, and then shot him twice again in his head.

The article stated Sperrazzo was a known gambler; although he claimed he was a partner in the Atlas Employment Agency. He had been a prime suspect in the shotgun murder of his brother-in-law, Angelo Graziano, nine years earlier. Graziano was ambushed by a man with a shotgun near Superior Avenue. The Graziano murder was never solved.

The informant also told agents that about three months earlier, Brancato had attended the funeral of a friend of his, Bob Guciardo.

On November 2, the Shaker Heights police informed the Cleveland FBI that they had interviewed John Fotopoulos, a.k.a. John Fotos. Fotos stated that he was a partner with Mike Sperrazzo (AKA: Barbut Ralph) in the Atlas Employment Services. Fotos told police that Mike came to him a couple of years ago looking for a partner to get into business with him. Mike told Fotos to bring in some new business and he would accept him. He did so, and they became partners in this firm, which hired out common labor to businesses.

In December, Frank Brancato, along with his new partner, Joseph Licata, purchased an old bar and renamed it the Seaway Club at 2525 Superior Avenue in the heart of downtown Cleveland. Licata was the brother of his daughter–in-law Dolly. After a legal battle with city officials for several weeks about certain building permits dealing with structural issues, the remodel of the location went on, and by December of 1959 the new place was open for business. The men spent over $5,000 remodeling and updating the building.

The men enjoyed a very busy holiday season, with friends and customers coming into their club and enjoying the background music, featuring records by Frank Sinatra, Dean Martin, Elvis Presley, Perry Como, and many other popular entertainers of that year. The waitresses were all dresses in skimpy servers' outfits to give the club a strip-club atmosphere, and the place was well-decorated to give the joint a classy look. The ladies worked hard to earn their tips. The club needed to look great to attract showgirls when they got off work at 2 in the morning.

The high spenders in Cleveland would enjoy having a great time with showgirls, as well as being seen at the new club.

On December 18, John Scalish was convicted in U.S District Court for conspiracy to obstruct justice, and was sentenced to five years in prison and fined $10,000 for his part in the 1957 Apalachin meeting. This ruling would soon be overturned on appeal.

In late 1959 Frank was using a little-known Irishman named Danny Greene as his personal bodyguard and driver when needed. Greene would often use other ethnic Irish gangsters to act as errand boys and muscle to enforce the Mafia's influence around the city of Cleveland during the 1960s over the garbage-hauling contracts as well as other Mob-influenced rackets.

Greene seemed to enjoy fighting and showed off his talents often in bars and on the street. After seeing Greene in action one night at Frolics Bar, Frank believed Greene could be very useful in helping him to retrieve debts that were owed to him from gamblers who could not or would not pay back their debts.

Years later, Greene started working for the Cleveland Solid Waste Trade Guild, where he was hired to keep the peace. Impressed with his abilities, mobster Alex Shonder Birns would later hire him as an enforcer for his various numbers operators.

Brancato learned to regret his decision to bring Danny Greene into the Cleveland mob by the late 1960s. Greene's history has been well-documented by Cleveland author Rick Porrello in the book *To Kill the Irishman*. The book became a popular movie that was released in March of 2011.

CHAPTER TWENTY

Bottle Clubs

1960

O n January 14, the *Cleveland News* reported that twenty of the Apalachin delegates had been convicted in Federal Court, New York City, on December 18, 1959, of conspiracy to obstruct justice. Later in the year, on November 28, 1960, the *Cleveland Press* reported the U. S. Court of Appeals in New York had overturned the conviction of the twenty men who were alleged leaders of a so-called nationwide crime syndicate.

According to FBI files, the "Seaway Bottle Club," owned by Frank Brancato, was raided by the Cleveland Police Department in the early-morning hours of Sunday, January 24.

A "bottle club" is a bar where guests would have to pay $5 to $6 to become a member. Then they would bring in their own bottles of whiskey, which would be locked in a storage locker, ready for their next visit to the club. Their guest could also request that the club buy their liquor, and then store it for them in their personal locker. Individual drinks could not be sold without a costly liquor license, but guests or club members could bring in their own bottle of whiskey.

Members of the Cleveland Police Vice Squad spoke with Brancato while he was in custody about these clubs. Although there is a question concerning the law governing bottle clubs at this time, there is no ruling which requires such clubs to have a liquor license to operate. This question is currently in front of the local Cleveland prosecutor for his review.

In their investigation of the remodeling work that was completed on the club, they found a large two-way glass or mirror that measured six inches by six inches located in the upper part of the white front door.

On Saturday, the day before the raid, the Cleveland Press

reported that the city officials, state liquor agents, and the police asked the owners of the plush club to vacate the premises.

The police accused Brancato of being the backer of the club. Brancato denied the allegation and explained, "There is nothing on paper anywhere that would connect me with this place." Brancato then told police, "If they thought the place was mine, then they had his permission to go through the house and wreck it"—which they did not do.

Police officials said two club officials are related to a well-known hoodlum. One man was Frank Brancato's son, Joseph Brancato, and the other was Joseph Licata, who were both plumbers by trade. Joe Brancato was the president and Licata was listed as the secretary.

Frank Brancato told police "he was advised by the lawyer who drew up the club papers that this club was perfectly legitimate, as has been the case with other such clubs presently in operation in the City of Cleveland."

In their investigation, the city building inspectors found that the heating, electrical and plumbing permits had not been properly obtained. The building also had a lack of proper exits, a faulty chimney, improper wiring and storage of combustible materials.

It was noted in the FBI file that Brancato was seen leaving the club in the early morning hours. According to their file, he was a Prohibition-era hoodlum with a long police record. When entering the club, the police found a hat check girl, a barmaid, a host, and bartender who were relatives of Brancato (his son Nasher and son-in-law John, Ninfa's husband). That pointed them to the strong possibility that Brancato was a major sponsor of the operation known as the Seaway Social Club.

In the Salt Lake City, FBI office agents received "reliable information from an informant" in Las Vegas on February 12. A female clerk informed them on February 9 that she was unable to locate a record of Frank Brancato, who was to have been registered at Wilbur Clark's Desert Inn Hotel in Las Vegas. She was not able to locate or copy a voucher or a registration card that Mr. Brancato… registered at the hotel from November till December of 1959. The FBI also did an alphabetical checklist of guests daily who had used the hotel for the same period of time, and found no record of Brancato staying at the hotel.

Even before Brancato's Seaway Bottle Club could open for business on a full time basis, he was told he could not operate his club after the building inspector's condemned the building for "being badly decayed"

After doing some major alterations to the Seaway Social Club, before all the proper city permits were issued on February 18.

That evening, a fire destroyed most of the club.

Luckily, no one was in the club at the time when the fire broke out. There was, however, a family of five living next door. Moss and Rose Williams, along with their children, who were seven, five, and twenty months old, were watching TV. The police and firefighters had to go into their home and save them from the blaze.

The newspaper told its readers that locker clubs do not need state licenses, and are exempt from state inspection. For this reason, the police were opposed to locker clubs.

It was the second time in a month that the Seaway Club was condemned by the city building department.

The *Cleveland Plain Dealer* reported on February 19 that Frank Brancato was working on reopening his club. Brancato was a known club member and his son Joe was to have been the owner of the club. The news story said the city building division aides reported that the Building Standards Division had overruled the inspector's original recommendation and Okayed the building for use as a club.

"The Seaway Social Club," located on 2525 Superior Ave., was shut down in January after the police and state liquor agents questioned Joseph Brancato and Joseph Licata, who are listed as president and secretary of the Seaway Club. The actual use of the building was for a home office, shops, a warehouse and a club.

The owner of the building, Irwin Greene, was given permission and permits to repair the building.

The nightclubs, or bottle clubs, are places where customers would bring in their own bottle of whiskey or beer, and there would hold it in a locker for the customer. This practice made good sense to many customers. "BYOB" is an acronym most commonly meant to stand for "bring your own bottle," "bring your own booze," or "bring your own beer." BYOB is often placed on an invitation to indicate that the host will not be providing alcohol, and that guests are welcome to bring their own. It is also frequently used by regular bars, restaurants, or strip clubs which do not have licenses to serve liquor or alcoholic beverages in general. In some jurisdictions, licenses for strip clubs and liquor licenses are mutually exclusive.

Another article in the *Plain Dealer* dated February 19, written by Fred Mollenkoff, reported:

The Superior Avenue Seaway Locker Club that Brancato owns and where his son Joe is listed as the president will be able to operate, despite serious building code violations.

There were very strong recommendations against the club operating by the city building inspectors. Harry J. Fransen, secretary of the board, flatly denied the allegations "The board's order was only that the building could be used for its original purpose, if the owners complied with building laws."

On Monday, February 20, the *Cleveland Plain Dealer* had an article written by Fred Mollenkopf, which said:

A member of the building department, William Gulton, and the secretary of the Board of Building Standards consistently passed the buck yesterday on who authorized the Seaway Club to operate if it complied with building laws.

Gulton's department has granted a permit to Irwin Greene, the owner of the building, to change it into a private club. Greene is known as a former member of the Zoning Board of Appeals to the Building Standards Board. The report found a permit issued on Thursday, several days before this announcement came to the public's knowledge.

One of the inspectors, John Drees, who inspected the damaged building, called it "a hazard to life and limb."

Inspectors looked over the club in January after police and state liquor agents discovered the plush interior. They questioned Joe Brancato, who was listed as the president, and Joe Licata, listed as vice president. Police noted, "The two club officials are related to a well-known hoodlum."

The building inspectors found heating, electrical, and plumbing permits were not obtained, as well as a lack of proper exits, and improper wiring and storage of combustibles.

On Sunday, February 21, the *Cleveland Plain Dealer* reported:

Two Cleveland Councilman; called the Seaway Club a threat to the entire city.

The club will be able to operate until the Building Commissioner and the councilmen bring this matter up with cities Chief Counsel Joseph H. Crowley.

The owner of the building was Irwin Greene, who was formerly a member of the Cleveland Zoning Board of building standards, (which) would oversee appeals for building violation.

One of the councilmen is listed as Wilson Latkovic. ... The Seaway Club is inside his ward. The other councilman is Leo Jackson. He was quoted as saying, "The bottle club takes away all control over illegal liquor activity."

Both councilmen reported that they have had calls asking what effect on the neighborhood and on the city itself this kind of club will have.

Jackson responded, the handling of the Seaway Club building permits violation was a familiar story in which there is confusion in interpreting the building code laws to suit individual cases. "The locker clubs take away all control over illicit liquor activities."

The *Cleveland Press* reported on February 25, 1960:

Damages caused by a fire hit a newly remodeled bottle liquor club of Frank Brancato, Joe Brancato and Joseph Licata.

The FBI speculation is that Licata is possibly the nephew of the Los Angeles criminal boss, Nick Licata, since both men are from Brooklyn.

The story said firemen had to break a padlocked door to get into the smoldering blaze in the rear of the Seaway Club.

The article said when Brancato got on the scene, he was overheard saying, "We just got our permits, and now we have to start all over again."

The fire started about 10:10 p.m. in a shed wall near a heater, spreading up to a second-story roof.

After the fire was extinguished, Battalion Chief John Sammon ruled out the possibility of arson.

Cleveland Law Director Ralph Locher said he thinks the Legislation Service Commission should look into the liquor club problems that are taking root here and all over the state. Locher also reported that he felt that this would be the best first step toward getting state legislation that would cover locker clubs.

On February 26, The *Cleveland Plain Dealer* had an article written by Fred Mollenkopf which said the Seaway Club building had been condemned for the second time in one month, due to structural damages. ... All permits allowing the building to be remodeled or fixed were revoked.

According to the fire Chief John Salmmon, the fire definitely started in a rear room under a water heater, and it apparently was going for some time until it went up a rear wall, (and) up through the second floor, where it damaged the rafters and the roof.

The building inspectors discovered that the work had been done without permits.

The Board of Building Standards is looking to condemn the building.

Cleveland police were relieved to hear the club could not be reopened. They were alarmed to hear Brancato was the operator of this club. Locker clubs require no liquor license and are not subject to a state inspection. The Seaway club would never reopen.

The FBI continued to make semiannual inquiries into Brancato's banking history, to determine how much money he had in accounts and what he owed to financial institutions. They would log them into his history and background information to keep track of his financial picture. At no one time for over fifteen years did Brancato have over $4,000 in assets in any bank in Cleveland. His automobiles over the years were all leased, and he never owned one of them outright. He would always put a small down payment, from $500 to $2,000 at the most.

They were possibly looking for a reason to deport him or charge him with income tax evasion, like so many others in organized crime had been. The banks were listed as the Shaker Savings Association, The Cleveland Trust Company, GMC Financial, National City Bank and the Cleveland Retail Credit Men's Company. They also found that he only held one life insurance policy, for $1,000, with the Metropolitan Life

Insurance Company.

Brancato was stopped driving his vehicle on May 4 by Cleveland police. Inside his 1959 Lincoln Continental with him were three men who residents of Detroit, all of whom were described by Detroit police as belonging in the hoodlum category. Police denoted on the report that Brancato should be considered armed and dangerous.

A source informed the FBI in May in regard to the funeral of Thomas E. Gerak Sr. at Hopko Funeral Home, which took place on March 25. The source told agents Gerak was in apparent good health but was quite a carouser, and "lived it up to the hilt." He was believed to have an association with Brancato.

Gerak had been sitting at his kitchen table, drinking a cola, when he suddenly keeled over and died almost instantly. Tom Sr. was a well-known fence among the criminal element in Cleveland. Gerak's father was Charles, and had been in the rackets for a number of years, and had always been known as a "slugger" in the old days.

An informant told agents that he believed Babe Triscaro was a longtime hoodlum, fence and racketeer and a "labor slugger" in his own right. The informant told agents that he believed Triscaro was a "messenger or errand boy" for the Cleveland group in Las Vegas, and had made several trips throughout the United States and into Mexico, possibly to see Frank Milano for them.

On July 14 a source told the Cleveland office of the FBI that Frank Brancato had attended a stag party at the Quad Hall Hotel the previous week. Brancato was responsible for bringing in seven Canadian exotic dancers who were hired to do the entertaining for the evening, and the girls were available for "tricks." The young, attractive girls would strip down to their bras and G-string. The event was held in the dining room in the rear of the building, and that there was plenty of muscle in the area to protect the two hundred guests, who were mostly men, but there were several women in attendance who enjoyed the show.

Later, guests were invited to go up to the mezzanine for a craps game or they could go up to room 418 for a large-stakes craps game, where the informant was told the pots could get upwards of $10,000 or more at one time.

The source also told them Frank Visconti was attending this

affair, and had opened up another seafood restaurant at 79th and Causeway in Miami, Florida. Sam Cardinal was also in attendance for this affair.

On September 8, FBI agents reported Frank Brancato was seen in a heated argument with Shonder Birns, a known numbers man in Cleveland, at the Frolics Lounge on Vincent Street at 10:52 in the morning. The agent went said he could not determine what their argument was about, but both men were very angry with one another. The heated discussion lasted about twenty minutes before Brancato got up and left.

On September 19, the *Cleveland Press* and the *Cleveland Plain Dealer* reported an attempt had been made to organize the hospital employees in Cleveland with the incorporation of a new union. Papers were filed by attorney Henry Levine. Hospital Workers Local 500 was targeting Saint Luke's and Huron Road Hospitals. The purpose of the union was to organize about 115 of the non-professional employees of hospitals, convalescent homes, and sanitariums. They were, signing up orderlies, housekeeping, and nurse's aides in Cuyahoga County. The men starting this union were listed as Ignatius (Nasher) Brancato, a bartender (Frank Brancato's son), and Angelo Amato Jr., who was employed at an Eastside factory, and Sam J. Veechio, who was named as the secretary of the new union. None of the three men had any union background or an education in union affairs.

The AFL-CIO regional office said they had not been contacted yet by either man to start this union. The FBI became interested in his report, since they were not sure whether Frank Brancato would become a part of this union organization.

Another informant told agents Brancato told his son to sever any connection with this union, which filed and received a state charter to operate a non-profit organization in September.

A confidential informant told FBI agents that an unknown bookmaker who books horse and would not be considered to be a big-time bookmaker, was causing some concerns in other bookmaker circles because he had been reportedly turning over some of his slow accounts for collection to Brancato. In the past 3-4 weeks Brancato had been seen several times at the Sahara Motor Hotel on Euclid Avenue with John Scalish's brother-in-law, Angelo Lonardo. The club was becoming a hangout for some of the higher echelon Italian hoodlum element.

A *Plain Dealer* article on October 21 reported:

Three officials of the hospital union that conducted a strike at Huron Road hospital were jailed last night as the police sought a solution to the two eastside bombings. Held for questioning at city jail were Angleo Amato Jr., Sam Vecchio, and Walter Marinelli.

Inspector Richard Wagner, detective chief said, "The men will be held for questioning while their alibis for the time of the bombings are checked out."

On October 30, Frank's good friend John DeMarco suffered yet another heart attack and was taken from his Shaker Heights home to Mt. Sinai Hospital in Cleveland, where he was confined.

CHAPTER TWENTY-ONE

1961

According to the *Cleveland Press*, on January 31, 1961, Brancato's new Seaway Bar on East 9th Street and St. Clair lost their liquor license for twenty-eight days after the club's manager, Nick Zate, who was drunk, started to threaten customers with two pistols and was selling liquor between the hours of 1 a.m. and 5:30 a.m., in clear violation of the Ohio liquor laws. It was the third violation for the Seaway Bar, the first being in October 1959, and the second on May 7, 1960.

The FBI documented that during January and February of 1961, Frank Brancato visited the West Coast to see some of his old and dear friends, Nick Licata, Tony Milano, and Tom Dragna. Frank once again went with his close friend Sam Cardinal. The visit was for the wedding of Sam's niece in Los Angles. They visited Los Angeles, San Diego, and San Francisco and planned to end their trip in Las Vegas, staying at the Desert Inn Hotel for several days. The two friends then made plans to stop in Mesa, Arizona, or Hot Springs, Arkansas, on their way back to Cleveland, as they did yearly, but on their way home they hit several rough storms and decided to skip Hot Springs and drive straight back. They arrived in Cleveland on February 20. The Cleveland FBI believed, but could not prove at this time, that Brancato had to check on the Cleveland Syndicate's investments in these cities and possibly do some additional business for Scalish.

The FBI continued with their extensive file on Brancato, updating it quarterly. He still had his every-Sunday-morning meeting at either the Damante's barber shop on Chagrin Boulevard or at LaMarca's barbershop on Kinsman.

My cousin Dorothy told me she and her sister Virginia would often go with our grandfather on these Sunday-morning meetings. They would stop at LaPuma Bakery and pick up cookies and Italian pastries and then visit several relatives after the meeting. Dorothy would often stay in the front of the barber shop while the men went into the back for some time. She recalls how she enjoyed and relished the time she spent with our grandfather.

The Cleveland FBI had filed several petitions with the court to get approval to place an undercover microphone in the barber shops so they could hear the conversations that Brancato, Scalish, and DeMarco had weekly. They must have had trouble getting these warrants, since the FBI records never disclosed any wiretaps, warrants, or any recordings of their conversations. It is speculated that every time their request was made, it must have been denied by a different federal judge.

The shops were of a public domain and not unlawful establishments where illegal operations or drug trafficking were taking place. If the FBI could have shown just cause that this was taking place, the courts would have been happy to give them their warrant. Frustrated, the FBI could only watch and observe the weekly Sunday-morning meetings from a distance in their parked cars.

On weekday evenings, Frank Brancato was seen almost nightly visiting the Blue Grass Lounge and the Royal Oak Motel, both located in Maple Heights. Then he would often hit the downtown clubs—Frolics, owned by Lonardo, and Mickey's Lounge. Both were known strip clubs.

Frank was known as a very good tipper to the waitresses. With a $20 bar bill, he would often give the waitress a $5 or $10 tip. He always got the best service from the girls and the bartenders in the bars that he would visit.

When the clubs would close down, he would finish his night at Captain Frank's Seafood Restaurant. Often he would be seen going with two to three attractive young girls from the clubs on his arm. They would sit and have a late-night dinner until around 3:00 or 4:00 in the morning. Some of the time they left by themselves, but many times Frank left with one of the attractive young women.

The *Cleveland Plain Dealer* reported on March 14:

The Cleveland City Council has given the green light for the sale of liquor at Captain Frank's Seafood House on the north coast. This will be the first time in eight years of business, since May 5, 1955, when the restaurant caught fire and was partially destroyed. It was rebuilt, but Frank Visconti lost his liquor permit.

Visconti, the so-called owner of the seafood house, has finally been able to surmount this major hurdle, but still has to obtain a liquor permit from the State of Ohio.

The vote was taken during the evening session of the city council and was supported by all except one member of council.

Visconti told the newspaper that he has the $15,000 that is being held in escrow for the liquor permit and is just waiting for approval from the State Liquor Department. Once he is given his permit, he is considering spending approximately $60,000 to remodel the restaurant once again.

His lease is up on August 1, 1962, and he will then renegotiate another lease with the City of Cleveland, which owns the property.

A source informed the FBI that on April 25, Brancato attended the wake of Joseph Poliafico, the father-in-law of John DeMarco, at Biondo's funeral home, along with his sons, Nasher and Joe.

Other hoodlums in attendance were Shonder Birns, Anthony Milano, and Frank Visconti, Milt Rockman, Dominic Sospirato, and Sara Triscaro, the wife of Babe.

At this time the FBI was unsure of the relationship between Joe and Salvatore Poliafico, who was on trial earlier in 1954 for a big drug trail dealing with the cities of Cleveland, New York, Buffalo and Philadelphia. Frank's lawyer, Henry Levine, was Salvatore's attorney as well. Poliafico was found guilty and sent to jail for a period of fifteen to twenty years.

An FBI report stated on their daily surveillance of Frank Brancato from May 3 until June 1 that he had a normal routine. Frank would leave his home on Westview between 9 a.m. and 10 am. He would go to either Damante's or LaMarca's barbershop for a shave. He would then generally go to Cardinal Tire on Woodland Avenue and park his Cadillac on the side of the building, where he would stay until lunchtime. From there he would often then go to Captain Frank's Seafood House, then go back to Cardinal Tire for a few more hours.

From there he would go to the Northern Ohio Food Terminal, where he would play pinochle for several hours. He would then return to Cardinal Tire and would either go home for dinner or go back to Captain Frank's Restaurant for dinner. After dinner, Frank would go to the IAB Club in Little Italy to play pinochle once again with some of his old friends from the hill until 9 or 10 p.m.

After that, he could often been seen downtown on St. Vincent

Street, hitting some of the girly joints. After closing, he would once again show up at Captain Frank's for a drink or light bite to eat with some of the showgirls from the clubs. Brancato would normally get home by four or five in the morning.

Agents noted that on Thursday nights, he only went to the Manager Hotel and played cards there most of the night. They were not aware of who he played cards with, but were trying to find out.

A source informed the FBI in May that the word was out, and many of the men in the Cleveland Mob were starting to wonder whether they could trust Danny Greene.

On June 26, an informant told FBI agents that he had heard Frank Brancato recently had passed the word to his Cleveland associates to stay away from Greene. According to this informant, Frank specifically passed the word for everyone to stay away from Greene's car. He advised them all that Greene had long been suspected by Frank and his associates of being a police informant. They further felt Greene had extremely rotten morals and Greene was of the opinion that they were finally going to "be done" with him.

The police informant was not aware of whether the word sent out actually would indicate that a bomb would be placed in Greene's car, but he believed something like that would happen to him—if not now, then in the near future.

In Youngstown, Ohio, on July 17, Vincent DeNiro was murdered in a car bombing in a feud with Charles Carabbia and his brother, who were attempting to take control of the racket operations through the Mahoning County.

These men had been feuding since January 1, as the Carabbias tried to take over the pinball and gambling operations in Mahoning County that DeNiro had controlled for several years. The Carabbia brothers tried unsuccessfully several times to muscle in on DeNiro, trying to take the cut that belonged to the city prosecutor.

Frank was a well-known gambling factor in Mahoning County and had been acquainted with DeNiro in the past, but the bombing was definitely not the doing of the Cleveland Syndicate.

After the murder, it was reported that a white 1960 Pontiac had been seen in the area of the bombing. This type of vehicle was owned by Dominic Senzarino, a known associate of Carabbia. Senzarino would later be murdered in 1990.

FBI reported that a well-known source advised them on August 7 that back in early July, Donald King, a black policymaker, met with Brancato, Angelo Amato Sr., and Angelo Amato Jr., along with Shonder Birns and Vincent DeNiro, at the residence of Angelo Amato Sr. At this meeting, according to the source, Amato Sr. reportedly told DeNiro that if he did not take their numbers layoff, they would take care of him. Amato Sr. reportedly had said, "You know, the finger is on you anyway."

On September 6, an informant advised the FBI that he had received information that DeNiro was murdered over an argument with Tony "Dope" Delsanter, who would become the boss in Warren, Ohio, in the 1970s, and who attempted to control the Mahoning County rackets through the Mahoning County Prosecutor's Office.

The informant stated that Delsanter and DeNiro had been feuding since January 1, as Delsanter attempted to take control of the pinball machine business in Mahoning County, by using a police detective to confiscate these machines on the grounds that the business establishments were paying off cash for free games won on the machines.

The informant stated that DeNiro fought this out with Delsanter, and Delsanter was unsuccessful. He stated DeNiro had had control of the gambling operations in the city of Campbell for several years, and after January 1, Delsanter tried to muscle his way in on his operation, but once again was stopped. Delsanter then tried to muscle his way into the barbut games held in the Youngstown area, thereby taking a cut which was due to pay for the help with the city prosecutor.

The informant advised the FBI that during this time, DeNiro was fighting with Delsanter without any outside help from the Cleveland Syndicate or Frank Brancato. He was evidently in good standing with Frank Brancato.

The informant stated that the murder of DeNiro was definitely not the doing of the Cleveland Syndicate, as those individuals do not go in for extinction. He stated when the Cleveland Syndicate decides to eliminate an individual, they are certain that only the proposed victim is eliminated, and no bystanders are wounded.

An informant told the Cleveland FBI that he had heard the Cleveland Syndicate knew for certain that Phillip James Mariner, a.k.a. "Fleagle," was the man who made the bomb that killed DeNiro, and that Dominic Senzarino, a.k.a. "Junior," placed the bomb in DeNiro's car. Mariner was due to be released on bond from the Mercer County Jail. Mariner would also be murdered in 1970s.

By September 8, the *Cleveland Plain Dealer* ran a story saying that Ohio Attorney General Mark McElroy had met with U.S. Attorney General Robert Kennedy about the new laws that had been passed in Ohio to stop gambling activities in their state. After the session with Kennedy, McElroy informed the reporters that he and his aides would be drafting up the model anti-gambling laws, which "would detail new proposals for federal legislation to attack syndicated gambling operations in the nation."

McElroy told reporters he was confident that the new laws in Ohio would take more than $300 million out of Ohio racketeers' pockets each year.

Bobby Kennedy called the new laws in Ohio "the toughest in the nation." He was looking to do the same and raise the penalties for all the promoters and kingpin racketeers with heavy fines across the country and prison time of up to ten years. This bill also makes possession of certain gambling equipment a crime.

The FBI was advised on November 15 by an informant that he had always heard and believed it to be true that Frank Visconti, who operated Captain Frank's Seafood Restaurant at East 9th Street pier, was merely a front man for Frank Brancato. The source also advised them he had heard Brancato had all the money in Captain Frank's Restaurant. The source stated he had heard Brancato and his friends play cards in a second-floor room at the restaurant every Friday night.

The FBI was notified by an informant on December 14 that, in his opinion there is a good possibility Frank Brancato has a financial interest in the Cardinal Tire Company. The source revealed that a number of local truck drivers have been falling behind in their payments for their tires. According to the source, Brancato had been calling on some of these drivers in an effort to collect what they owed for their tires.

The source revealed he had heard that either Birns or Brancato had requested that Donald King and his two friends who ran numbers turn their receipts over to Birns. According to the source this occurred sometime prior to February 1961. It was reported that these three men were giving their receipts to Danny Greene, who was now a Birns man.

The same FBI informant went on to tell agents that it had been definitely established by the Cleveland Syndicate that on the orders from Tony "Dope" Delsanter; placed Ronald Carabbia in charge of the death of DeNiro. He also stated that immediately after the murder it was reported that a white 1960 Pontiac had been seen in the area of the bombing. This was the type of car Dominic Senzarino owned and operated.

The informant told the agents a representative of the Cleveland Syndicate had fairly well established with him that the above information of these two representatives of the Cleveland Syndicate was in Youngstown at the present time. Brancato is one of these men, but he had not heard of the name of the other man. These men were not staying at a motel or hotel in the area. Brancato was possibly staying at the home of Mike Romeo, who was the son of Brancato's trusted old friend, who was now a former wine shop owner in Struthers, Ohio, and residing in or near Poland, Ohio. The informant told the agents Brancato and either Charlie Cavallaro, a.k.a. "Cadillac Charlie," could not have been involved. Brancato had forced a successful Youngstown vending machine operator to cut the Cleveland Family in on one-third of his profits.

By 1970 the Cleveland Family had given control to the Pittsburgh Family and was now receiving about 25 percent of the profits from the Youngstown vending machine and the gambling rackets in Pittsburgh. Angelo Lonardo would often bring the money back to Cleveland monthly. The amount was believed to be in the range of $5,000 to $6,000 per month, and went as high as $23,000 for one month.

The informant mentioned Brancato and Cavallaro supposedly had gone to see Delsanter. They interviewed him at great length concerning his relationship with DeNiro and stated that Delsanter seemed to be scared to death. He was afraid to talk to anyone about this incident. Brancato had always been friendly with Delsanter in the past, but with the new development he did not know how to handle the situation.

The FBI documented that Frank had been seen several times at the Theatrical Restaurant in downtown Cleveland, The Blue Grass Lounge by Northfield and Warrensville Road in Maple Heights, and the Royal Oak Motel. Whenever Frank walked into these bars, he always had his drink of choice, Chivas Regal Scotch, waiting for him, whether it was at the Theatrical with Angelo the bartender, or James at the Blue

Grass, or Thomas at the Royal Oak. Agents continued to include in their reports that Brancato was a known felon and was to be considered to be dangerous and armed at all times.

CHAPTER TWENTY-TWO

1962

On February 18, 1962, an FBI agent working surveillance at the Cleveland Hopkins Airport observed John DeMarco arriving by plane from San Francisco at 6:15 a.m. The agent observed Brancato waiting in the lobby area for the plane to arrive

At 6:35 the plane arrived at the gate. DeMarco walked up the ramp to the main lobby with someone next to him. The agent did not recognize the man, but he was noted to be a large man, about 250 pounds, in his mid-fifties, and about 5'8" tall. The man was later identified as John Miceli.

DeMarco introduced Miceli to Brancato and they spoke for several minutes. The three men left the airport and were followed by the agent. They got into a 1962 Cadillac bearing Ohio license plate JJ 9831. It was later learned that the car was registered to the Teamsters Joint Council Number 41 located on East 22nd Street.

As the FBI continued with their surveillance of Brancato, they noted that on March 19, he had lunch once again at Morris Wexler's Theatrical Restaurant on Vincent Street with Scalish and Joe Polo, who was president of the Hotel Service Workers Local 274. The agent noted that he had been told Brancato owned over twenty suits that cost $100 to $200 each and that he enjoyed having several pairs of shoes made for him, which he would pass along to his sons.

Brancato always starts his day at Cardinal Tire Company around 10:00 a.m. where he parks his Cadillac on the side of the building and is there for two to three hours. He then goes to play pinochle daily at the Northern Ohio Food Terminal on East 40th Street and plays with men who work at the food terminal, where the games run about twenty to thirty minutes long and the guys play for $20 to $50 a hand. Some evenings (Frank) could be found playing cards at the IAB Club in Little Italy with friends from the neighborhood, while other days they have followed him to other locations, where he stays for several hours playing cards.

Other stops for Brancato included normal visits to The Egg Place Restaurant, owned by Tony Buffa on Broadway, the Tasty Barbeque on Vincent Street, Sweeny's Little Club on Chester, the Frolics Club, owned by Angelo Lonardo on Vincent Street, and Mickey's Lounge Bar on Vincent Street. The Fulton Fish Company located on Woodland Ave, The Val-Taro lounge on Broadway, and Miceli Dairy Products Company on East 90th Street. At times he has been seen there with his friend DeMarco and other times he shows up by himself and does not stay longer than thirty minutes.

On March 23, 1962, an informant told FBI agents that he believed Frank Brancato was still going strong and visiting the Northern Ohio Food Terminal on a daily basis to play pinochle with several men, one being Martin Rini, who was a retired produce man. The source mentioned in relation to the other hoodlums in the Cleveland area, Scalish, DeMarco, and street boss Brancato appear to be of influence and in charge of the Italian group in Cleveland, but the top man of this group is still Anthony Milano. The source stated that he had nothing really factual on which to base his opinion other than being an Italian himself, and having been around the Cleveland area, where a great number of Italians gather. He was under the impression that Milano was still the boss and gave all the orders.

On March 23 FBI agents observed Brancato and DeMarco drive up to Miceli Dairy Products Company on East 90th Street and park their car in the Kroger Building next door to the dairy. Both men entered the building and stayed for only ten minutes. Both men left and were seen driving down Buckeye Road. Agents noted that this had lately become a weekly stop for the two men.

The FBI interviewed Frank Brancato on March 26 at Cardinal Tire Company, where he was asked if he knew Samuel Finzzao from Detroit and Salvatore Peritore of New York.

Brancato admitted knowing both men, and that his father and Peritore's father were compares back in Sicily. He occasionally sees him when he visits his sister in Brooklyn and they occasionally call one another with the connection of a death or another occasion. He spoke with Peritore last when he called to invite him to the graduation of his daughter.

When asked by the agents if he knew what Peritore did for a living, Brancato answered he believes that he has had interest in the Longshoremen's Union on the New York waterfront, and considers him a good friend.

As far as Finzzao goes, he contacted him back in 1958 as a favor for a girl who danced at Mickey's. Her husband was in trouble with the law in Detroit and needed some help. Brancato phoned him to see what he could do for him, but Finazzo called back a few days later and told him the husband had already pled guilty to the crime.

The Cleveland office of the FBI received a teletype message form the Director of the FBI, J. Edgar Hoover, on April 9.

Information is in regard to Brancato, should be reviewed thoroughly by your office for any possible leads related to your investigation of Brancato criminal activities inasmuch as he has been selected as a key hoodlum figure being afforded an all-out investigation attention under the Criminal Intelligence Program.

On May 2, the Cleveland office of the FBI received a teletype communication from the Director of the FBI in regard to Frank Brancato, which read:

A review of your recent communication regarding this matter indicates a need for development of a highly confidential source and quality criminal informants that will furnish substantial information regarding Brancato and his hoodlum activities and operations.

You should immediately review your investigation of Brancato to determine new avenue of investigations. Further pinpoint possible locations for highly confidential sources and submit requests to the Bureau for permission to conduct the necessary surveys.

This matter should be given your immediate attention. Copies of this document were sent to the Attorney General's office and the cities of Cincinnati, Detroit, New York and Pittsburgh offices, in the likelihood that Brancato's investigation will continue in these cities as well.

On May 10 an informant told the FBI that in his opinion, Brancato was deriving most of his income from legitimate enterprises in which he was a silent partner. In his opinion, Brancato had a piece of Captain Frank's Restaurant, the Fulton Fish Company, the Cardinal Tire Company, Rivera Supper Club and perhaps many others, all in

Cleveland. The source told agents that he did not believe Brancato was involved in any gambling activities at that time, not because it was above his status in the community, but because it would involve being confined to that activity for a long period of time. He believed that Brancato enjoyed moving around the Cleveland area too much and did not like being confined to any specific place or duty.

On May 22, the Cleveland FBI office interviewed Frank Visconti in regard to his relationship with Brancato. Visconti told agents that he no longer owns his restaurant, Captain Frank's, by himself, and in fact, he and his family were presently incorporated as a family business. He owned a boat named "Captain Frank" which was registered with the U.S Coast Guard. He said he had known Frank Brancato for about thirty-five years and had been very closely associated with him. In fact, his wife and Frank's wife were best of friends and very close while they were alive. His relationship with Frank Brancato was mostly social, except for the time when they were in the shrimp business together.

Visconti told agents that Brancato did not have any interests in the restaurant, but he acted like he did. Visconti admitted to agents that the place came alive when Frank visited. He said, "Frank brings in a lot of customers and helps improve our business. (He) normally comes to eat dinner about 6:30 p.m. or so, and stays for a while. He will then go and play cards on Mayfield Road in Little Italy until midnight or so. He will then hit the girlie joints and have a good time, and when they close at two in the morning, he will come here with many of the showgirls, bartenders, and other friends."

Visconti said Frank was extremely well-liked by the Italian community and "would give you the shirt off his back if you needed it." Visconti told agents that he knew of an instance where an individual came to Brancato to borrow some money and Brancato did not have it, but he went to some of his friends to borrow the money from them and lend it to these individuals. In other words, "If Frank did not have it, he'd go and get it for you." Brancato had done a lot of favors for a lot of people in Cleveland. Brancato's close friend and *compare* was DeMarco. Until apparently three years ago, John was on the payroll of the Fulton Fish Company as a salesman. Visconti said he believed John was connected in some way with the Miceli Dairy Company, but was unsure whether Frank was connected with either of the businesses.

On May 26, 1962, the FBI intercepted and documented two letters that were going to Frank Brancato's home address. The first one was from the Atlas Insurance Company and the other from a Charles Monastra, who lived at 3476 East 153rd Street in Cleveland Ohio. The records from the Cleveland Retail Credit Men's Company, as checked by agents on May 28, reflected that Charles Monastra was born on August 24, 1901, in Italy. A credit report as of June 19, 1956, reflected that Monastra was divorced from his first wife, Grace Leanza, on February 21, 1955, and had one daughter, Antoinette, who lived with him. Monastra was employed as a core maker at the Consolidated Iron and Steel Manufacturing Company in Cleveland. He previously was employed at the Federal Machine and Foundry Company for thirty-five years. His credit rating was listed as satisfactory. Monastra had no arrest records in his file. Agents could not determine the connection between the two men.

The Cleveland FBI office informed the Director of the FBI on May 31, 1962, that a source had informed them Brancato knew that he was "hot," and that the FBI were investigating him very closely. He was behaving himself lately. The Cleveland office noted they would make arrangements to pick up Brancato shortly for an interview.

On June 4, the FBI Cleveland Office interviewed John Fotos, who said if Frank Brancato was getting a piece of his game, it would have to have come from Sperrazzo, but it certainly was not coming from him. Fotos told agents that he never questioned what Sperrazzo did with his share of the profits. Fotos informed them that they were partners in the Atlas Employment Company and that he had left the barbut game in 1950. Sperrazzo continued the games on his own until his death. As far as Brancato goes, in having a piece of the game, he said he only knew Brancato by his reputation and that he had never given Brancato any money at all, nor was he ever muscled by any individual while he operated the barbut games. Fotos also stated that although the dice game of barbut was originated by the Greeks, the games have been operated by both the Greeks and Italians. In northern Ohio, the games were all run by Italians at that time.

On June 4, during an interview with the Cleveland FBI agents, Frank was asked whether he had any connection or financial interest in the Corbo's Italian Spumoni Company, located on East 150th St. and Kinsman.

Frank replied that he did not.

When asked if he had any interest, financial or otherwise, in the Miceli Dairy Products Inc., Brancato replied he definitely did not; that he visited the place occasionally because his good friend and compare DeMarco worked there and he went to see him. Brancato also stated he went there whenever he wanted to buy some cheese, because he could get it at a wholesale price.

Brancato then told agents, "The Cardinal Tire Company has an account with Miceli Dairy and I sell tires to them for their trucks." Frank reiterated to agents that he did not have any financial interest in any business, and that his only source of income was derived from the Cardinal Tire Company.

Agents then asked Brancato whether he made a trip to Youngstown, Ohio, shortly after the death of Vincent J. DeNiro, who was murdered in a car bombing which occurred in Youngstown on July 17, 1961."

Brancato replied that this was absolutely untrue, and that he specifically recalled that the last time he was in Youngstown was approximately one month before DeNiro was killed. "On this occasion I went to Youngstown to see an old friend, Charles Malfitano, who was born in Licata over seventy years ago," Brancato explained. "Malfitano was going back to Italy about this time, and I wanted to see Malfitano to give a little money to give my sister and her husband, who were still in Italy." Brancato told agents he knew DeNiro very well and had a very high regard for him and considered him a very good man. "As a matter of fact, I obtained Malfitano a job in the office as a bookkeeper."

Brancato stated to agents that while he had no positive information, in his opinion, the murder of DeNiro was more or less a family affair. Previously DeNiro had accidently shot and wounded Sandy Naples in Youngstown, and one of the Naples brothers, Billy or Mike, may have murdered DeNiro in retaliation.

Agents then asked Frank what he and several other individuals were doing in Mansfield, Ohio, approximately one month ago.

Brancato explained he had been contacted by a friend who needed some help in the Mansfield area, "So Carl Rospo and Dominic Lonardo and I went down to see what we could do."

Agents then asked Frank whether he went down to Mansfield to put in a fix.

Brancato smiled and said, "Well, we went down to get the right attorney." Then he indicated, "If I should get into any trouble, I would be subject to deportation." (He said) he treasured his U.S. citizenship and was making every effort to abide by all the laws of the state and county and to stay out of any kind of trouble."

The FBI reported that their intensive investigation of Brancato failed to reveal any current violations of law. Informants and daily surveillance reflected that he spent most of the days at the Cardinal Tire Company and frequented restaurants and places of entertainment and often played cards. In Brancato's place, agents strongly recommended that DeMarco be selected as a target for intensified investigation.

The Brooklyn, New York, FBI office interviewed Frank Nogara, who said he was born in October 28, 1899, in Licata, Sicily. He arrived in the United States in 1924 and resided in Brooklyn, New York. He had been employed as a longshoreman since 1924.

Nogara told agents that his wife Caroline was in bad health due to a heart condition. She was once married to John Brancato, Frank Brancato's brother, but he died about forty years ago, in late 1923. Nogara advised agents that his friend Charles "Chito" Balsamo and his wife flew in from Cleveland and stayed with him for a week and flew back to Cleveland. Nogara told agents that he had never met or spoken to Frank Brancato, but knew of him and could not offer any information about his income or his address.

Brooklyn agents contacted and interviewed Salvatore Peritone on his relationship with Brancato. Peritone told agents Brancato had not lived in Brooklyn for many years, and that his mother and Brancato's wife, V, were sisters. They often called one another to see how they were doing and when he came to Brooklyn, Frank stayed in different hotels. He always came over for dinner and to visit. When agents asked if he knew what Brancato did, Peritone simply said no, they did not discuss this and he did not know who he worked for. Peritone told agents that he had been questioned once before by law enforcement because he knew a man named John Oddo. He told them he was a close friend of his in the past but did not know what he was doing now. He was then asked about John Aiello. He told them he worked with him years ago in the Melarmo Dress Company, but did not know where he lived.

In July 1962 the FBI continued to observe Brancato and DeMarco at LaMarca's or Angelo's barbershop on Sunday mornings.

My cousin Bill told me stories of how he would often go with our grandfather on a Saturday morning and while Grandpa got a shave at Damante's barbershop, he would visit a car dealership next door.

Billy would often go inside and look at the cars. At the age of twelve, that was what he was most interested in. Billy would sit in the cars and act like he was driving them. Many were Buicks and some were a vehicle called a Rolls-Royce. The manager would always kick Billy out with a harsh, mean voice.

One Saturday, while Billy was sitting in a Rolls-Royce playing, Grandpa Brancato walked in to get little Billy. The manager walked over and asked, "How I can help you, Mr. B?" knowing very well who he was talking with.

"I am just getting my grandson," Frank said. "I hope he has not been a problem for you."

"No, Mr. B., he is always welcome to come in and sit in the cars if he wishes," the manager replied. Frank soon left with little Billy holding his hand.

By the end of July, FBI agents had inquired for any accounts that Frank Brancato may have had with them. The financial firms investigated were Merrill, Lynch, Paine Weber, Bache and Company from National City Bank, Ball, Burge and Kraus and Merrill-Turben and Company, both associated with Union Commerce Bank in Cleveland.

Brancato continued to play cards at the Northern Ohio Food Terminal virtually daily, and both men visited Miceli Dairy Products Company and stayed anywhere from three to fifteen minutes at a time. Then they had lunch at Captain Frank's Restaurant. Occasionally with them was Joseph Anthony "Jesse" Logatto, who was born on October 4, 1905, in Brooklyn, New York. Logatto had a long police arrest record that dated back to August 24, 1929, where he was interviewed as a suspicious person and then released. He was currently working as a Teamster at Thistledown Race Track.

On August 24 an informant told the FBI in Cleveland Brancato had warned DeMarco that he was being followed by agents twenty-four hours a day. DeMarco told Frank, "They even follow me to the bank." The informant also told agents Brancato told him that Visconti had just returned from a trip to Italy and had become very ill. He was currently in the hospital. Brancato told him that while in Rome, Frank had met up with someone and that Visconti was looking to buy a home and to start an American-style restaurant in Palermo.

On September 9, the Cleveland FBI updated the Director of the FBI in regard to Brancato. Brancato's new entertainment spot in Cleveland was The Swing In Bar on West 25th Street and had a combo which played updated music like the twist and other popular songs.

The source told agents that many unattached females visited the club, and Brancato enjoyed being with the women and the younger crowd. The informant then told agents from August 30 to September 6, Frank had visited relatives in Brooklyn and attended a wedding that was held in the Burgundy Room of Junior's Restaurant on Dekalb Avenue in Brooklyn. He spent some time with his sister Mary, who was very ill, before returning to Cleveland.

On September 18 an informant advised the FBI that Angelo Amato Jr. was living on Fairhaven Road in Mayfield Heights and was the son-in-law of John DeMarco.

The source advised agents that Brancato continued to be seen on the streets in the vicinity of the girlie shows and would be seen between 3:00 and 4:00 in the morning at Captain Frank's. Brancato frequented the Swing In Bar, which was frequented by many of the local entertainers and musicians, "and they do some pretty wild versions of the twist." The source advised agents Brancato planned to attend a clambake at the Cameo Lounge in Sandusky, Ohio, the next night, and he would probably bring DeMarco, since the Cameo Lounge was a customer of Miceli Dairy Products Company. The owners, John and Joe Miceli, were longtime friends of Brancato and DeMarco.

An informant advised the FBI on November 24 that Brancato would be visiting a friend in New York with John Miceli on a business trip. It was his understanding that this friend was in the cheese business and they should return by the November 27.

On September 18, Cleveland FBI agents observed Brancato and DeMarco at the wake of Joseph Artica. Agents noted that Artica was an old neighborhood friend of both men and was employed in the trucking business.

On November 30, Brancato was interviewed by FBI agents at his place of employment, the Cardinal Tire Company. Frank was asked if he knew Charles Cavallaro. Brancato replied that he did not, except by his reputation, and added it was his understanding that Cavallaro was engaged in some sort of gambling activities in the Youngstown area. Cavallaro was once thought to have participated in the bombing death of Vincent DeNiro. When asked if he had any idea who would have bombed him and his young son Thomas, Brancato replied that, in his opinion, the bombing was a tragic thing in that Cavallaro and his son Thomas were involved, and that whoever was responsible for this crime should be caught and punished without mercy.

On December 4, Calegro Charles Malfitano was interviewed in Youngstown by local FBI agents in connection with the unsolved bombing murder of Charles Cavallaro, a.k.a. "Cadillac Charlie," and his son, Thomas Cavallaro, age eleven. Malfitano told agents he was seventy-three years old and was born on December 17, 1889, in Licata, Sicily. Malfitano was a bachelor and held an interest in the National Cigarette Service in Youngstown and was in partnership with Scalish. Vincent DeNiro was involved in the business until his death in July 1961. Another partner was believed to be Carl Rospo. Malfitano told agents he entered the United States on December 19, 1923, and that he was contemplating returning to Italy during the summer of 1963, where he would establish permanent residence with his unwed sister.

Malfitano told agents that he had known Charles Cavallaro for over twenty-five years. He was acquainted with DeNiro and Sandy Naples, who was shot to death in March of 1960. DeNiro had been a victim of a shooting, but he survived.

According to an FBI report, and also noted in Allan May's book, *Welcome to the Jungle Inn*, Mike Farah was killed by a shotgun blast in June of 1962 and William Naples was a bomb victim in July 1962. Agents asked how he had been able to know all of these men, and was also presently on a friendly basis with other Youngstown hoodlums. Malfitano said he just happened to make their acquaintance while residing in Youngstown.

Malfitano said he had no idea who could have caused the killing of the aforementioned individuals and stated that he did not know the identity of the person or persons who had been operating the barbut game in Youngstown area, or anyone who was booking numbers. He did state, however, that he was previously arrested for booking numbers, and was placed on a two year probation, and that he had never booked any numbers since.

Malfitano was then asked if he had met Scalish, DeMarco, or Brancato. He stated that he had. He was then asked if he knew whether Scalish and DeMarco had attended the Apalachin meeting in 1957. Malfitano told agents that he had read about this in the newspapers. Malfitano said that at no time was there anything discussed regarding any illegal activities. He said he did not believe any of these people were involved or connected in such activities, and they were all legitimate businessmen. He said Scalish was connected with the Buckeye Cigarette Company and DeMarco was connected with a cheese business.

Malfitano said the last time he saw Brancato in Youngstown was about six months earlier, and that he did not know or inquire about his visit. Brancato had also visited Youngstown on several occasions. He said Frank kept his nose clean and did not interfere with anyone else's business, so he would not know the reason for his visits.

On December 5, 1962, FBI agents investigating a telephone call to Brancato's home listing in Akron, Ohio, found it to be that of Carl Rospo, who lived on North Main Street. Agents noted the Akron Credit Bureau advised agents that in their file for Rospo, started in 1929, a newspaper clipping was contained in his file from the Akron Beacon Journal dated July 2, 1938. This clipping reflected that Rospo was arrested as a suspect in the 1935 shotgun slaying of "Big Mike" Saviolis, the number-one numbers racketeer in Akron. The article indicated that Rospo was released on July 27, 1938, for insufficient evidence. The file stated Rospo was retired and was a bartender at an Italian Club in Akron. The file said Rospo was born in Italy on June 7, 1897. His first recorded arrest was in Akron, Ohio, on March 17, 1920. He was charged with a highway robbery. The case never came to court and was nullified in May of 1920.

A source informed the FBI on December 6 that on November 25 and 26 Brancato and DeMarco, who, he believed, both owned a portion of Miceli Dairy in Cleveland, had visited the Pollio Dairy in Campbell, New York. The source stated he had not heard why both men went for the visit.

On December 6, a source advised the FBI Brancato had been seen quite often the past summer at the Lakeside Yacht Club in Cleveland, along with Scalish. To his knowledge, the men were ever together, and that neither man owned a yacht. The source continued to tell agents that

Brancato was going to take his sister Sara, who had been visiting with him and his family, back to his other sister Mary, who lived in Brooklyn. She would return to Italy and was planning to spend the holiday season in Brooklyn.

On December 18, a source informed the FBI that Brancato was seen at the opening of a new nightclub in downtown Cleveland called Leo's Restaurant on East 24th Street and St. Clair. This club would later become a well-known African-American entertainment venue renamed Leo's Casino. This club would become the well-known Cleveland connection to the "Motown sound."

CHAPTER TWENTY-THREE

Hawaii

1963

On January 23, 1963, a source informed the FBI that Frank Visconti had opened a new Las Vegas restaurant called "The Lido" and Angelo Gelo Amato was a partner with him. Visconti had leased this from an Asian man and they were only operating the bar area at this time.

Visconti told the source he believed he could get all the wholesale and retail fresh fish business out of Las Vegas. He could do very well financially in a setup like this, since there was currently no one in Las Vegas who knew anything about the fresh fish business. The source told agents that he did not know whether "Uncle Frank" Brancato was a partner with Visconti, but he had always been suspected to be part owner of Captain Frank's.

On February 16, Brancato attended the marriage of Angelo Amato's daughter at the old Mounds Club, which is now known as the LaVera Party Center on Chardon Road in Willoughby Hills.

On February 22, a source informed the FBI "Uncle Frank" was seen at a new club named Wolfie's late in the evening, where he had a couple of drinks and spoke with a few of the strippers and left. The source also stated Brancato had been seen several times at Fulton Fish Company on Woodland Avenue. He and others believed Brancato had a piece of this company.

In late February, a female source reported to FBI agents that she had heard Brancato had flown in an unidentified private aircraft from Cleveland to Montreal, Canada, to gamble. The flights started on February 18. She told agents she did not know whether Brancato was going to engage in personal gambling for his own enjoyment, or if he was going there in connection with gambling activities of a business nature.

On March 1, the Miami field office of the FBI contacted the Cleveland office about the letter they had sent out with a photo and fingerprints in regard to "Brincardo," which they spelled wrong. Frank Brancato is the man they mentioned in their update. The Immigration and Naturalization Service in Cleveland had a continued interest in Brancato since, if he should be convicted of a crime involving moral turpitude or if he should leave the country for any reason, he would be deported.

On April 9, an FBI agent observed Brancato drive up in his new 1963 gold-colored Cadillac. They noted that it had a television in it. Frank arrived for the wake and funeral of Carlotta Polizzi, which was held at Biondo's Funeral Home on 116th Street. Also making an appearance were Scalish and DeMarco, Milt Rockman, and Frank and Dominic Lonardo.

The FBI sent an urgent update to the Director of the FBI on April 24. Their continued surveillance of Brancato noted that John DeMarco became a member of a new corporation called "Ohio Pizza Products, Inc.," located at 2721 East Ninetieth Street, also known as "Miceli Dairy Products, Inc." At this time the FBI believed that both Brancato and DeMarco may be silent partners in this new business venture. The new corporation intended to manufacture pizza products and ship them mainly to grocery stores throughout the United States.

On April 30, a source advised agents that he believed "Uncle Frank" Brancato was on the payroll of the Frolics Club, a girlie joint. According to his information, Brancato showed up at the club every Monday night, which was payday, and picked up his "salary" in cash for lending protection to these clubs.

On May 2, the Director of the FBI; J. Edgar Hoover sent an urgent message to the Cleveland special agents in charge. The director asked for the team in Cleveland to look at developing a highly-placed confidential source. By doing this, it would help to obtain quality information regarding Brancato's activities as a hoodlum.

You need to concentrate on any other investigative avenues if the bureau has any hope to develop a case against Brancato and his friends. You must develop any new sources of information and obtain permission to pursue this investigation before you conduct the necessary surveillance. This matter should be given your immediate and personal attention, as this is of high importance.

On May 5, the FBI reported that they found another large dice game or barbut game in Cleveland, located at the Ohio Plating Company on Second Street and High Street. The game was being held on the third floor. They noted seeing Brancato going into the building and staying for several hours. Among the guests were DeMarco, Logatto, Cassaro and Frank Lonardo.

Later, an informant told the FBI that he believed "Brancato has a piece of the action in these games." Brancato visited New York to attend the wedding of his friend Angelo Lonardo. Agents noted that Brancato had also met with Charles Cassaro, a known Cleveland bookmaker.

On May 23, the Cleveland burglary squad had Joe "Skinny" Faragone under surveillance. They noticed he met up with Frank Brancato in a parking lot. Skinny got out of his car and into Brancato's car and they spoke for several minutes. Faragone had a criminal record and operated the Best Labor Company. He ran a plush card room on Eagle Street and Woodland. This meeting indicated to police that Brancato and Faragone may be partners in this card game.

On June 4, 1962, the FBI interviewed John Fotopoulos, a.k.a. John Fotos, who had operated barbut games from the late 1940s to the early '50s. His partner at the time was Michael Sperrazzo. They both were employed at the Atlas Employment Company on West Superior Avenue. The men became friends and started this Greek dice game, but now it was run by the Italians in Cleveland.

When asked if Brancato was a partner, Fotos told them that he was not aware of Brancato being a partner of his portion of the games, but if Sperrazzo was paying Brancato out of his share of the profits before he was killed, he did not care one way or another. Brancato never tried to muscle his way into the games, as far as he knew.

The FBI then asked whether Brancato could have had Sperrazzo killed in 1959; he said he did not know.

On June 6, the Director of the FBI in Washington sent a teletype message to agents in the Cleveland field office:

Since you have not been able to establish a highly confidential source inside the Cleveland organization which will be able to penetrate the hoodlum society, we are informing you that the daily surveillance messages on Brancato can now go to weekly updated messages, but we ask that you continue to monitor DeMarco and Scalish, since all three of the men are connected.

If we intensify our investigation on these men, we can hope to establish a connection between all the men and their illegal activities to prosecute them all properly.

According to the *Cleveland Plain Dealer* on June 7:

The first Senate bill dealt with increasing fines and penalties for bookmakers, and makes it a crime for a building manager or agent to allow them the use of rooms for gambling purposes. In the second bill passed there are three main sections. First would be if a person is convicted of allowing the use of a premise for gambling, (they) would be subject to a fine and jail time. At the present time, the fines could only range from $5 up to $55 and the jail time of ten days to six months for any number of offenses. The new fines for the first offenses would call for fines up to $500 and six months in jail. Additional convictions would be fines of $500 to $1,000 and from one to three years in prison.

The second portion of this bill includes managers and agents of the building owners and would be included under the ban against allowing the use of rooms for gambling. The third section of this bill sets the penalty for a first offense of selling a lottery ticket up to $500 and six months in jail; additional offenses could be from $500 to $1,000 and jail time up to three years. Governor Michael DiSalle signed this bill into law on Monday as the first measure in the anti-gambling group, which was aimed at the numbers racket.

In a FBI file documented on August 26, the *Saturday Evening Post* had an extensive article on the Mafia. It said the Mafia may be referred to *La Cosa Nostra* or the Syndicate, and was known as the "Outfit" to most insiders. Others mentioned in this article from Cleveland were John Scalish, Morris Kleinman, James Licavoli, John DeMarco, George Gordon, and Scotty Glotman.

In questioning an informant, the FBI asked if he knew who the top men were in Cleveland. The man answered that John Scalish was number one, and depending on who you spoke to, some people believed it was Brancato as the number-two man and some thought it was DeMarco. "I personally think it is Brancato," the source said. When the informant was asked about the Apalachin meeting in 1957, the man told agents that he knew Scalish and DeMarco were captured and prosecuted, but he believed that Brancato and Frank Embrescia had escaped capture, since they arrived in New York the next day. He said Embrescia was in a partnership with Scalish in the Buckeye Cigarette Service Company in Cleveland.

The FBI in Cleveland had their list of top men: John T. Scalish was the boss and a partner in the Desert Inn in Las Vegas. He was probably not only getting "skim money" off the top from Vegas, but he probably had points, or interest, through Morris Kleinman and DeMarco from Cleveland, along with George Gordon of Miami, and the late Scotty Goltsman of Cleveland. All had a piece in one way or another of the Desert Inn and Beverly Hills Country Club.

The informant told the FBI it was understood that Scalish divided the money between the Milano brothers, Brancato, and DeMarco also, as a share for their help. Scalish was considered to have a piece of the Beverly Hills Country Club, which formerly operated in Southgate, Kentucky. The source believed Scalish was the "big man" in the Midwest and inherited his status from his late brother, Tom Scalish, who died in an auto accident in 1947. Tom had inherited it from Al Polizzi, who was living in Miami, Florida. The Cleveland Outfit was run by Scalish and his capo and street boss Brancato, consigliore DeMarco, and associate Nick Satullo.

The FBI informant told them the Outfit in Cleveland wanted nothing to do with narcotics or drugs in general. The informant said that there were considerable differences between the Italians and the Jews. This had resulted in a number of murders and beatings as they fought to control the numbers rackets in Cleveland. It finally ended with the help of Dalitz, who was then living in Las Vegas and was credited with making peace between them by giving Scalish and his crew a "piece" of the Desert Inn.

On September 5, a source informed the FBI Cleveland office that everyone was aware that Scalish and DeMarco went to the Apalachin meeting, but actually there were two other men who went with Scalish and DeMarco. At first he declined to tell agents who they were, but later, during questioning, he told them he had heard through the grapevine that Brancato and Frank Embrescia went to the meeting and escaped being caught.

The source also told agents that he was a friend of Dominic Moio for about fifteen years. The last time he saw him was back in late August. He was acting very strangely, as he was worried about being deported. Moio called Angelo Amato for a job in the early summer to work in his concrete business. Angelo put him to work as a cement finisher, but that only lasted a few weeks because of his age. Other men were complaining that Moio was not doing his fair share of the work, so he just quit.

The source told agents Moio was at one time a very good friend with Amato, and that Amato used to go to Canton to get some "good buys" on jewelry. Through this friendship, Moio met Brancato at Amato's home in Cleveland.

Dominic Moio was a suspect in the Youngstown murder of Cavallaro and Billy Naples and was brutally killed in September 1963.

On September 15, the Cleveland FBI file stated DeMarco was undergoing open heart surgery in Cleveland and might not survive the delicate operation. His dear and trusted friend Brancato, who would normally be at his bedside, had left for Las Vegas on United Airlines Flight 711, which left Cleveland at 6:45 p.m. and would arrive in Las Vegas at 10:10 p.m. Brancato left with his friend and possible bodyguard Visconti. They both were holding reservations on a Western Flight 3 from Las Vegas to Los Angeles on September 23 The flight were scheduled to leave Las Vegas at 9:24 a.m.

Cleveland agents noted that Brancato not staying in Cleveland for DeMarco's operation was very important, and that this trip must be of high importance for their illegal activities.

Upon hearing this very important news update, the Cleveland FBI office thought they finally had a break to link Brancato and Visconti with Scalish and their organized crime operation, which would help the INS to once again try to deport Brancato back to Italy, a job they had failed to do for several years now.

The next page of teletype from the FBI with the same date stated that the two men then had a United Airlines Flight 763 from Los Angeles to Chicago leaving at 12:40 a.m. on October 3, which would arrive in Chicago at 6:15 a.m. Then they would take another flight that would leave Chicago at 6:50 a.m., arriving at Cleveland at 8:50 a.m. on October 3.

The report said the two men might get special bookings in Los Angeles for Hawaii, since their close friend Jimmy Fratianno revealed to them that the two planned to go to Hawaii.

The letter noted that both Brancato and Visconti were well-known in Las Vegas and at the Desert Inn and the Stardust Hotel. Fratianno believed they were going to meet up with Brancato's friend, Angelo Amato, who owned and operated Gelo's Lounge Bar in Vegas. Brancato and Visconti were scheduled to stay at the Stardust on September 16, according to the Clark County Sheriff office and Special Agent Dean Elson of the Las Vegas FBI.

On September 16, the Las Vegas Clark County Sheriff's Office followed as both Brancato and Visconti checked into the Stardust Hotel and were registered in room 701. Both men had been observed later that night gambling at both the Desert Inn and the Stardust Hotel. They informed Las Vegas FBI agent Dean Elson on September 18 that they had heard both men possibly could be leaving Las Vegas on Sept. 19 or 20. On the evening of Sept. 19 both Brancato and Visconti went to the Clark County Sheriff's Office and registered as ex-felons in the city. Both men were fingerprinted and photographed.

The informant said he had heard Scalish had been very happy with the income from the Desert Inn and "it has exceeded his wildest dreams." He indicated Brancato and DeMarco shared in this monthly income.

On September 17, the FBI field office in Los Angeles sent a teletype message to the Cleveland and the Las Vegas offices. Using a legal wiretap on September 16, they heard Brancato phone Nick Licata (underboss) in Los Angeles and inform him that he would be coming out to visit him after he finished his business in Las Vegas with Frank and Angelo.

The Las Vegas field office informed the other agents that they would try to obtain an updated photo of Brancato and Visconti and one for Angelo Amato. The Los Angeles field office informed them that they had a very good liaison with United Airlines and they would obtain the flight information as soon as possible and pass it along to the other field offices.

The purpose of the trip to Hawaii was unknown at that time, but they felt it was very significant, since Brancato left the bedside of his dear friend DeMarco in Cleveland to face his heart operation without him.

The Los Angeles FBI noted that both Brancato and Visconti met up on September 23 with Nick Licata and visited with him at the Casablanca Hotel.

The FBI had an extensive file on Nick Licata, who had endeared himself to L.A. Boss Jack Dragna. Dragna had been able to convince Joe Zerilli of Detroit, Michigan, to call off an earlier murder contract on Licata.

Licata was accepted as a member of the L.A. Family and became close to Dragna's brother, consigliore Tom Dragna. On March 25, 1932,

Licata had become a naturalized citizen. He resided in Inglewood and owned several apartment buildings, including the one he lived in. Licata owned several bars and taverns and operated as a bookie and loan shark. He normally worked out of a mob hangout on La Brea Avenue in Hollywood and a club called Five O'clock in Burbank.

On the evening of September 24, the Cleveland office of the FBI received a radiogram from the director of FBI operations in Hawaii, saying that both Brancato and Visconti had arrived in Honolulu as scheduled at 3:10 p.m. They registered with only one room at the Waikiki Biltmore Hotel, as members of a Berry Tour group.

It was noted that the Biltmore was a very nice and exclusive hotel on the island, and expensive for most people. The report continued to state that they would follow and observe both men while they were in Hawaii and make follow-up reports as needed.

On September 24, an FBI file was sent from the Honolulu office to FBI field offices in Cleveland, Los Angeles, and Las Vegas. FBI agents in all their cities were excited and hopeful that Brancato was in Hawaii to make some type of an agreement or to arrange for either drug shipments, since this is what Visconti has been imprisoned for many years ago, or to possibly set up gambling joints or underground casinos in the island, or even possibly arranging to launder money from the casinos in Las Vegas in the islands. Time would tell, and they made it a priority for the Honolulu agents to follow closely and report activities as needed.

Brancato and Visconti landed in Honolulu via United Airlines Flight 91 from Los Angeles at 3:05 p.m. The Hawaii visitor's bureau passenger forms that were filled out by both men are being held and secured by the State of Hawaii Agricultural Office with the other passenger declarations. Copies of Brancato's and Visconti's forms will be sent to Cleveland as handwriting specimens as soon as possible.

Based on the handwriting from hotel registration forms later examined by FBI agents, the information was filled in by Visconti, with the exception of Brancato's signature. They are registered with the Berry Tour 400 Group 22.

Agents observed that the tour was divided between the Waikiki Biltmore and the Princess Kaiulani Hotels that are located one block away from each other on Waikiki. Brancato and Visconti are booked to stay at the Biltmore, since both names appear on the *form typewritten, which means they have planned this trip at least fourteen days ago. If it was later than that, their names would have been in pencil. Agents continued to follow both men to their hotel and noticed they both registered and were assigned to stay in room 408, which they occupied together. When reviewing the signature cards, FBI agents noticed that they were filled out by Visconti once again, and the room rate was noted to be $4.50 a day per person.*

After arriving in their hotel room, Brancato made a call to phone 91105, which is registered to a Honolulu restaurant supply company. After going to the hotel bar for a few drinks, both men walked down the street to a La Scala Italian restaurant for dinner.

Agents observed that two men joined them and spoke with both men for several minutes, and then Visconti got up and left Brancato alone with the men at the table. While walking slowly past their table, one of the agents overheard them speaking in Italian and could not understand what they were saying, but they spoke in a quiet tone to one another. No one seemed to be upset; they seemed to be smiling and happy, so special agent believes it had something to do with business of some sort. Visconti came back after ten minutes and both men left twenty minutes later and walked back to their hotel and arrived about 12:30 a.m.

Special agents discovered that neither Visconti nor Brancato came to the meeting of the tour group on activities planned for the island vacation. One tour was leaving at 9:30 that morning on a charter bus tour around the main island. Agents noted that Brancato and Visconti had made reservations to go island-hopping and would leave on Sunday and return on Wednesday afternoon, in time to join the departing group tour at the international airport.

Frank Visconti dropped of a roll of film to be developed at the Alii Camera Shop in the Hotel Biltmore lobby. Agents took possession of the developed film and transmitted a copy of eight out of the twelve pictures to agents in the Los Angeles office for possible identification of the other men and women in the pictures, then returned them for Visconti to pick up the next day.

Agents noted that Brancato had on white slacks with a black jacket and Visconti had on light green slacks and a white sports shirt.

At 6:50 p.m., agents followed both men into the lobby of the Biltmore, were they met up with a woman about forty or forty-five years old, with dark hair and medium complexion and a nice flowered-print dress. It is possible she was Hawaiian, agents noted. The three walked into the bar and sat down and had a few drinks together. At 7:15, Visconti got up and went into the lobby and paced back and forth for several minutes while he checked his watch several times to see what time it was. At 7:20 p.m. Visconti left the front lobby and went back into the bar and met up with Brancato and the female, still seated at the table. At 7:25 the three left the bar and went out the front entrance and stood around like they were waiting for someone to pick them up on Kealakekua Avenue. After several more minutes of waiting, the three went back into the lobby and stood around for a few more minutes.

The FBI agent felt that he was "made" by Brancato. He left the lobby and came back at 8:10 p.m. as he kept his eye on the front lobby. When he came, back all three had disappeared, apparently having been met by someone and departed from the rear exit onto Koa Street.

Other agents were not able to find the three and believed they met up with others at a secluded bar or restaurant. FBI agents later identified the young lady as Laura Castro. After further investigation they found that Laura Castro was also known as Laura Castello and had lived in New York several years earlier, before moving to Hawaii and changing her name.

On September 25, the two men and the woman were followed as they did some sightseeing around the island in the woman's red 1961 Oldsmobile convertible. They stopped several times for drinks and to have lunch and then dinner on the cliffs near Diamond Head. They did not meet up with anyone, from what the agents could tell from their surveillance.

On September 26 FBI agents followed the men once again. Visconti received a call from Las Vegas, but he was not in. Later in the afternoon, the FBI obtained the recording from the man who called him. It was Angelo Amato, and he asked Visconti to call him back when he got the message.

With this information the FBI felt confident that there could be a drug smuggling operation going on between Visconti and Amato. Visconti then went to the counter to look into a charter to the other islands. The young woman at the counter told them that if they still wished to visit the islands, they would have to do it in one or two days, since they were booked to fly back to the United States on October 2. Visconti politely told her he would think about it and let her know.

On September 27, FBI agents were advised that Brancato and Visconti were planning to leave Hawaii on October 2 on United Airlines flight 94-R at 3:15 p.m. and would arrive in Los Angeles at 11:15 p.m. Los Angeles agents could pick up on the surveillance from there.

FBI agents were still pinning their hopes on the possibility that Brancato and Visconti were in Hawaii to make drug trafficking connections to help with the importation into America, but mainly into Los Angeles again, based on the fact that Visconti had been arrested for drug trafficking several years earlier.

Agents made notations about the men going out to dinner and who they met up with, including the fact that they bought a few drinks for some young girls. One time Visconti brought a $100 bill to a cashier to have it broken down. The agents noted it was a San Francisco Federal Reserve Note and included the serial number. The agents were concerned that it could be counterfeit, but after it was tested, it was found that it was not.

Both men were seen going to Maui, and both men purchased a large amount of men and women's jewelry. Agents believed they were planning to bring the jewelry back to the States and resell it for a profit, since they were noted to be very expensive gold chains and watches. They ruled out gifts for relatives or friends because of the cost.

An FBI file indicated that on September 29, Visconti received a phone call from Cleveland, Ohio, at 9:36 a.m. It was Mary, the manager of Captain Frank's Seafood House. She mentioned that she did receive the packages, all except for one that he had sent to her.

Frank told her to go ahead and cash one of the checks, and he would look into the matter when he got home. They spoke about how the business was doing for several minutes, and then Mary mentioned to Frank that she was planning to live in Hawaii after she retired from the seafood house. The agents believed this was a code to let both men know to be careful and that the phone was possibly being recorded by agents.

The FBI file indicated that Visconti received a special delivery express air mail package the next day from Captain Frank's Restaurant in Cleveland, Ohio. The size of the envelope was approximately nine inches by twelve inches. The contents were not known by agents, but they hoped that through their audio surveillance in the room of the two men, they would hear what the package held.

It was revealed later that the envelope held bookkeeping statements from the restaurant. The financial statement told the men that the bar and liquor profits for last week was $1,413 and the restaurant and food profit was over $500. Both men knew that Visconti received a weekly financial statement by Wednesday, no matter where he was in the country. Visconti IRS records showed that he filed his taxes every six months. The statement also showed the man who purchased Visconti's old Las Vegas seafood house was behind in his payment of $20,000 and the payments had been slow in coming to him.

Brancato returned from a dinner date with a young woman, where they dined at a very high- class restaurant named Michele's.

On September 30, both men had arranged to take a tour of the Wahiawa, Oahu, pineapple fields and left with the tour at 10:57 a.m. The Hawaiian FBI agents went on the tour as well, and followed closely behind the two men all day. They hoped that there would be a meeting up with someone to help them build a case against both men. While going through the massive maze of pineapple plants, Brancato and Visconti met up with what agents believed to be a Hawaiian native. They spoke for several minutes and the man then gave Visconti a light brown envelope. Not knowing what was inside the envelope, they continued to follow Brancato and Visconti. They made no other contacts while on the rest of the tour. Later, the agents hoped that they would once again get lucky and hear the men talking about what the envelope had in it, but sadly, the men did not speak about this in their room later in the evening.

October 2, the Hawaii FBI Director sent a decoded radiogram to Los Angeles, Las Vegas, Kansas City, and Cleveland. It advised the cities that Brancato was wearing a dark blue or black suit with a white shirt and red tie with black shoes and was carrying a small light tan bag and a light colored tan topcoat. Visconti had on light tan slacks and a white open-collared sport shirt and was wearing white-and-brown shoes and carrying a small gray handbag. They had left Hawaii as planned on the United Airlines flight to Los Angeles. They then had a connecting flight on Western Airlines Flight 770, departing Los Angeles at 12:05 a.m. and arriving in Las Vegas at 12:55 a.m.

Agents asked that the FBI agents in Las Vegas to see if there were connecting flights to Kansas City or Cleveland. The director requested that agents in Los Angeles observe the suspects at the airport and that agents in Las Vegas follow them, if necessary. The Honolulu office would have no future involvement in the investigation.

FBI agents in Las Vegas picked up Brancato and Visconti when their Western Airlines flight landed. They took both men to the Federal Building to ask them a few questions. Special agents split up the two men into different interrogation rooms and asked why they went to Hawaii and how they were able to afford such an expensive trip. Both men told agents the same story that they went to Hawaii to look at real estate to open up a new seafood restaurant on Waikiki Beach. They did the same thing in Los Angeles and in Las Vegas. Both men said they were disappointed with Hawaii and how expensive the beachfront property was, but thought they had found good locations to purchase in Los Angeles and in Las Vegas.

When asked how they paid for their trip, Visconti told the FBI agents he treated Frank Brancato as a special birthday gift to him, since he was born in September. He said he was looking for a site to build a high-class seafood restaurant.

In a different room, Frank told agents that Visconti paid for his trip as a birthday gift. He said he came to Las Vegas because his cousin, Joe Agosto, told him he was interested in hiring him to help him in Las Vegas for $200 a week and that he was seriously considering his offer and moving to Las Vegas permanently. Agosto was in the building business with Joe Porrello Jr. in a company called Golden West Enterprises, Inc. He had been very busy lately and Frank said, "He needs a man like me to help him."

The FBI agents kept both men in the rooms and spoke to them about other illegal activities. Of course, the men knew nothing about what Nick Licata did in Los Angeles, or how he made his money. Both men were released by 4 a.m.

After returning to Cleveland from their Hawaii vacation, Brancato was seen at Mt. Sinai Hospital daily, staying for six to eight hours at a time, visiting his close friend DeMarco. According to an FBI informant, Brancato was acting as a bodyguard in the hospital to protect his friend.

NOTE: Frank Visconti is listed in the Federal Bureau of Narcotics "Big Book," while Frank Brancato was not. From 1935 to 1937, Visconti served time in Leavenworth on a narcotics conviction. In 1962, Visconti had sold his interest in Captain Frank's and in August

1962 he visited Palermo, Sicily, his place of birth. This all had to raise a "red flag" with law enforcement and the Federal Bureau of Narcotics, who were very active at the time. This was the time of the "French Connection" cases, and the government was looking at probably anyone "connected" to organized crime. Of course, Frank Brancato, as we know, never had any drug dealings, but that probably didn't stop the government from keeping an eye on him. Maybe that's what all the heavy surveillance was about.

CHAPTER TWENTY-FOUR

Daily Life

During their monthly meeting with an informant on October 7, 1963, the FBI asked him who would be likely to take over as the boss when Scalish died. The informant told them that because of their age and experience, Brancato could be considered at this time, but because of his health and heart condition, DeMarco likely would not be considered.

Ten years from now, it would be hard to say, but if both men were still around, "I see Brancato and DeMarco passed up because of their age and it could possibly go to Jack White (a.k.a. James Licavoli), or John Nardi, who is the nephew of old man Tony Milano and the president of Local 410 Vending Machine and Service Employees Union and a part of the large Teamsters Union. Another person who was up-and-coming in the Outfit was Pete DiGravo, who was active in a legitimate business called Doan Machinery and an illegal business as a loan shark. He had been moving up rapidly in recent years and making a name for himself.

The informant said he heard that Brancato, Visconti, and DeMarco were looking to become silent partners in a Las Vegas motel and that their friend Visconti would be the owner of the operation. Brancato was now driving a 1963 gold-colored Cadillac Fleetwood. The title was listed in Brancato's name. It was purchased from Central Cadillac for an estimated price of $4,857 cash. With the extras that were installed, including his television set, the total cost was estimated to be close to $7,400.

On October 12, the *Cleveland Press* said:

It is hard to believe that the Mafia crime syndicate would skip Cleveland to carry on a $150 million–a-year business in Detroit.

Strangely, the top Cleveland police can't even agree whether the Cosa Nostra, or Mafia, is operating here. Joseph Valachi, who has been telling the same Federal Investigation Committee of the many murders and gangland power struggles, earlier had named Scalish as a regional overlord. In later testimony, he said there were about forty La Cosa Nostra members in Cleveland. Statements already given by informers indicated that the McClellan Subcommittee on Organized Crime could profitably devote time to the Cleveland and Ohio situation.

Youngstown long has been disgraced by gangland killings over the years. Four of Youngstown's most notorious racketeers have been indicted in Federal Court here for income tax evasion and other offenses.

What, if anything, does Valachi really know about the Cleveland area, and the Youngstown crimes in general? Ohioans want more information from Valachi while he is talking.

Some people feel that Valachi was feeding information to the federal government before he came out to testify in court.

A source advised the Cleveland FBI on November 18 that he had never heard of the title La Cosa Nostra. In his mind, the organization had always been called the Outfit. As far as he was concerned, the leaders of the Outfit in Cleveland were Al Polizzi, who now lived in Miami, Anthony Milano, Jack White, Frank Brancato, John Scalish and John DeMarco.

On November 27, 1963, an informant told the FBI that he had recently heard a story about Brancato to the effect that a couple of "sharpies" pulled a past-posting operation on an Eastside bookmaker and took him for a couple of thousand dollars, two days in a row. From what he understood, one of the sharpies was a man he did not know, and apparently there were some difficulties between the bookmaker and the man.

The unknown man then went to see Brancato and told him his side of the story and asked if he would arbitrate these difficulties between him and the bookmaker. The informant understood that after listening to both sides of the story, Frank decided that the bookmaker was wrong and advised him to pay off the wagers made by the two men. The bookmaker reluctantly paid them off within two weeks.

On December 2, an FBI informant told agents that he had heard that Dominic Lonardo, who was originally from Youngstown, was now a cab driver and was friends with two brothers who would drive cabs, one during the day and the other at night. Lonardo was having problems with his old boss in Youngstown, Frank Amato, who was currently the underboss for John LaRocca.

Amato was believed to be running the Pittsburgh Mob at the time. It seems that Amato did not think that Dominic Lonardo was doing his part to make Amato money and wanted more money from Lonardo for him to stay in business in his town.

Knowing he could not make any headway on his own with Amato, Lonardo heard that his old friend in Cleveland, Frank Brancato, was becoming well-known as a negotiator for people in their line of work. He would always hear the complaint or "beef," and would make sure that everyone won.

One day Dominic drove up to Cleveland to meet with Frank Brancato and Tony Milano when he was in town at the IAB Club on Murray Hill. Lonardo explained his story to both men, and as a result, Brancato and Milano told Lonardo to go back to Youngstown and tell Amato that he was out and you (Lonardo) were now coming to Cleveland to work for them.

The informant told FBI agents that he was sure there was no payoffs made to Brancato or Scalish from Youngstown; however, Dominic Lonardo operated with the understanding that if something came up where some money could be made, such as a shakedown, he would contact Brancato in Cleveland, and Brancato would see that the shakedown was made.

The informant cited that up to three years earlier, a man in Pittsburgh owed $40,000 to a person in Youngstown, but refused to pay. He said within a couple of days, a couple of guys went down to see this individual and told him that Brancato and Scalish had sent them, and that this debt for $20,000 should be paid. It was then collected by the persons who had contacted him.

The money was then divided five ways, with Brancato and Scalish getting their share first. The source was then questioned as to how the Cleveland Outfit could put pressure on a person from Pittsburgh to collect such a debt. This person was considered to be Frank Amato, who was the underboss to LaRocca.

It was pointed out to the agent that, in the event this person had contacted someone like Brancato asking for help, what would have been the results? The source stated that what would happen would be Brancato, or possibly someone using his name, would approach the individual and put pressure on him to make the payment. Then, in return, if Cleveland needed help, someone from Pittsburgh would visit the individual and put pressure on them to pay up on their debt. In the end, both cities would win and get paid what they were entitled to.

On December 6, a well-known FBI informant told them that, in his opinion, "Uncle Frank" Brancato obtained most of his money from illegal shakedowns in which he actually did not come in contact with the person involved.

The informant told agents that, in a typical case, Brancato would send someone who would use his name. Brancato would put pressure on the individual, and if he did not pay, he would have to answer to Frank directly.

The individuals normally would pay up, at which time Brancato would get his cut from the debt. The informant stated that the only way a person could get close to Brancato would be to set up a big score for him, one that he could not refuse, because his cut would have to be too big for him to pass up. But even then, the informant said, Frank was always careful not to be physically connected with any deal, whether it was large or small.

On December 13, the FBI asked an informant about how many members of the Italian organization there were in the area. The man replied, "about one hundred." The main members were Scalish, DeMarco, street boss Brancato, Nardi, Nick Satullo, and James Licavoli, a.k.a. Jack White.

The source also revealed that Scalish was supposed to be a member of the national committee of the organization, but in his opinion, Tony Milano, a longtime member of the organization, was "still the big man."

The informant was asked whether he felt that Bill Lias of Wheeling, West Virginia, had any Italians behind him in general, or particularly Brancato. The source stated that he was not aware of any Italians being behind Lias, and had always considered Lias as "being a big man himself" in his own right. He said Lias supposedly had the Wheeling Chief of Police in his pocket.

On December 23, a female informant came to the FBI office in downtown Cleveland to let them know that she heard Brancato had made several personal appearances at the barbut game in downtown Cleveland, which, to her knowledge, was the first time in many years that Frank had appeared at the game. She said she heard the reason he showed up was because one of the players had created quite a stir over his loss of some big money. In order to quiet things down, Frank made a personal appearance and settled the matter right then and there with the man. When asked by agents what was said to the man, her reply was that she did not hear, but she was told the man picked up the rest of his money on the table and quickly left the game and the building, as if he was in a hurry.

She told agents the game continues to move around, from the old Ohio Plating Company building on High Street, where players needed to take a freight elevator to the third or fourth floor to enter the room, or to a hotel room, or another location Brancato would select.

At one location several weeks ago, it was three in the morning and there were still over sixty people gambling and having a good time. There would be anywhere from $1,000 to $3,000 on the table at one time. She said this game was run by the Greeks, and in order to participate in the game, players had to be known by either John Fotos or Frank Brancato.

This source also said she had heard that the cut of the house on each game was between two and a half percent to three and a half percent of an individual's winnings.

1964

In January 1964 FBI agents were informed that Frank Brancato now had a piece of John Fotos' barbut games operating in Cleveland, as well as other games that were operated by Bill Lias in Wheeling, West Virginia, in a club named Billy's. Bill Lias had told others that he had the Chief of Police in his pocket. Lias, a.k.a. "Big Bill," knew Brancato back in the bootlegging days. The informant said Brancato had been seen almost daily going into Miceli Dairy Products Company with DeMarco.

On January 2, the Cleveland police visited the Carnegie Businessmen's Club at 411 Woodland Avenue after receiving a complaint from a woman whose husband had lost large sums of money gambling in a barbut game.

Present at this club, along with many other men, was Frank Brancato, who was searched. Brancato was found to have over $800 in cash on his person. Brancato had also been seen at The Capri and the Three Coins Lounge. Both were well-known downtown Cleveland night spots.

No other action was taken against Frank or anyone else in the club at that time.

A police source said he had heard that the following day that Frank came around to see the man and asked him what all the trouble was about. The man told Brancato what had happened to him. Brancato listened very patiently and even sympathized with the man in order to let him "get it off his chest." The source told the police that apparently Brancato was able to calm the man down, and in his opinion, probably gave the man some money to compensate him. He was not sure whether the man was happy or not when he left the meeting with Brancato.

The source also told police that Brancato had been seen at the upstairs bar at the American Night Club on Euclid Avenue.

In January of 1964 an informant told the FBI that he heard in late November of 1963 that, on one occasion some time ago, Frank had been convicted of perjury following the killing of two men on Mayfield Road in Cleveland. According to the story, Frank was believed responsible for the shooting, and he was actually wounded.

Agents told the informant that they were well aware of this, and the information was useless to them. The informant went on to say that they (the FBI) did not know this about Brancato's crime: While Brancato was in the Ohio State Penitentiary, he received a notice one day from a guard to come to the residence of the warden as soon as possible.

Brancato dropped what he was doing and went to the warden's residence, which was connected to the prison. Brancato was still wearing his prison garb.

Present in the warden's home when he arrived were the warden, the city prosecutor, and a city judge from a small town near Columbus, Ohio, which, in the informant's knowledge, could have been in the Washington Courthouse. Brancato had never met these men before.

During the meeting, the prosecutor told Brancato that he had his release papers in his pocket, but "it would take some money."

At first Brancato did not trust these men, but after thinking about it for several minutes, and more convincing from the three men, Frank finally made his decision. He told them that "if they would drive him to Cleveland to a particular address and let him out, he could come up with the money."

Soon after this comment, the prosecutor and the judge put him in their car. The two men took Frank, still wearing his prison uniform, and drove him directly to Cleveland, to the address Brancato gave them.

Brancato left the car without any handcuffs or shackles, and returned thirty minutes later. He gave the two men $15,000 in cash. (In today's terms, that sum would be worth $247,677.)

The two men simply thanked Brancato and drove off, leaving him on the sidewalk, still in his prison uniform. Brancato told others that he never actually signed any papers to obtain his release, and he never heard from the men again.

FBI agents reported the weekly Sunday meetings continued at Damante's or LaMarca's barbershop with Scalish, Frank, DeMarco, and an new person, Jesse Logatto, who reportedly was a parking lot attendant at the race tracks in Cleveland, but was better known on the streets as an associate of Brancato.

From what other informants had related to the FBI, Brancato often seemed broke, with no money to his name, but he still went to many nightclubs each night. He would venture to the Three Coin Lounge on East 9th Street or the Club Caravan on Chester, both located in downtown Cleveland.

Brancato also had been known to go to the new Capri Nightclub or the Carnegie Businessmen's Club on Woodland Avenue. It would not be hard to find Frank with anywhere from $800 to $1,000 in cash in his pocket at any one time. He still enjoyed having younger women on his arm and showing off the attractive women to his friends.

On January 11, two FBI agents went to Brancato's home on Westview at 9 a.m. They knocked on the door and found Frank's daughter Bella answering the door. Of course, they knew she and her family lived with her father. The agents politely asked if Mr. Brancato was in.

Her response was, "Yes, please come in." Both men came into the home, which was very well furnished with a nice brown leather couch, two chairs, along with a beautiful mahogany coffee table, and end tables with beautifully decorated lamps. The men were greeted by Frank, who asked the two men to join him for breakfast.

Both agents said, "No, thank you."

Frank insisted, and told his daughter Bella to make the men some eggs, sausage, and toast as he poured coffee for the men. He sat down at the kitchen table with them as they all enjoyed their coffee.

One of the agents asked, "Why do you have a red mark on your forehead, Frank?"

Bella was heard laughing by the stove as she made the agents their breakfast. Frank looked at Bella, then back at the agents, and told them that one day, back in September, he took his little grandson Frankie, Bella's son, who was born with club feet and needed to wear leg braces for several years, to the Cleveland Indians game at the stadium. They were giving out these little mini-size baseball bats to all the young kids at the game.

One agent told Frank he remembered that game, because he had brought his own young son to the same game.

Frank continued, ever since that day, his little grandson would, at least once a week or so, hit him in the forehead when his mother told him to go wake up Grandpa.

Both agents laughed, along with Bella, and in front of Frank. He laughed along with them, and said, "every time the little shit hits me in the head, I hide the bat from him; but he somehow finds it and does it again to me when I am not expecting it. I can't win."

After they all enjoyed a good laugh and their breakfast, the three men left, and went downtown in the agents' car to the Federal Building in downtown Cleveland.

The agents first made some small talk and wanted to just ask Brancato a few questions, which they had done for many years. The first question to him was, "Who is Laura Castro?"

Brancato said she had been a girlfriend of Frank Visconti for many years. He tried to meet up with her at least once or twice a year, either in Los Angeles, or he would go to Hawaii to meet up with her and her son.

"Frank, talk to us about the old days; how was it?" was the next question agents asked.

"I am not sure what you are asking about, but I remember how there used to be a crap game at East 40th Street and Woodland in the area of the Northern Ohio Food Terminal back in the 1940s." Brancato mentioned he had one-fifth interest in the game and Morris Kleinman, a well-known Miami and Las Vegas gambling figure, also had one-fifth interest in the games.

Frank told the agents that several years earlier, as a result of a bad run of luck, he lost over $90,000 in the games and was about broke when he went to see Al Polizzi in Miami and wanted to borrow $15,000. Al's reply was, "Okay; you can get it from my brother-in-law."

Brancato told them he was working on the last $2,250 of this $15,000 loan and he threw it all on the table at one time, then he split the table. Brancato told the agents that his luck changed immediately on that one roll.

Within the next three hours he won back $25,000, and by the end of the night he eventually won back the $90,000 that he had previously lost, plus about another $25,000 extra.

Brancato told agents that he had always been friendly with the late Lou Rothkopf, who was a well-known Cleveland and Las Vegas gambling figure. He became quite despondent over the loss of his wife, who had been blind for many years, and it was sad that Lou had committed suicide.

Next, FBI agents asked Frank about his friend Frank Milano.

Brancato said he had been told that "Frank Milano is in very bad shape physically, and spends about nine months a year at his place in Mexico, and the other three months in Las Vegas with his family. I am sad to say I do not think he has much time left with us."

"Frank, how is Tony Milano doing in Los Angeles?"

"I am sorry I was not able to see him when Frank V. and I went on vacation to Hawaii. He was either in Las Vegas or in Cleveland at the time, and we just missed each other. But I hear he is doing well, and in good health."

Agents then asked Brancato about DeMarco.

Brancato answered; "I am sad to say my good friend is not feeling well at all. The doctors are now simply trying to build up his body to a point where he can go back into the hospital for another operation involving the removal of a cyst on his bladder; I will miss him dearly when he dies."

228

One of the agents then asked him about George Gordon. They knew him to be a well-known gambling figure and racketeer who now lived between Miami and Las Vegas.

Brancato answered he was sorry that he was not able to see him when he was in town the previous week. "But I am not that friendly with him, and it would have been a visit out of respect."

"Frank, how is Al Polizzi doing?" was the next question asked by agents.

"Al is doing very well and is in good health, from what I understand. He has a good business going on in Coral Gables, Florida. I believe it is a construction company, but I cannot remember the name."

"How is your son Nasher, and what is he been doing?

Brancato responded, "Nasher and his father-in-law have opened up a restaurant, "The Night in Paris Club," on Ivanhoe Road in Euclid, Ohio. It is doing very well so far, but it takes a while to get a place going in the right direction. Nasher can do it, I am sure.

While speaking with an informant, the FBI agents asked him whether the Outfit these days might be doing any muscling-in work for any local bookmakers with regard to making collections.

The informant told agents, "Scalish would definitely not sanction anything of this type today, because he does not want anybody rocking the boat. There is no rough stuff going on in Cleveland without Scalish's permission." The informant said that did not mean, however, that some Italians and some members of the Outfit did not do work of this type, but it would not have Scalish's approval. He went on to say for example "an individual like Mr. B., the capo, would move in on anybody he could or wanted to and Scalish would not necessarily hear about it, and would not even want to know about it. Frank B. can just about do whatever he wants to do in Cleveland."

On January 27, an informant told agents it was his understanding that Charles Cassaro owned and operated the Square Newsstand on Public Square and that, in years past, he always worked for Brancato whenever Brancato had anything going on in the way of a gambling joint. He stated, for example, Cassaro had worked for Frank B. when he had the gambling joint on East 93rd Street a number of years earlier. Brancato was also seen getting into a car owned by union official Babe

Triscaro.

The FBI noted on February 3 Brancato made a phone call from his home phone to a phone number located in Buffalo, New York.

On April 3, the Buffalo office informed the Cleveland office that the Buffalo phone number was listed to Carl Rizzo. A check was made of Rizzo's records with the Buffalo Merchants Credit Association by local agents on January 7, 1964. He was residing on Busti Avenue. Rizzo was a maintenance employee of the Board of Elections, and earlier was self-employed in the City Cigarette Service. He had a satisfactory credit rating.

On February 4, 6, and 23, the Cleveland FBI office received reliable information telling them that there was a barbut game being operated on East 2nd Street and High Street in downtown. It was doing very well, and Frank Brancato had a piece of the action, and "has some pretty good rollers" lately.

According to the FBI file on Brancato, the Cleveland police were making arrangements to raid a barbut game in the heart of downtown Cleveland in which Brancato had an interest.

On March 2, a source informed the FBI that the old barbut game Brancato was running a few weeks ago had now moved to the first floor of the Ohio Plating Company. Players had to enter by the door from the front, where there was a doorman present. Then it was necessary to walk up three flights of stairs to where the game was being held. The game usually started about 2 a.m. and broke up between 6 or 8 in the morning. Sometimes it might go on until early afternoon if it was a Sunday. The source told agents, "The games have been slow lately, and... not too much money is being gambled."

An article in the *Press* on March 23 said: Padlock Orders Closing the Three Vincent Avenue Joints Sought in Common Pleas Court Today by the State Liquor Director Donald Cook and Attorney General William Saxbe.

Targeted were Frolics Bar, operated by Max Brook, with Angelo Lonardo, Mickey's Lounge Bar, operated by Charles Lakis, and the 730 Lounge Bar, operated by Oliver Cohen.

According to the FBI, they believed Brancato was a known silent partner in the Frolics and Mickey's Lounge bar, but they were uncertain about his involvement with the Gay Nineties bar. The closings were because the three bars were common nuisances to the community. "We have long been concerned that these and similar permits premises in this infamous district spawn the seeds of abuse of the public order, decency, and sobriety," Cook proclaimed.

On March 23, the Cleveland Police Department raided a barbut game on High Street in the late-evening hours. There were twenty-eight players in the room standing around talking; however, there were no arrests made, since apparently someone had notified the organizer involved with the game. The police were unable to locate any physical evidence in the room, such as dice or a cup used to roll the dice. Police obtained the name and address of all the players in attendance and would make this information available to the FBI as soon as it was typed up.

It was now Easter Sunday in the year 1964. I can remember when Mom and Dad took us (their four children) to Captain Frank's restaurant to eat dinner. It was a very unique experience for us all to go out for dinner, but yet on a holiday, now that was something special. We were all very young. Jim was about twelve, I was nine, Joann was about six, and little Karen was about one year old. Everyone was all dressed up in their best Sunday and Easter clothes for this special dinner out. I cannot remember ever being in the downtown area before, and especially on the lakefront. It was cold and windy, and yet it was such a very new and exciting experience for us all.

Dad, Jim and I had dressed in suits and ties, while mom, Joann and Karen had very soft and pretty spring dresses. This was a rare treat for us all, since not many families could afford to go out to dinner on Easter, let alone to a fancy restaurant like Captain Frank's. Captain Frank's was located on the pier on the great Lake Erie shoreline and on East 9th Street.

As we walked in, the lady who was the hostess greeted us with a hello to my mother, like she knew her, and said, "Jennie, your table is ready; follow me," as she walked us over to a table facing the lake. The lake was a little rough that day, with about three-foot waves. How did she know my mother's name?

Dinner was a real treat and a wonderful experience for us all. The restaurant was elegantly decorated, and was filled with guests enjoying their holiday dinner like we were. I know Mom had lobster and Dad, Jim, and I enjoyed a steak, while JoAnn had chicken. Dad did not like seafood at all, so mom hardly ever made it, even if it was just for herself.

After dinner, the strangest thing that I had ever seen in my young life happened. The waitress brought Dad and Mom the check for our delicious dinner. Mom simply turned it over and wrote, "Thanks, Dad, for a wonderful dinner. We enjoyed it very much and are sorry you could not have joined us. Love, Jennie."

I asked my mother, "Doesn't Dad have pay for our dinner?

Her answer was simple: "Grandpa is treating us." She smiled as we got up to leave.

At this time in my young life, we were all told that our grandfather sold tires for a living and worked for a company called Cardinal Tire. I did not think much about it, how selling tires could make a person so much money that he would be able to dress in a nice suit. I do not remember him wearing the same one twice. He always drove a nice new Cadillac every time we visited with him. We always commented; "he traded it in when the ash tray was dirty."

We did not know at this time that our grandfather was a man who had so much influence and power in the city of Cleveland. Many men looked up to him with great respect or asked for his guidance; while others looked at him with fear and terror in their eyes and hearts if they dared to cross him or his friends. We had no idea what the Mafia was or did at this time in our young lives.

CHAPTER TWENTY-FIVE

'The Judge'

The *Plain Dealer* ran an article on May 12, 1964, which reported:

A court order barring solicitation for prostitution and for drinks was slapped yesterday on the Frolics, one of the three Short Vincent girlie-bars the State Liquor Department wants to close. The order was issued by Common Pleas Judge John V. Corrigan, pending a full hearing on the liquor department's request to permanently close the Frolics.

Attorney General David L. Kessler of Columbus represents the liquor department, and the other two girlie show joints listed are Mickey's Lounge and the 730 Lounge Bar, both on St. Vincent Street.

On May 15, the Buffalo office of the FBI contacted Carl Rizzo at his place of employment, the Erie County Board of Elections office in Buffalo, New York. Rizzo told agents that he would be willing to appear in the Buffalo office later that afternoon.

Later in the day, Carl Rizzo appeared at the Buffalo office of the FBI. He advised them that he was presently employed as a clerk at the Erie County Board of Elections on West Eagle Street. Rizzo said he was born on July 28, 1915, in Marion, Illinois, to Peter and Lucy Rizzo. He stated that his brother was Michael Rizzo, who was fifty-six years old. Rizzo said he was married to Mary Sperrazzo, the sister of the late "Barbut Ralph" Rizzo. He formerly worked for his brother-in-law, Salvatore Sperrazzo, at Rogers Corner Restaurant. Prior to that, he said he operated a vending machine business, which he later sold.

Rizzo said he and his wife maintained regular contact with friends and relatives in Cleveland and in the Youngstown area. Rizzo stated that his sister was once married to Angelo Amato, a cousin of Frank Brancato.

Joe Lonardo and Rizzo's brother had been victims of a gangland slaying several years earlier, and he said his brother-in-law had been gunned to death in Cleveland a few years ago. Rizzo said he did not know any of the circumstances surrounding these murders, and had made it a point not to ask questions concerning such matters while visiting Cleveland or Youngstown.

Rizzo informed the agents that he knew both Salvatore and Joseph Brancato, nephews of Frank, who formerly operated the Flamingo Room at the Richford Hotel in Buffalo. To his knowledge, Joseph still resided on Hoyt Street in Buffalo. Rizzo would not or could not furnish any further information concerning the Brancato brothers. He emphatically denied that he had ever been in business or associated with the Brancato brothers. Rizzo told agents he enjoyed working for the Board of Elections, and all of his time was spent on the political campaigns for the Republican Party in Buffalo.

On May 26, an informant told the Cleveland FBI that Brancato had been invited to a wedding on June 6 in Brooklyn, New York. The daughter of Salvatore Peritore was getting married, and being a longtime friend of Peritore, Brancato was sure to attend. Others invited from Cleveland were John Scalish, John DeMarco, and Frank and Tony Milano. The informant believed that only Brancato would attend, and the others would just send an envelope with a gift of money for the young couple.

A source stated that on the evening of July 12, Brancato and DeMarco attended the wake for Josephine Vecchio, the wife of Angelo Vecchio, a close friend of both men. The source told agents that the Vecchios were members of the Lodge of St. Angelo of Licata, as were both Brancato and DeMarco.

On August 3, a source told the FBI that within the past two weeks Brancato, Scalish, and Anthony Milano, as well as an unnamed well-known Akron, Ohio, Italian racket figure, had made a connection with the Ohio State Parole Board member in Columbus, whereby they would be able to get anyone out of prison in Ohio for the right price.

Anthony Delsanter of Warren was involved in this matter as well. They were contacting families of incarcerated individuals who had money, to determine whether they were willing to pay to have their relatives released. They had made contact with Ohio Governor Rhodes' administration office in the past.

On September 8, a source informed the FBI that he believed Brancato still had certain interests in Wheeling, West Virginia, through

Bill Lias, a well-known racket figure. The source said that, in his opinion, Brancato only got "peanuts" out of Wheeling, and had an interest in a Steubenville game. He said Frank had gone down there when a gambler had difficulty paying a debt to Lias.

According to FBI files, Frank Brancato was brought downtown for questioning once again on September 18. At his interview, agents tried to create a situation whereby some confusion and general talk might be generated among the other members of La Cosa Nostra in Cleveland. This was a common practice used by the FBI known as "tickling the wire."

Brancato was informed that an individual had come to one of the federal agents in another city, and had told them a story about how Dr. Romano, a well-known Cleveland surgeon, had been murdered in 1936. The agents told Brancato the informant indicated Dr. Romano was murdered in the residence of Frank Milano, the onetime national head of the Outfit, and then his body was taken from Milano's home and dumped in an Eastside suburb.

Brancato was then told by agents this person furnished information to the effect that John DeMarco was one of actual murderers, "and although this person did not indicate you, Mr. Brancato, you were present at the time of the murder."

Brancato became very upset and proclaimed, "I was in jail at the time Romano was killed." The agents' well-thought-out plan seemed to be working. It got Frank mad, and they already knew this to be true, but they hoped Brancato would immediately carry this story back to DeMarco, and that a situation would create tension. Then there would be confusion, and suspicion would spread regarding the possible identity of the informant.

When asked to evaluate the information they just gave him; Brancato responded, "I do not think there is any truth to it, and… it was probably some disgruntled individual who has an axe to grind with DeMarco, and possibly with me."

Agents then asked Frank about the Gay Nineties Bar. Brancato just answered that it was a shame what happened to that nice joint. It was always a great place to have a few drinks, and enjoy the girls and the show, to have some fun and a relaxing evening. But now, in the basement, there was a bar for "queers," and it was almost impossible for females and males to get in unless they were queer.

What about the Roxy Musical Bar? Agents now asked

Brancato told them, "The old vaudeville days are over, and it is disappointing that the place will be closing down soon, and that the building will be torn down as a part of the new Erie View project."

Brancato liked to reminisce about the old days, and told agents how he used to run whiskey in the late 1920s from Cleveland to Wheeling, West Virginia, in a truck to a Polish fellow whose name he could not remember. At the time he used to run a big barbut game in Wheeling. Frank told the agents the reason he ran the whiskey down to Wheeling was that he could get more for it. In Cleveland, he was lucky to get a few bucks, but said he never did sell any in Cleveland.

Back in 1929, I wanted to go back to Italy to see my family, so I let Jesse Logatto take over my runs to Wheeling for me while I was gone. On Jesse's first run to Wheeling, he stopped for something to eat, which I told him never to do. When Logatto went to leave the roadside diner, a police officer stopped him and asked him what was in the truck. Logatto told him nothing, but when the officer looked inside for himself, he found the whiskey. After several minutes of silence, he told Logatto he would like $300 to let him go. Logatto told him he did not have that kind of money on him, and if he could make a phone call, he would try to get it for him. The officer had no problem and Jesse called me to get the money.

I told him to stay there, and then I called a Polish man that I had been doing business with, and the man told me he would take care of the police officer. I phoned Logatto back and spoke with the police officer on the scene. The police officer settled for $200, and Jesse Logatto had no other problems on the remaining trips down to Wheeling, West Virginia.

Frank then told the agents that he was having a problem selling his home on Westview. He originally wanted to get $34,000, and it was now down to $29,000, but he still owed $10,000 on the mortgage. "Now that my wife has gone, I have no more use for the house... it has bad memories of the good life we shared."

Agents then asked Brancato, "What can you tell us about Danny Greene?"

"In my opinion, Greene is no good; he drinks too much and goes around with some of his longshoreman cronies, getting drunk and

breaking up bars.

On one occasion I asked Greene if he would help an ex-convict friend of mine to work as a longshoreman. When my friend went to see Greene, Greene told the man he needed to give him $400 for a fee to join the International Longshoremen's Union (ILA).

Frank went on to tell the agents that this was not irregular, and that everybody who went to work and joined the union must pay this fee, which was legal.

I then called Greene and asked him, since this guy just got out of prison and he was not in the position to come up with the $400 fee, (if) Greene could put him to work and take so much money out a week from his paycheck until the $400 was paid. That damn Greene turned me down cold on my proposition. I thought it was very fair. My ex-con friend did not get the job that he needed to stay straight. Danny Greene is getting too big for his britches.

Some time ago, Greene and some of his friends went into the Three Coins Bar, which is owned by a friend of mine, and one of his so-called toughest goons tried to pick a fight with an eighteen-year-old kid who was just sitting at the bar, minding his own business... The goon came up, apparently to pick a fight or beat up on this kid for no reason at all. The goon quickly found out he picked on the wrong kid, because he knocked out several of the goon's teeth, and Greene's group left the bar. Sometime later that evening; Greene and his men came back to the bar and did considerable damage to the front door with an iron bar.

Another time, Greene and his men went into a bar inside the Garfield Heights Hotel and tore up the place, again for no reason. The owner of the bar called me, and asked if I could come down and look at the damage that Greene and his men did to his place.

I went over and was amazed at the damage I saw. The owner wanted revenge for the damage that Greene and his men did to his place, and he wanted retaliation. I suggested to my friend that I would advise against this, and I told him to forget about it, and I gave him $1,000 to help in his new remodeling project."

I would also see Danny Greene with his bodyguards by his side inside Captain Frank's a lot, and he would always want to buy me a drink or two. Occasionally I would accept, but I knew it would be best to stay away from him. I have no use for Greene any longer, and one day, he will get what he deserves.

Agents thought Brancato seemed pleased that Danny Greene had been having problems and that he had to resign his ILA post. By 1964, Greene's members had had enough. Some of them got in touch with Sam Marshall of the *Plain Dealer*.

A job shakedown on Cleveland's waterfront is forcing longshoremen to work thousands of hours without pay. Workers are being compelled to give up an estimated $30,000 or more a year, former officers of the International Longshoremen's Local 1317 told the Plain Dealer.

Greene scoffed that the complainers were "all dissidents." But the series quickly brought investigations by the U.S. Attorney, the Internal Revenue Service, the Labor Department and the Cuyahoga County prosecutor.

It also emboldened the members: ninety-two of them signed a petition asking the International to remove Greene as president.

The ILA quickly sent a team to Cleveland and found, among other things, that Greene had failed to make payments to the union's welfare fund and had planted "bugs" throughout the union hall to record what members were saying about him.

The officials immediately stopped payment on all union checks and removed Greene from office.

On September 15, a source informed the FBI that a few years earlier, James Licavoli and Vince DeNiro had started out together in the vending machine business and in the numbers racket in Youngstown. He said this partnership was doing well, but ran into difficulties when DeNiro accused Licavoli of selling narcotics. A number of arguments ensued.

The informant explained DeNiro would give a certain order and later, without DeNiro's knowledge, Licavoli would countermand it. Then, to add to the difficulties between these two, Licavoli tried to move in several of his brothers as partners in the operation. This ultimately became so bad that Licavoli and DeNiro split and went their separate ways.

The informant reported that Licavoli, an old-time Italian, spent many years in Cleveland and was unable to make a name for himself in the Italian element. He then went to Youngstown. In Youngstown he became friends with DeNiro and financed DeNiro in the numbers racket and became a partner of Vince's in the cigarette vending business, as well as the numbers business, right from the beginning.

According to the informant; Licavoli and DeNiro continued to have difficulties with one another. About this time, Licavoli stated taking DeNiro to Cleveland to talk with DeMarco and Brancato in order to discuss DeNiro's difficulties with Licavoli and what could be done about them. The informant revealed that DeNiro gradually drifted into the control of the Cleveland Syndicate in this matter.

Then Calegaro Malfitano, who originally was from New York, and who had to come to Cleveland, and who definitely was a Syndicate man, wound up in DeNiro's Youngstown organization. In the informant's opinion, the Cleveland Syndicate, represented by DeMarco and Brancato, told Licavoli to find Malfitano a spot. There was also a possibility that Malfitano might have obtained a piece of Licavoli's interest in DeNiro's operation.

On September 28, an informant came to the FBI field office in Cleveland with information about Brancato, saying that he always made a lot of money as he continued to instill fear in people.

The informant added that he did not believe at that time Brancato would actually use muscle himself, but would probably get some younger people who did the work for him.

Brancato was an old-time member of the Outfit, and he never used the name of Scalish, the boss, when he was straightening out a beef between two men or putting pressure on anyone.

Brancato had started to be called "The Judge" by many men in Cleveland, and was very much respected. Brancato had a reputation for being very fair when ruling or helping with these difficulties. By only using his name, some of Brancato's men would cause fear in someone who owed money to one of Brancato's friends.

Brancato had also been involved in solving differences for Akron Mob guy Carl Rospo, who was known to be connected to the Cleveland Outfit. Brancato had to go to Akron once when Rospo called him to help him solve a $7,000 claim from a friend of his against a construction contractor, who could not build the house that Rospo's friend wanted built. Brancato soon ordered that both men meet up with him to discuss this problem. After listing to the two men and both sides of the story, Brancato told the contractor that he needed to repay the $7,000 or he would face penalties. Brancato did not mention what those penalties would be at the meeting, but there was no question that the contractor understood his meaning.

Carl Rospo had a connection or was in partnership with the owners of the Sicilian Super Club in Northampton Township near Akron, Ohio. It was well-known as a Mob hangout. Rospo had been in ill health and would later die in November.

According to a memo from the Director of the FBI to the Cleveland office dated October 19 and information obtained on October 6, regarding the recent interview with Frank Brancato, the chief lieutenant of Cleveland rackets boss Scalish:

The interview... conducted by agents of the Cleveland Office in connection with the Interview Program indicates your office is continuously giving considerable thought in carrying out the objectives of this program. Your plan... to create a situation whereby something confusing will occur and general talk might be generated among other members of La Cosa Nostra was well conceived. In this regard, you should closely follow this situation and be alert for any indications that the Brancato interview has created some discussions among the hoodlum element in Cleveland, and has perhaps caused some degree of confusion between the men.

To further enhance your effectiveness related to this program, you should continue to adopt and utilize new approaches and untried methods wherever possible, and keep the Bureau advised of any situation developing as a result of your efforts.

An informant reported to the FBI on November 6, that he had heard DeMarco and Brancato were interested in building a motel in Las Vegas, Nevada. He stated that he had also heard that a possible partner in this venture would be Visconti. Possibly Brancato would be a silent partner, since he could be named in a gambling operation.

On November 13, an informant told the FBI he had learned that Frank Brancato had called on one of the officials of the Forest City Material Company, a large building and home-improvement center, at their new Brookpark store recently, and tried to persuade Forest City to put in cigarette machines from the Buckeye Cigarette Service Company, in which Scalish was a partner. Forest City had the Buckeye machines in all of their other branches. These accounts were handled by Frank Embrescia, who was a partner as well.

The source told agents he thought it was odd that Brancato would be soliciting this business for Buckeye, and was of the opinion Brancato was possibly doing a simply favor for Scalish.

On December 30, an informant told the FBI that on December 26, a pretty good-size barbut game was going on at East 2nd and High Street in Cleveland. There was a large number of people, approximately 70,000 in Cleveland that weekend for the Browns-Colts Championship football game on Sunday. The barbut game lasted all of Saturday night and ended only two hours before the kickoff, about 11 a.m. or so.

In this exciting 1964 football season, the Browns went 10–3–1 and reached their first title game in seven years. The Browns throttled the heavily favored Baltimore Colts with the fabulous Johnny Unitas. The Browns won 27–0, with receiver Gary Collins catching three touchdown passes to earn him the MVP award. Other great Browns players on this team were Jim Brown, quarterback Frank Ryan, place kicker Lou Groza, and running back Ernie Green. The Browns would go to three more NFL title games in Brian Collier's eight-year tenure as head coach, including years after the great Jim Brown's retirement.

In the informant's opinion, neither Brancato nor John Fotos showed up at any of the games, but everyone knew they both had a piece of all the games. Nasher Brancato, Frank's son, represented him, and John Fotos had some Greek guy representing him, to ensure the games went on properly and to ensure that the two men got their proper cut of the profits.

The informant added that players of the games knew they would not be arrested, since Fotos had paid off people who were high up in the city to ensure police protection. No other downtown games could operate unless they get their okay from Fotos himself first, or he would contact his people and their games would be shut down by the Cleveland police.

On December 14, FBI agents observed Brancato meeting a man at Captain Frank's for lunch at 2:05. After the meeting lasted for over an hour, both men left. Later, after running his license plate, the man was identified as Peter Salemi, the president of Central Excavation and Sewer Company. Agents believed that Brancato was making a connection and working on gaining some type of control in the labor unions.

CHAPTER TWENTY-SIX

1965-1966

Cleveland police reported on January 15, 1965, that Frank Brancato now drove a 1963 gold Cadillac which was parked in the driveway of James Licavoli.

On January 17, detectives from the Special Investigation Unit of the Cleveland Police Department gave Cleveland FBI agents a copy of a police report regarding surveillance of Frank Brancato. On December 24, he attended a Christmas party at the home of John Scalish in Gates Mills, Ohio. Attending the party were Brancato, Babe Triscaro, Angelo Lonardo, Harvey Kater, Milt Rockman, Frank Embrescia, an unnamed Teamster official in the Hotel and Restaurant Workers Union, and Mike Minaden, an official in the Laundry, Dry Cleaning and Dye Workers Union.

Early on December 25 (Christmas Eve), detectives revealed that at 3 a.m., Brancato left his home on Westview Road and was followed by detectives to the home of Angelo Amato Sr., who lived on Throckley Avenue. He stayed for only one hour, and then Brancato left and returned home by 4:30 a.m. The police speculated that the men were dividing up money from a large-stakes crap game that had taken place that evening.

On January 26, the Cleveland police advised that, until recently, there had been a shoeshine stand located on East 9th Street, a few doors away from Vincent Avenue, run by a couple of Greeks. The stand had just moved around the corner into a space occupied by a dry cleaning establishment.

It is believed both places apparently accepted wagers as agents for different bookmakers in town. Brancato had been seen visiting the shoeshine stand on several occasions. The men had been calling their bets into a different bookmaker until recently. A source told police that Brancato informed him in no uncertain terms that they now would have to call all of their wagers to Charles Gruttadauria a.k.a. Charlie Carr, rather than the bookie they had been using. The source told police he had heard the Greeks apparently complied with the request.

On January 27, FBI agents revealed to the City of Cleveland Police Department that Brancato drove to Brooklyn, New York, on December 31. He visited his sister Angelina and her family for the new year, and stayed to see relatives of his late wife, and did not return until January 11. Agents noted he did this several times a year and had seen his sister, as well.

Brancato continued to go to their Sunday-morning meetings at the barbershop with Scalish, DeMarco, and Logatto. James Licavoli and John Nardi had started to attend some of these meetings. After his morning shave at one of the barbershops, Brancato continued to make his daily appearance at Cardinal Tire Company, and then went to the IAB club on Mayfield Road to play pinochle with some of his old friends on the hill. Some days he would visit Miceli Dairy Company with DeMarco as well, but they only stayed a half-hour to an hour, at the most.

In the evenings he would go to the Carnegie Club or his son's Night in Paris Lounge on Euclid Avenue. He had also been seen going to the Holiday Inn on Route 90 in Wickliffe, Ohio. Brancato had also been seen going into the Howard Johnson Hotel on South Marginal, where he stayed for one to two hours, several times a week. The Cleveland police believed he was running a floating crap game with his son-in-law, John Brancato, who kept the game moving to different locations to ensure the game was not found by police.

On January 29, a source told the FBI that, in his opinion, DeMarco and his close friend Brancato were longtime Outfit members. Both men were together in "Little Italy" almost daily, and they spent a great deal of time at the IAB club on Mayfield Road. In his opinion, he would consider La Cosa Nostra or Mafia to be synonymous with the expression the Outfit, and Brancato would definitely be considered as being a top member of La Cosa Nostra, the Italian Outfit, or whatever else you would like to call it.

On February 5, an informant advised the FBI Brancato had been seen the previous evening at the opening of the Tender Trap, a new liquor spot and restaurant on Broadway in Garfield Heights. In a few weeks the club would be renamed "The LaScala Super Club." The informant told agents that Scalish, DeMarco, and Jesse Logatto attended the opening, along with Pete DiGravo and James Licavoli. It was believed that Angelo Amato was part owner of the new restaurant, along with Tony Buffa, who was a well-known fence, but he did not know for sure if Brancato had a piece of the restaurant or not.

On February 9, an informant told the FBI Brancato was currently visiting the Pearl Road Businessmen's Club on Pearl Road. It had become a well-known after-hours bottle club, similar to the Seaway Club Brancato used to operate before it was closed down by a fire and the police.

On March 6, a source told the FBI that Brancato continued to be at the LaScala Supper Club almost nightly. The owner was Angelo Amato, an old-time racket figure and a close friend of Brancato. In his opinion, he wouldn't be surprised if Brancato had a piece of this club. He informed agents Brancato had also been seen at the Encore Room, a nightclub at Chagrin and Lee Roads in Shaker Heights. Frank normally had a very attractive young woman on his arm.

On March 21, the FBI heard from another informant that a new nightclub in the heart of Little Italy had opened up the previous week. It was called Toys. It was owned by Pete DiGravio, and all the Mob guys went into the place. Brancato had been there several times a week, but he only stayed for an hour or so. Brancato acted when he was there as if he had a piece of the action in the place.

On April 3, while the FBI was watching who went in and out of Captain Frank's Seafood Restaurant, they noticed Frank Brancato made his normal lunchtime visit about 12:35 in the afternoon. After he placed his top coat and hat into the coat-check room, he was approached by a white female who was about forty or forty-five, about 5'5" tall, with short, auburn hair, known as Mary, the manager. She greeted Frank with a friendly smile and a kiss on the cheek and handed him a white envelope. Brancato then opened up the envelope and fanned out the money, which the agents could see clearly. There were some bills that were double figures, as well as other denominations. The envelope was a Captain Frank's Restaurant envelope, with the name of "Frank B." handwritten on the outside. Agents strongly believed it was Brancato's share of the weekly profits.

Cleveland FBI agents were informed by a reliable informant that a new crap game was going on inside the "Orion Club" on Miles Avenue. The game was getting a lot of action lately. The stick man was John Brancato, Frank's son-in-law, and he had heard Brancato got 50 percent of the profits.

A "stick man" is the man who is in charge of the dice or Crap table. He will insure all bets are placed before he passes the dice to the next roller. He will then collect the dice and insured everyone is paid off before then the new set of bets are made before the next roll of the dice.

On May 4, FBI agents watched from a car outside Biondo's Funeral Home in Cleveland, Ohio, to see who would come to pay their last respects to Jesse Logatto, a longtime racketeer and Outfit man.

The agents at the stakeout were not surprised to see Brancato, who arrived in his 1963 gold Cadillac. They reported Scalish as the boss and DeMarco, Angelo, and Frank Lonardo, as well as Tony Milano showed up, along with several other Italian racket figures. Agents later found out that Logatto died of lung cancer.

FBI documented from a previous investigation that Brancato made several phone calls to a number in Akron, Ohio. The number was listed to a pay phone at the Sicilian Club in Northampton Township, near Akron. The Sicilian Club was a well-known hangout for Carl Rospo, who was a known associate of Brancato. He spoke with someone for several minutes.

On May 6, a source informed the FBI that the barbut game at East Second Street and High Street had closed down because of "heat" by the Cleveland Police Department. The game was going to move and open up later in the week and would be held on the second floor at 1372 West Sixth Street. Brancato was also operating a large dice game at the Orion Club on Miles Avenue, and was being visited by some very well-known gambling figures.

On May 31, the Cleveland office of the FBI noticed this article in the *Cleveland Plain Dealer*. The subhead was "Liquor Rackets Boom at Bogus Bottle Club." The article reported:

A Westside cheat spot masquerading as a plush bottle club has been selling liquor after hours and on Sundays for the last six months without state permits. The Plain Dealer placed reporters in an undercover investigation over several months and found the joint selling whiskey illegally to anyone and everyone.

Police continue to report they have been hard pressed to find the same evidence that would allow them to close down the club.

Local restaurant and lounge barmaids and bartenders in more than a dozen area nightclubs in downtown Cleveland area were found to be shilling for the place and sending customers, including

Plain Dealer reporters, to the cheat spot after their nightclubs closed down for the night.

(Frank) Brancato, a well-known racketeer from the days of Prohibition, hangs out there very often and has even been seen working in the place. The operator of the cheat spot is an old hand in the Cleveland bottle clubs. He is Louis "Lumpy Lou" Raffa. The name of this joint is the Pearl Road Businessmen's Club on 4281 Pearl Road.

The Pearl Road Businessmen's Club is the latest liquor racket of its kind since the 1960-1963 periods, when more than a half-dozen bottle clubs sprouted up in Cleveland and some were (believed) to have been operated by Brancato.

Most of these clubs were closed down because of violations (of) building codes, and a few others were found guilty of illegal sales of liquor. Brancato and his associates operated the well-known Seaway Club until it was closed in 1960.

After several phone calls from the citizens, the Cleveland police say they know of this Pearl Road Bottle Club but they cannot do anything about it, because their undercover men have so far not been able to prove the rumors (that) illegal liquor is sold for cash.

The Plain Dealer undercover reporters had no such problem in their investigation. Reporters bought drinks at Lumpy Lou's bar for cash, despite a sign over the bar proclaiming the club did not sell liquor. Another sign confirmed set-ups and the mix cost 90 cents. But the reporters bought drinks several times as guests of other members and then as members themselves.

A membership in the club costs $5, plus $20 or so for a fifth of liquor the member rarely sees. The member signs a phony-looking agreement that the club will buy the liquor for the member, and then the members pay the club.

Drinks were poured freely from bottles grabbed at random by the bartenders, not just those supposedly to be for the members. Reporters found that several bottles did not have name labels on them, as well.

Despite little name labels pasted on the back of the bottles, the bottles are refilled from other bottles indiscriminately. This in itself is a violation of Ohio liquor laws.

Many of the customers were well-dressed men and women who seemed to be professionals, while others were single men and women who told reporters they were bartenders, barmaids, and waitresses from other restaurants, and they enjoy coming here to relax and have fun after work.

The real action at the club begins after legitimate taverns and nightclubs close down. The reporters bought drinks from 3 a.m. until 9 a.m. almost every day in the week, including Sunday morning. Other members told the reporters they could get into some high-stakes gambling in the basement on Sunday afternoons, when the club was closed to members.

The drinking is in a plush layout on the modernistic, forty-foot-long bar that seats twenty-five people. There are twenty-four tables in the place, seating up to eighty people, and most mornings the joint is jammed. The club has carpet on the floor and candles on the table. There is also a small dance floor with a jukebox in the corner and the club is dimly lit.

There are about forty locker containers lined up near the front door, and more than one member's name and bottles are listed on the outside of the small locker doors.

The front door into the restaurant looks to be made of steel, and has a one-way see-through mirror, through which Lumpy Lou checks those coming into the joint.

Those outside could only see a reflection of themselves. Anyone who enters who is not a member immediately gets a guest card from Lumpy Lou's wife. The couple greets nearly everyone who enters into the place.

There is another door made out of steel as well, that the guest must pass through before they enter the bar area. The double-door system is protection against sudden entry from the police.

The police are having problems providing evidence of an actual cash sale for liquor. Donald Cook Director of the Ohio Department of Liquor, said, "The problem could be corrected if the cities... adopted ordinances outlawing such clubs, like Toledo and Akron have already done."

The *Cleveland Press* reported on June 2:

Safety Director John McCormick today gave his approval to an ordinance that would outlaw bottle clubs in Cleveland.

Bottle clubs are semi-private clubs that serve drinks from a bottle supposedly owned by members. Since technically no sale of liquor is involved, they need not obtain a state liquor license or abide by closing hours or other state regulations governing taverns.

This new ordinance is aimed at the Pearl Road Businessmen's Club, located at 4821 Pearl Road. The club is operated by Louis Raffa, who formerly operated the after-hours joint called the Mayfield Road Businessmen's Club on Mayfield Road, which operated for three years until the police were able to obtain evidence to close down the club.

Police strongly believe that Raffa is working for (Frank) Brancato, a well-known gambler in Cleveland. McCormick admitted to The Press, "This ordinance has never been tested in court."

By late June, the Cleveland FBI office finally observed the Cleveland Police Department was getting harder on illegal gambling by raiding floating crap games, poker and barbut games.

One night the games would be held at the old Ohio Plating Company or at the Food Terminal Building. Then they would be moved to the Orion Club on Miles Avenue.

The police continued to focus on Brancato's Pearl Road Businessmen's Club. The floating games could be at the Howard Johnson Motel on South Marginal Road one night, located next to the Cleveland WJW Channel 8 TV station, now known as Fox 8. The next night it could be at the Am-Vets Club at 992 Broadway in Bedford, or in a room at the Holiday Inn in Wickliffe, Ohio.

These games, operated by Frank Brancato with his son Nasher and son-in-law John Brancato, continued to move around quite often, because the heat from the Cleveland police was now on all illegal gambling operations.

On July 30, a source stated a crap game had been raided by the Oakwood Police, since they did not have "the green light" to operate along with the Ohio State Liquor Department at the Mayfair Club on Aurora Road. Some people believed it was a part of Brancato's operation, but he was too streetwise to have not obtained the Oakwood "green light" to operate the game, so it must be an independent operation. Arrested were Joe Lonardo and several others.

This same source told agents that on August 23, Brancato and Visconti visited Las Vegas once again. They stayed at the Stardust Hotel and were there for some type of business venture.

On September 2, FBI agents asked the same source if he had ever heard of a card game called romika. The source said he had heard of the game, which is played with two decks of cards, and he believed this game was played on Bolivar Road in downtown Cleveland and particularly in John Fotos' place. John had a piece of the barbut games, along with the Italian Outfit through Brancato, and he would not be surprised if both men were involved with this game.

An FBI anti-racketeering report on September 27 revealed Frank's close friend John DeMarco was confined to Mount Sinai Hospital, where Frank was a visitor daily.

It was also noted that agents believed Brancato had an interest in a new card room. He was spending a considerable amount of time at the Eastwood Social Club, located on East 122nd Street and Woodland. Brancato had reportedly been assisting Shonder Birns, a local bookmaker, in collecting from bettors who owed Birns as a result of their gambling.

From the Cleveland office of the FBI to Director J. Edgar Hoover, a memo dated October 5 noted that a mention was made to a new card game known as romika, being played in Cleveland area. No prior information about the game had been found in the Bureau files.

Since this would be of interest in connection with our gambling investigation in regard to Frank Brancato or others, it would be appreciated if you would furnish the Bureau with full particulars and rules covering the operation of this game. Our interest would be how many decks of cards are used, number of players in a game, how bets are placed, and how a player can win or lose. Include type of stakes and any other information concerning this game. Please advise us if this game is common only to Cleveland, or whether it is played in other parts of the country, possibly under a different name.

1966

On February 14, 1966, an informant advised the FBI that it was his understanding that Frank Brancato had no particular use for Leo Moceri or Ernie LaSalle, a.k.a. "Fusco." Both were well-known La Cosa Nostra members residing in or near Akron, Ohio. This source revealed that (either) Leo Moceri or Jack White had been able to get Brancato overruled in the death of his friend Mike Farah about five to six years earlier. Farah was killed by a shotgun blast from a passing car while he was in his back yard in Warren, Ohio.

The informant explained Farah and Brancato were extremely close and when the "hit" was out for Farah, Brancato tried very hard to intercede for Mike Farah with John Scalish, but Moceri and Jack White were able to overrule him, and Scalish gave his approval for the hit.

On March 18, an FBI informant advised them that he had heard in Steubenville, Ohio, Mafia Boss Dino Cellini came to Cleveland and visited with Brancato and John DeMarco every month in Murray Hill. The informant was unsure whether it was to give them their share of the profits from his gambling interests from his area of Ohio, but in his opinion, it had to be.

The same informant said he and a bunch of the younger Mob guys called both Brancato and DeMarco a couple of "dons" and were waiting for the old men to just die so they could move up the ladder in the Outfit, but none of them had the "balls" to try to kill either man.

On April 7, a source advised agents that he had heard the barbut games currently operating in the downtown area would be, in his opinion, owned by Frank Brancato. He would get seventy-five percent of the take and the other twenty-five percent would go to John Fotos.

The source also told agents Brancato was seen having dinner at the Sicilian Club in Akron. When Leo Moceri came in, Brancato just got up and left the club.

An FBI informant told them on April 12, Brancato discussed with other Cleveland racket figures the possibility of setting up a gaming operation on the top floor of the Garfield Hotel, where he planned on offering card, crap, and barbut games. Brancato said that if it did materialize, he would like to have Tony Panatela; a reported Mafia member and numbers man, to run the games.

On July 15, an informant advised agents he had observed on July 13 Frank Brancato, Frank Embrescia, and Al Polizzi at the Hunky John's card room, located on Mayfield Road in the heart of Little Italy. Joining them was Jack White, along with Tony Randazzo, a known Mafia member, who now resided in Miami. The men were playing cards together most of the night. The source was told that Embrescia and Polizzi were in town for an upcoming wedding, but did not know who the wedding was for.

On August 3, an informant told the FBI he had heard Sam Poliafico had made several comments related to the recent newspaper publicity pertaining to Scalish receiving $50,000 per month from Las Vegas gambling interests in the Desert Inn. The informant told them White indicated Brancato and DeMarco even received a share of these funds from Las Vegas. The informant said the Stardust also "kicked up" money every month, but the amount was said to be much smaller, only about $30,000 per month.

The Desert Inn had many high rollers, or what Vegas liked to call "whales," and they made a bigger profit margin. The Stardust was a casino for the working man, and they had regular gamblers who could only afford to spend much less.

The informant heard that out of the "skim money" given to the Cleveland Outfit, Scalish got 100 percent of the profits. It is believed he then gave 20 percent to Moe Dalitz, 20 percent to John (George) Angersolo, who lived in Miami, and 20 percent to Frank and Tony Milano. Then he divided his 40 percent, with a few of his men. For example, if his cut was $50,000, Scalish gave $10,000 to the Milanos out of respect. Then out of his cut of $40,000, he gave 10 percent to Brancato and DeMarco.

The informant went on to say he had heard that even James Licavoli might get a smaller cut if the skim money was higher, but normally Licavoli did not get anything. This same informant added that he had heard Brancato got seventy-five percent of all the profits from John Fotos' barbut dice games and Fotos got only twenty-five percent of the profits.

On August 10, a source told the FBI that he had recently learned from a close friend of Babe Triscaro, who was a real estate developer, that if anyone desired to borrow funds from the Teamsters, he first had to see Frank Brancato, who represented Scalish and Triscaro.

On September 2; FBI agents were advised by a local source that he had heard people in New York were upset about the publicity about the Las Vegas "skimming" operation. Alex Shonder Birns, a well-known

Cleveland racket figure who was close with Scalish and Brancato, both well-known La Cosa Nostra members, was being dispatched within the next couple of days to contact George Gordon in Miami, Florida, to discuss the possibility of Gordon getting in touch with Edward Levinson of the Fremont Hotel, to call off his lawsuit against the government.

The source indicated it was the feeling of the "Cleveland people" that the government pressure in Las Vegas was just the beginning, and they were fearful that the entire Las Vegas gambling industry might be adversely affected and eventually ruined.

Later in the day, FBI agents heard from the immigration inspector from the Immigration and Naturalization Service in Cleveland, Ohio, that Shonder Birns had telephoned them and indicated that he may be going to Miami, Florida, on September 3. If he did go, he would wire the INS from Miami. INS agents noted that on September 6, Shonder Birns had informed them that he did, in fact, go to Miami, Florida, on September 3 and returned on September 4.

On October 17, the Cleveland FBI learned from an informant that there was a new gambling place in Warrensville Heights. It was the old Veterans and Auxiliary Association on Warrensville Road, where craps and blackjack as well as poker were being played almost nightly. The source said Brancato reportedly had a piece of this operation as well, and for his piece of the profits, Brancato gave his protection and permission to run the operation without the Outfit's interference. Brancato still made visits to Angelo Lonardo's Highlander Motel for breakfast and would often meet John DeMarco and his son Carmen, then it would be off to Captain Frank's, and had been seen at the Hunky John's card room on Mayfield Road.

On November 1, the same informant advised agents there was a dice game being operated by Angelo Amato, a well-known Eastside gambling figure, at the Vet's Club on Warrensville Center Road, across from the Randall Park Race Track.

The informant goes told agents this was a commercial-type game where all the players would shoot against the house. He understood Brancato had been given an interest in this game, but did not have to invest any money in the operation.

The FBI informed the Warrensville Heights Police Department on November 3 about the information they had received about the dice game at the Vet's Club. Agents also asked for their help in watching the building and the activities that were going on there.

On November 4 at about 8:30 pm, FBI agents saw Frank Brancato pull up in his 1966 Cadillac and park in the Maplewood Funeral Home, next door to the Vet's Club. He walked to the side door, where he pressed a button and gained entrance into the building. The agent noted the door sounded like it was made out of steel.

The FBI continued to keep their eye on this operation for the rest of the year. They made notes of all the license plates being parked outside the Vet's Club and the men who went inside to gamble in this illegal club.

CHAPTER TWENTY-SEVEN

1967-1968

On January 5, the Cleveland FBI was informed by a reliable source that Frank Brancato was upset because he had felt for a while that one or more of the employees in one of his weekly dice games at the Vet's Club might be stealing or skimming money from him.

Brancato told the source he was thinking about putting someone he trusted into the joint to watch over his investment—someone like his son Nasher or his son-in-law John Brancato. There had been quite a bit of heat on these games from the local police lately, and Brancato had been thinking of moving them to a different location or closing the games down for a short time, or perhaps permanently.

On February 7, the FBI learned from another informant who had visited Brancato's Bottle Club on Pearl Road and noticed Brancato in the lounge area. He overheard Frank talking with a woman and telling her he had a very good, legitimate business going on here, and he did not feel the heat was off enough to start commencing with gambling at the club, but if things remained relatively quiet, he was planning to start up a high-stakes dice game at the club in the near future.

On March 1, a police detective observed Brancato in the Theatrical Restaurant and Lounge late in the evening. As Brancato walked toward the bar, the young bartender, Angelo Rich, handed Brancato his drink like he always did, scotch on the rocks with a splash of water, without Brancato even asking for it. He noted that this was the third time in two weeks that Brancato had showed up at the restaurant to meet Angelo Amato Jr. The detective stated the significance of this action meant that Amato and Brancato must be back in action somewhere, or they were planning on a new location after the closing of their dice game that was being held at the Veterans Club.

The Cleveland FBI reported in March that Brancato was finally able to sell his home on Westview for $29,000, but he claimed he had lost money on the deal after he paid off the home mortgage loan that was still on the property.

On March 8, the Cleveland Police Department advised the FBI that their department recently, upon receiving several complaints concerning a card game held at the Garfield Hotel, located on 38th and Superior. When the police arrived they went into the Garfield Hotel and straight to the Tuckers Room and chased out a small group of ten men, including Frank Brancato and Tony Panzarella, a known racket figure.

The detective told the FBI the guys were playing romika, a card game, and that there was no money found on the table. They said they must have been keeping track of their bets by some sort of accounting system that allowed them to have no money on the table at any time. Several days later, the Cleveland police learned the game had just been moved to the Watson Motel down on Euclid Avenue.

A police detective also advised the FBI that Frank Brancato had been seen playing cards at the Versailles Motel on Euclid Avenue, as well the Tuckers Room, and was alleged to have an interest in the Eastwood Social Club on East 122nd and Woodland Avenue.

On April 14, the *Cleveland Press* announced to the city the new location for a great entertainment center, with a lounge and an informal atmosphere, which was owned by Larry Mako and a well-known popular local entertainer in the city of Cleveland named Scott Reed.

The Blue Grass would have a dining room able to seat up to three hundred guests at one time. It would be located south of Libby Road near Rockside Road. It would have two banquet rooms, one for smaller affairs that would accommodate one hundred people, and a larger one that could hold close to two hundred people. It would have dancing and entertainment nightly, with the Jimmy Belt Trio providing most of the music. The Blue Grass would also feature Scott Reed as the main singer in the lounge. The Blue Grass Motor Inn, a five-story motel, would be built next to the restaurant within the next five to six months.

On April 26, FBI agents were advised by a source that Brancato had been seen frequently at "The Scene," a new discotheque located inside the Belmont Hotel on Euclid Avenue. The source indicated he had heard Brancato might have a piece of this club, while he had heard from other people that he did not.

By this time, Frank learned he lost yet another sibling, his brother

Salvator to cancer.

On May 16, an informant advised the FBI that John Fotopoulos, a.k.a. John Fotos, and Frank Brancato had started up yet another game and moved their barbut dice game to a new location on Prospect Avenue in an upstairs room. The sign on the front door said "AN Benevolent Association" and the players just walked in through the front door.

On June 1, FBI agents were told by a source that Brancato continued to frequent the Garfield Hotel on Prospect Avenue and played romika. The source stated other well-known criminals and numbers figures were at the game when it was "hit" by the local police, just because they had heard Brancato and Tony Panzarella (a well-known numbers man) were present in the game.

On June 7, an informant came to the FBI with information on yet another "negotiation" that Brancato did in the city of Cleveland. The informant stated Frank settled a dispute between an unknown Mob guy and John Nardi, nephew of Tony Milano. Nardi allegedly beat up this guy and both men had been seen frequently at The Scene and at the Capri Lounge on Euclid Avenue as the tension between them continue to grow. The source stated the man came to Frank with a black eye and mentioned that he had been in a fight with Nardi. The man went on to tell Frank he was going to kill Nardi.

The source then stated Frank was well aware that the man in question was a bad actor and had a bad attitude when he got to drinking. He asked the man what the beef was about. The man told Frank he did not know, whereupon Frank, in the role of a peacemaker, went to see Nardi. Nardi then informed Frank the real reason for the fight was that the man was fooling around with his friend's wife. The source stated Nardi likewise told Frank if this guy did not stop this, he was going to kill him. The source said ultimately Frank brought the two men together for a meeting and after the "sit down" and talking things out for about an hour, the two men shook hands and agreed to forget about the incident.

The source went on to say that, in addition to settling this beef a week earlier for a man named Arnone in Akron, Frank settled another argument for someone else several weeks earlier. Arnone is well known to Brancato. Arnone was at the race track and got into an argument with a well-known bookmaker in the city over the debt that Arnone owed to the bookmaker. The man who owed the money went to Frank for help and guidance. Frank went to the race track personally with Arnone and spoke with the bookmaker to see whether they could settle the debt and make peace between the two men. After talking in a private room, the three men made an agreement and the beef was settled.

The source stated to the FBI that in all of these negotiations, Frank had never made a threat of any kind to anyone, and as a matter of fact, had been quite nice and calm and helped both parties to settle the beef properly and without any violence.

On September 18, an FBI source said the previous day at 3 a.m., he entered Lumpy Lou's Bottle Club on Pearl Road and one of the people standing at the bar was Frank Brancato, who had been seen there quite frequently. The source said Brancato now drove a 1967 Cadillac and had been at the club for several hours and stated that he must have had a piece of the large crap game that was going on in the basement. The source said in his opinion, it was a large-scale dice game. Brancato was watching everything that was going on at the table.

The source went on to tell agents he went up to Brancato and asked him if he could borrow some money from him. Brancato asked if it was to buy drinks and he told him yes, it was. Brancato turned to the bartender and told him to give him whatever he wants. The source told them he ran up a $30 tab after receiving the okay from Brancato. The informant said Brancato would often seat and help the customers when needed, and for a man that some have said does not have a piece of the action, he definitely acted as if he owned the club.

In July, a source told agents Brancato and Frank Embrescia came up to a man who was a known loan shark and grabbed him by the collar. The man explained to both men that Nasher had owed him $100 from last year and that all he wanted was his money back with no interest. The source told agents that Brancato gave the man $120 in cash and told him in no uncertain terms that he was to never lend money to his son Nasher again, under any circumstance. According to the source, Frank took care of the rest of his son Nasher's obligations with several loan companies in the city, thereby allowing him to get back to work at both the Thistledown and Northfield race tracks.

On August 8, Cleveland FBI agents observed John DeMarco, Frank Brancato, John Scalish, and Milton Rockman meet once again at LaMarca's barbershop on East 154th Street and Kinsman Road. Agents believed this was an important meeting, since Rockman attended.

On October 13, an informant advised the FBI he had heard

Brancato and his son-in-law John had occasionally rented rooms at the Howard Johnson Motel near downtown Cleveland and reserved several rooms at the Blue Grass Hotel to hold professional-style poker and dice games. The source also told the FBI Brancato had been negotiating for a place in Summit County, which he believed was on Old Route 8 near the intersection of Route 82, for a dice game. The informant told them Brancato had been trying to make arrangements to move their dice game operation to Burton, located in Geauga County, but had been unable to do so thus far, because the prosecutor there was currently arguing with the mayor. The informant told the agents he had heard from a good source that Brancato had been getting regular treatments at the Cleveland Clinic and it was not certain whether it was because of gout in his feet or for his arthritis in his lower back.

On October 13, a different informant advised agents Brancato had been trying to make arrangements to move his dice game operation into Burton, Ohio. The source also advised them a friend of his, who until recently had been employed in the money room of Cleveland's two race tracks, would be quitting both tracks in order to commence booking on the west side of town on West 25th Street. The source revealed he would have to put up some money for the bankroll and Frank Brancato would provide "the fix," and that one of Brancato's men would be working with him.

This same informant told agents Tony Buffa, a well-known Cleveland fence, continued to play cards with Brancato and Panzarella at the Garfield Hotel.

On November 27, the FBI received information that a plan was under way for Brancato to set up a location in Bainbridge, Ohio, in Geauga County, to operate a crap game. The source told agents it would include his son Nasher and his son-in-law John, along with Frank Majestro.

According to the source, Nasher had made contact with an unknown local source to get the okay to operate this game. The source went on to say that this group was not particularly interested in transit players, since they had their own steady group of players, such as businessmen and an assortment of professional people, and some women who like to gamble and could well afford to lose and would come to wherever the games were being held in the city.

The man also informed agents that this game would be under way in a very short time. The informant told agents from what he had heard, the new location would be on Route 306 north of Chagrin Falls and past two stoplights north of Lake Lucerne on the northeast corner. There was a liquor license for sale and the place was not open for business yet.

1968

On January 18, an informant told FBI agents Frank Brancato had been having a real rough time physically and had been in the hospital over the holiday season. He was then discharged from the Cleveland Clinic, where he had spent several weeks in the hospital, having undergone a prostate operation. He was considered to be very weak.

On February 8, an informant told FBI agents that at approximately 11:00 in the evening on February 6, Frank visited a big dice game in Geauga County on Route 306 and Route 422. There were quite a few men in the building, as well as several women. The man observed Brancato in the room watching the game. As he watched the dice game, he was told that both Frank Brancato and John DeMarco owned the game. The men were planning to add other casino games like roulette, poker and blackjack to attract more people, and especially women.

The building was an old white southern-style home with several pillars in the front. There was a large white sign in front of the place, which was painted over, and there was a small sign underneath a larger sign, which stated, "Kinsman Social Club, Members Only."

The informant said the game had only been in operation for several weeks. Several players said the game had not had too many players yet. Virtually every night they had operated had been a winning night for the house, with the exception of one night, which turned out to be a winning night for all the players. The principal game was craps. The source revealed he left at four in the morning, and things were still going strong.

On February 27, an FBI informant told them Brancato had not been feeling well lately once again, and had been seen going in and out of a doctor's office and the hospital. The informant said he had not heard what was wrong with him, or whether he was still having issues with his earlier prostate operation.

On March 12, the *Cleveland Plain Dealer* ran a front-page expose on the gambling place Frank Brancato ran in Bainbridge Township known as the Kinsman Social Club.

Because of the adverse publicity and reaction to articles in the Cleveland newspapers about the gambling joint, Frank decided he had no choice but to close the operation down after only being open for four short weeks."

The source said Frank told him he would have to move the location of his gambling operation, which would cost him both time and an excessive amount of money. Frank was not sure whether a new club was going to be worth the trouble.

By this time, in 1968, my cousin John Bisco was out of the Army after serving two tours of duty in Vietnam. With help from Grandpa, John headed for Las Vegas and within two weeks was working at the Stardust Hotel, learning how to deal all the card games in the casino, along with working the very popular crap table and roulette wheel.

John stayed in Vegas for one year and decided to come home to Cleveland and see what opportunities he would have. By 1974, John was back in Vegas and working at several casinos as a dealer until he retired in 2009 and moved back to Cleveland.

By April, Frank Brancato was driving a new light-yellow 1968 Cadillac Fleetwood sedan. An FBI source said he had heard Brancato had an interest in the new Cleveland Bottle Club in downtown Cleveland.

Whenever a beef or concerns came up in the gambling world, only Brancato was to be called to help moderate and negotiate the peace between the men involved. Brancato had become a respected and trusted ruler and a fair man, and his decisions were always final.

On May 4, the *Cleveland Plain Dealer* ran an article that said after the Ohio Supreme Court had turned down a rehearing of a March 13 ruling upholding the municipal banning of bottle clubs, Lt. Ernest Wilcox decided to have a talk with Louis Raffa. Raffa was believed to operate the Pearl Road Businessmen's Bottle Club for (Frank) Brancato. Raffa told Lt Wilcox he would close temporarily, but insisted he had not given up the fight to stay open.

The Cleveland newspapers The *Plain Dealer* and The *Press* reported that on June 21, 1968, 42-year-old Pete DiGravio was enjoying a game of golf with three friends at the Orchard Hills Golf Course in Chesterland, Ohio, when suddenly he was shot to death on the 16th hole. Six shots had been fired by a sniper.

Police brought in many different people for questioning, including Frank Brancato.

Through an informant, the police found out that DiGravio, who was believed to be a loan shark, had been visited earlier by an unknown man who told him the Outfit wanted 10 percent of his profit.

DiGravio quickly refused the man's request. Several days later he was shot while enjoying the game of golf. Police were not able to solve this murder. The Cleveland Outfit once again had proved they would not tolerate men like DiGravio working in Cleveland without kicking up a portion of his profits.

On July 11, an FBI informant advised them he had heard Frank Brancato had been operating for the past two weeks near Geauga Lake Park in Geauga County. (Geauga Lake Park was a well-known amusement park in northeastern Ohio.) The informant said an individual told him about the dice game and described it as being located in a house at the rear of a motel, possibly on Aurora Road. The source told agents it had at one time been noted for being the location of a house of prostitution.

Brancato had been seen working in the house and was behind this game. The games seemed to be very large and profitable for the Outfit. The local police did not seem interested in what was going on in the building. The informant told the agents that, for a man of his age who was said to have been very sick, Brancato still got around the city a lot.

For the rest of the year, Frank Brancato took it slow, but was still seen at his normal spots around the town. He did not seem to be himself, however; he looked older and more sickly to many of his family and friends.

CHAPTER TWENTY-EIGHT

Waste Hauling Takeover

According to Rick Porrello's book, *To Kill the Irishman,* in June of 1968, Joe Messina came to Cleveland from New York to help the Cleveland Outfit organize the very profitable waste-hauling business.

Messina joined forces with Brancato, who by now had been sent an associate from a friend in New York, Carmen Semenoro, to help enforce the takeover of haulers who would not cooperate with their request.

With the backing of Brancato and the Cleveland Outfit, Messina was to help organize all the waste-hauling business in Cleveland.

Several other businessmen in Cleveland started trying to organize the waste-hauling industry and founded the Cleveland Solid Waste Trade Guild. The main idea behind the Waste Haulers Trade Guild was to stop all the undercutting between all the other smaller trash haulers, take over their routes, and then set a fair price for all haulers.

Frank Brancato found out that Joe Messina was more concerned about his own rubbish hauling firm and not organizing the hauling industry, as was the original plan. Brancato had heard that Messina was using his name to take over routes, which infuriated Frank. Frank decided to have Danny Greene move in to take over the organizing job.

On August 29, an informant told the FBI he had heard back in late May or early June that John Scalish had requested some help from his friends in New York. Scalish asked for them to send someone to work with his street boss, Frank Brancato. The person would come to Cleveland to help organize the activities of all the different trash haulers in the city. Joe Messina was the man who came to Cleveland and helped Frank Brancato, along with the union organizer from the Teamsters, Babe Triscaro.

On September 8, Brancato was seen at Cleveland Hopkins Airport, where he picked up his close friend Al Polizzi, along with his wife and son, on their return from Coral Gables, Florida. This informant said he had heard Frank had an interest in the new "Scene Lounge" where many young people tended to go for an evening out. It had become very popular night spot in Cleveland.

By this time, in 1968, my older cousins, Dorothy, Virginia, Frank, John, or Bill, would often go to either Captain Frank's or to the Blue Grass Lounge for dinner and drinks on the weekends. Many times they would go together or meet some friends of theirs. My older cousins always enjoyed the entertainment, fabulous food, and the drinks, and were treated like kings and queens, as the men and women who worked in the restaurants all knew their grandfather was "Mr. B." Before they left the restaurants, they would tip the servers very well, then they just simply signed the back of the bill, "Thanks, Grandpa. Love, Dorothy" (or Virginia, Billy or John). It was easy for them to have a great dinner and enjoy the best that Cleveland had to offer with a grandfather like Mr. B.

On October 7, a source revealed to the FBI he had heard Frank Brancato and Danny Greene met at Captain Frank's on October 4 to discuss the trash haulers. In their meeting, Greene seemed more concerned about what was happening with the International Longshoreman's Association, or ILA.

Brancato asserted to Greene, "At the present time it is in bad shape, due to the threatened strike against the entire eastern seaboard by the ILA." The source said Frank told Greene that the time would be very bad for any trip to New York, and that he needed to stay focused on the trash-hauling situation in Cleveland.

On October 22, an informant advised the FBI that Danny Greene had been contacted by Frank Brancato, who advised him that he had some word from New York concerning Scalish's request to be able to contact someone there concerning the present situation in trash haulers. The source stated Brancato advised Greene that he had "something good to report:" a man would be coming to Cleveland to meet with him and that after this meeting Greene would have to go to New York, at which time he would get in touch with Joe Messina, who was in the Genovese family in New York. Messina was active in loan sharking and had investments in numerous other places.

The source continued to tell agents Brancato had become fairly friendly and close with Greene of late, and that Brancato had a room key to Greene's offices, known as Emerald Industrial Relations, Inc. in room 220 in the Pick Carter Hotel.

The source told agents Frank had helped Greene get this company started and would use one of Greene's rooms to rest when he was in the downtown area, or to just kill some time. As noted in Rick Porrello's book, *To Kill the Irishman*, it was Frank Brancato who had helped Danny Greene start up the Emerald Industrial Relations, Inc. For a hefty price of $2,000, a contactor would hire Greene's firm to ensure that there were no conflicts or job shutdowns or long delays by the unions in Cleveland. With men like Babe Triscaro and Jackie Presser working with the Outfit, they could control what was being built and how fast the job got done in the city. The $2,000 was considered to be a "consultation fee" to these companies.

According to Porrello, affidavits were presented to a federal judge, charging Greene with labor racketeering and a violation of his parole, which prohibited him working in or with a union for another two years.

It looked like an open-and-shut case for the authorities, until the judge suddenly and without an explanation announced that he was dismissing the charges and allegations against Greene.

It would be a full year before they heard the truth about why their efforts were in vain.

"It is hard to say no to J. Edgar Hoover," the judge explained.

It seems the information they were getting from Greene was so valuable it even warranted the protection from the FBI director himself.

Years later, once again, the FBI would be embarrassed by the infamous; "Whitey Bulger" case, which turned out to be a disaster for the FBI.

James Joseph "Whitey" Bulger, Jr. (born September 3, 1929) was a former organized crime figure from Boston. Local folklore depicted Bulger as a Robin-Hood-style bandit dedicated to protecting the neighborhood and its residents.

Bulger allegedly masterminded a protection racket targeting drug kingpins and those running illegal gambling operations. Based upon the testimony of former associates, federal prosecutors indicted Bulger for nineteen murders.

Beginning in 1975, Bulger served as an informant for the FBI. As a result, the Bureau largely ignored his organization in exchange for information about the inner workings of the Patriarca crime family.

Beginning in 1997, the New England media exposed criminal actions by federal, state, and local law enforcement officials tied to Bulger. For the FBI especially, this has caused great embarrassment.

On December 23, 1994, after being tipped off by his former FBI handler about a pending indictment under the RICO Act, Bulger fled Boston and went into hiding. For sixteen years, he remained at large. For twelve of those years, Bulger was prominently listed on the FBI Ten Most Wanted List. Then, on June 22, 2011, Bulger was arrested outside an apartment in Santa Monica, California.

1969

In an FBI document dated January 19, 1969, Frank Brancato is named as a leading La Cosa Nostra member in Cleveland. It continued to claim Brancato was considered to be the number-two man to Scalish and had received money regularly from Scalish. Brancato was also known to be close to Mike Farah, part owner of the Jungle Inn of Warren, Ohio, who was killed on June 10, 1961, the subject of a Mob contract hit.

The following references are listed in Brancato's FBI file captioned, Top Hoodlum Program pertaining to the criminal activities of Brancato from the 1940s to April 23, 1969, in the states of Arkansas, California, Hawaii, Nevada, New York, and Ohio.

Brancato was a Mayfield Road Gang member and is one of the leading LCN racket figures in Cleveland area and is a lieutenant to Scalish. He has associated with other known hoodlums in Cleveland and meets regularly at LaMarca Brothers and the Damante's barbershop on Sundays. It was alleged that Brancato went to the 1957 Apalachin meeting in New York, along with Scalish and John DeMarco other LCN members, even though he was not arrested or found in the area at the time of the raid.

Brancato gained prominence and strength during the bootleg days by being involved in several murders.

Brancato has received most of his money through shakedowns and had interests in several crap games, card games and business establishments, including a restaurant and barbut games in Wheeling, West Virginia.

265

Several of these places he had played cards personally or had a direct interest in the games. Some of these games were raided and closed down, although some games are believed to have been operated with the approval of certain police officers and possible payoffs to high officials in those cities.

Brancato has been interviewed several times regarding his activities and the activities of his friends and fellow hoodlums.

From January 1969 until July, Brancato has been seen at several different locations, from his normal shave in the morning at Damante's or LaMarca's barbershop to their Sunday-morning meetings with Scalish and DeMarco. From the Highlander Motel, owned by his good friend Angelo Lonardo, to the Capri and Scene lounge to The Penthouse Lounge, located inside the Versailles Motel in downtown Cleveland. He has also been seen at the Blue Grass Motel on Northfield Road (and) the Blue Fox Restaurant on Clifton Boulevard in Lakewood. Brancato would often be seen playing cards at Avaroff's, located on Bolivar Avenue in downtown Cleveland, and of course, he is always seen at Captain Frank's Seafood house on East 9th Street.

On February 28, the Cleveland FBI was advised once again from an informant that Brancato had left Cleveland on February 12 for Brooklyn, New York, where his sister Angelina's husband Amedeo Casuccio had passed away. Brancato stayed for several days and also attended the funeral of his old acquaintance and former boss, Vito Genovese, who had died in prison on February 16.

A source revealed to the FBI on April 17 that there were several indications Brancato still had an interest in Captain Frank's Restaurant. He regularly got income from this location.

An article written by Paul Lilley in July 16th in *The Cleveland Plain Dealer* was headlined, "Dan Greene Moves to Round Up $25,000,000-a-Year Rubbish Business.

Greene has entered into the commercial rubbish business and is looking to try... price fixing the industry. (He) has several police reports of intimidation against him.

Greene's new organization is called the Cleveland Trade Solid Wastes Guild. It was chartered by the State of Ohio on June 6 this year. The informant claims Greene is trying to standardize the efforts of all independent and private collectors and insists that it is purely voluntary. Greene claims that "some of the 'big guys' in town told me these men needed help in organizing, and that I was the man to help them." Greene never mentioned who the 'big guys' were, but the Cleveland police and FBI strongly believe it is (Frank) Brancato on the orders from (John) Scalish. This same method was used successfully in other major cities, including New York.

By this time in 1969, my older cousin, John Brancato, the son of Ninfa and John, received his discharge from military service and was home from the Vietnam War. John stayed in Cleveland for a few months, and like our other cousin, John Bisco, he headed west for Las Vegas. John Brancato drove for over forty hours and when he arrived he met up with grandpa and was given the Penthouse suite at the Stardust Hotel where John stayed with our grandfather and Frank Visconti. For several days grandpa introduced John to many of his friends in town before he helped him get into Caesar's Palace as a dealer. Unlike my other cousin, John enjoyed the glamor and excitement of Las Vegas, the warm climate and his new job. He decided to stay there for the rest of his life. His mother Ninfa, along with my other cousins, Dorothy, Rosie, Frank, and Joe, would soon follow him.

On July 30, the *Cleveland Press* ran an article written by Paul Lilley, which said:

John Scalish, who is the so-called head of the Cleveland Mafia and the man who has taken over the old Mayfield Road Mob, and some high-ranking Teamster officials, are targets in the federal government's anti-racketeering probe.

Although the federal government has refused to reveal the other names in addition to Scalish, we believe it will include William Presser, President of Joint Council 41, Louis "Babe" Triscaro, president of the Excavation and Building Material Construction Drivers and Race Track Employees Local 436; John San Filippo, a business agent for Triscaro; Frank Brancato, a known bootlegger, (and) gunman who won a long battle against the government on a deportation trial and is suspected to be the number-two (Mafia) man in Cleveland; John DeMarco, a partner with Scalish in the cigarette machine business and the possible consigliore for the Cleveland Family; Frank Embrescia, partner with Scalish in the cigarette machine company; Angelo Lonardo, who operates the Highlander Club and is the brother-in-law of John Scalish and a cousin to John DeMarco; and Milton Rockman, another Scalish brother-in-law and a partner in the cigarette machine company.

The federal government intends to do a complete and thorough investigation into all of these men.

Mentioned were Teamster bosses Presser and Triscaro, who for a long time have been reported to have been close with Scalish and some of the other men who are listed in this article and whose names are frequently in the headlines for their racketeering activities.

A Washington source revealed, "There is no doubt whatsoever that Scalish is the La Cosa Nostra representative in Cleveland, and that DiGravio's slaying last October was the direct result of his shylocking operation and his mafia connections." Just two days before he was gunned down in gangland style, DiGravio told the reporter, "He had no Mafia connections and needed the Mafia like he needed cancer." Years earlier, in 1947, the Los Angeles police revealed details of a recorded conversation between Triscaro and Mickey Cohen, a known West Coast racketeer, during which Cohen identified Scalish as "the big man in Cleveland."

In November 1969 the FBI learned from an informant that Frank Brancato was now extremely close to Joseph Messina, a Cleveland-area rubbish and solid waste operator. "Mr. B" was responsible for bringing Messina into the Cleveland area as a part of his plan to help organize the waste-hauling operations in Cleveland. The informant told agents Brancato had to go to New York City and "take some heat" because of Messina's complaint to unknown individuals in New York that he was being isolated by Brancato in Cleveland.

The informant told agents that because of this complaint, Brancato found it necessary to go to New York and attempt to clarify the situation. This concern was worked out, and the two men remained friendly today. Both men continued to work together along with Danny Greene to try to organize the large waste-hauling industry in Cleveland.

On November 18, the FBI was informed that Carmen Semenoro, who lived in Warrensville Heights, Ohio, had been brought to the Cleveland area by Frank Brancato. The informant told agents that allegedly Semenoro was on the run, and was run out of town by a New York Family and was sent to Cleveland to see Brancato. Brancato was to help Semenoro and straighten him out.

Semenoro insisted that he be introduced to others as Carmine, and not Carmen, his birth name. Brancato tried to get him work at several locations, and in general, Brancato had been looking out for him.

The informant also told agents Brancato often stayed at the Pick Carter Hotel in downtown Cleveland when he had time to kill, or needed to relax, or to see a girlfriend. He always used room 220, which belonged to Danny Greene.

This was a very special holiday season for me. On Christmas Eve in 1969, my mother's complete family gathered at the home of our Aunt Bella and Uncle John for a symbolic holiday feast which is observed with the *cena di magro* ("light dinner"), a meatless meal.

Fresh fish was provided by Fulton Fish Company. A wonderful variety was served to our family and friends. Depending on what a family was able to obtain or afford at the time, it could be seven to ten varieties of fresh fish, from trout, perch, shrimp, mussels, and lobster, to octopus, squid, and eel.

On Christmas Day, Italians often serve tortellini as a first course, then possibly lasagna as the main course. Typical Italian desert cakes of the Christmas season are biscotti cookies, panettone and pandoro (a round-shaped heavy style of bread sweetened with honey, from Milan). It is served in slices, accompanied with sweet, hot beverages or a sweet wine, such as Asti Spumante or Moscato d'Asti. This huge holiday gathering, we all ate like kings and queens.

After the feast, the adults would always set up a table to play cards and drink for several hours, but more importantly, they enjoyed each other's company, and the bond of family.

Most of the grandchildren at this feast, like me, were in their young teenage years and beginning to understand what their grandfather really did for a living. As all the adults gathered around the large bar, they toasted to one another, and to their good health. They covered the entire corner of the basement and talked business, from what we could hear. When they spoke about something important they would almost whisper, and then, when we got caught looking toward them, the adults began speaking in a softer voice, one that we could no longer hear, or they would speak in Italian, but we knew they were talking business with Grandpa.

By now, we all began to know our grandfather was not a tire salesman, like our parents had told us for all of those years. Our grandfather was an important man in town, we could all tell. He was a man who held great power and authority, a man with many friends, and a man who had always been well-respected in the community.

Grandpa dressed as though he was an owner of a bank, or a president or a manager of a business. Grandpa would always be happy to see us and would welcome us with a kiss on the cheek, and when he left, we got a big hug and another kiss—almost as though he was not sure when we would see him again

1970

On January 26, a federal investigation case was initiated when a resident of Youngstown telephoned an FBI agent and made a formal statement.

The man advised agents that he was in debt to Francis Ross, a known racketeer for a sum of money. The man was contacted and threatened by a man who he had not heard of, named Carmine Semenoro. Semenoro told him the debt he owed to Ross was being collected by him, which caused this man fear for his life, as Semenoro had threatened to break both his arms and legs. The man told agents he would come in and furnish a complete and signed a statement against him along with the receipts for payment that he had made already to Semenoro.

In Youngstown, Ohio on April 3, a female informant advised the local FBI that she was very nervous and frightened. She felt that a tall man was threatening her husband at her home, due to the angry tone of his voice and his manner. The tall man then told her husband, "I'll give you two weeks." After that, both the tall man and the shorter man left her home.

The female advised agents she believed she would be able to recognize the taller man, since he did most of the talking, but not the shorter man. The woman furnished the following descriptions of the two men. The taller man was between 6'1" and 6'2", with dark hair and a medium to heavy build. He weighed about 175 pounds or more. The shorter man was in his late sixties or so, about 5'6" tall and weighing about 155 pounds, with balding, graying hair and glasses.

Based off the descriptions and information about Semenoro in their FBI file, they strongly believed it was Semenoro and Brancato who came to see this woman's husband.

Semenoro had been born on January 21, 1938, and had three arrests in New Jersey in 1967, for assault and battery, disorderly person, and for threatening a person with bodily harm. Semenoro had exhibited a gun many times, and had used brass knuckles in the past several times, and therefore he was considered armed and dangerous.

On April 14, the Cleveland FBI informed the Washington office they had received information from a source that Carmine Semenoro, who was a known associate of Frank Brancato and was a subject of an extortion credit transaction investigation, was planning to flee the Cleveland area in a day or so. The Cleveland Strike Force attorney had authorized filing a complaint and charging Semenoro with violation of the Hobbs Act before Cleveland Federal Judge Clifford E. Bruce. The arrest warrant was on the basis that Semenoro "did knowingly, willfully, and feloniously obstruct, delay and affect commerce, as in the terms described in the Hobbs Act. He used the wrongful use of a threat of force and violence, and has threatened bodily harm."

Semenoro was arrested on April 14 by Bureau agents at his Warrensville Heights. No weapons were found on his person or within reach in his automobile.

Semenoro appeared before Federal Judge Bruce and was jailed in lieu of a $100,000 bond.

The report noted that Cleveland sources have said Semenoro had been brought to Cleveland by Frank Brancato to act as muscleman to make collections for Brancato and his associates. Cleveland informants told the FBI Semenoro's arrest would have a disruptive effect on the Cleveland Mafia.

The FBI contacted other cities looking for any information in regard to Semenoro's activities and information where he could have been collecting debts beside Cleveland, but no information was gathered.

On April 15, Semenoro appeared before Federal Judge Clifford

Bruce and was represented by Attorney Elmer Giuliani as he made a motion to reduce Semenoro's bond. Giuliani mentioned he had been retained by Frank Brancato to represent Semenoro.

In the morning of April 28, the indictment was returned by the Federal Grand Jury in Cleveland and signed by Judge Thomas E. Lambros. The arrest warrants were issued for Frank Brancato, Michael Romeo, and Francis Ross. At noon Brancato was arrested by FBI.

Brancato told agents he had met Semenoro while having a drink at the Blue Grass Lounge about a month before Christmas. Brancato advised agents that he had become friendly with Semenoro, but he did not know him prior to the time Semenoro came to Cleveland. After having a few drinks with him, Semenoro advised Brancato that he came to Cleveland from New Jersey. Brancato maintained he did not have any knowledge of Semenoro or his associates prior to coming to Cleveland, and as far as he knew, they had no mutual friends or acquaintances in either New York or New Jersey.

Brancato advised agents he met a man a few weeks later that knew of Semenoro at the Blue Grass and said, "Semenoro is a satisfactory employee of his at the Monroe Lighting Company and is a salesman for him."

After Semenoro was arrested, Brancato advised agents that he called Dominic Lonardo, a friend of his, to see if he could help him with his bond. Lonardo told him the bond was too high; therefore, he made no further efforts to get Semenoro out of jail.

Brancato stated he did this because he was friendly with Semenoro and he had no obligations to Semenoro, other than being a friend. Brancato stated that as far as he knew, Carmine was a nice man and was trying to make a living to support his wife. Brancato denied hiring an attorney to represent Semenoro, and he did not know who was representing him.

Brancato said he had known Scalish most of his life, as he grew up with Scalish in Cleveland. He further stated he knew Scalish's family during his youth and considered Scalish his friend. When asked about the La Cosa Nostra, Brancato stated he did not believe in the LCN and that the Italian meaning for this is "my thing." He felt there was no organized crime being referred to as LCN in the United States. Brancato further stated the term "Mafia" in Italy was used to describe "tough guys," but has no meaning as far as organized crime. Brancato stated he knew Francis Ross, but knew Michael Romeo, the son of Paul Romeo, much better, and that Romeo was a resident of the Youngstown area, but he did not associate with him very often.

After Brancato's interview with FBI agents, he was immediately taken before Federal Judge Lambros, at which time his bond was set at $50,000. Brancato was represented by his attorney, Elmer Giuliani, and after the bond was set; Giuliani requested a bond reduction before Judge Thomas D. Lambros. Brancato's bond was lowered to $10,000 and Brancato was released the same day.

A side note was made in Frank Brancato's file that as a reported leader in the Cleveland LCN, Brancato had employed Semenoro to act as a muscleman in the collection of debts for Brancato and his associates. Cleveland sources advised agents that the arrests of Michael Romeo and Francis Ross would cause additional disruptive effects on the Cleveland LCN.

Semenoro had lived with Nasher Brancato for a few months when he first arrived in Cleveland, until his wife arrived, and then they moved to Warrensville Heights.

On April 28, A *Cleveland Press* article by Al Thompson reported:

Cleveland Mafia figure Frank Brancato and four associates were indicted by a Federal Grand Jury today for conspiring to extort cash from two Youngstown businessmen. The men were charged with racketeering, violation of the Hobbs Act, extortionate credit transactions and conspiracy. This article involved the indictment from the Federal Grand Jury, who teamed up with the Justice Department and the Strike Force investigating organized crime in Ohio.

Arrested were Frank Brancato; Carmen Semenoro, a New Jersey gangland enforcer who is held on $100,000 bond; Dominic Lonardo, a known associate of the underworld, who in 1968 admitted his part in a nationwide mortgage loan swindling ring; Michael Romeo from Campbell, Ohio, reported to be a small-time hood; and Francis Ross, an Akron businessman, whose company was used in the shakedown operation for conspiring to extort cash from two Youngstown businessmen.

The two businessmen who were involved with this shakedown were Richard Eden and William Manus of Diversified Homes, Inc.

The indictment alleged that these men threatened to use violence against the two Youngstown men if they did not pay off a business

273

debt of $3,300 that was owed to Francis Ross. Semenoro and Ross threatened to beat up both men and break their arms and legs if they did not pay up.

Back on December 12, 1969, Semenoro met up with William Manus at the Highlander Motel, owned by Angelo Lonardo in Warrensville Heights, and threatened "to cut off his legs and throw them in the horseshoe drive of his home if he did not pay the debt that he owed Ross."

It is believed Semenoro told Manus he would even take a payment of $50 a week until the total of $3,300 was paid.

Federal Judge Frank Battisti ordered Brancato and the four men's bond set at $10,000 each. Semenoro's bond was set at $100,000, even though Semenoro was in prison for an earlier crime, and a trial date had not been set yet.

The U.S. Justice Department's Special Organized Crime Strike Force here has alleged that Semenoro beat five people with brass knuckles and has threatened the lives of five others, and has bragged about killing two other men when he lived in New York.

Several other witnesses also reported they had received threats from Semenoro in the past, that their property would be bombed or their families killed if they did not pay up.

On April 29, the *Cleveland Press* had a large article written by Al Thompson:

Frank Brancato, who is seventy-two, is facing possible deportation if he is found guilty of the extortion plot against two Youngstown men. Dominic Lonardo... was currently in jail on another crime in New York, and was scheduled to be released from his probation in a few months.

Judge Clifford Bruce related how "Brancato is the brains of (the bunch)" and set Brancato's bond at $50,000, then lowered it to $10,000. ... Lonardo and Semenoro's bond was set at $5,000."

The indictments resulted from the work of the Justice Department, Crime Strike Force and the FBI. The FBI arrested Brancato three weeks ago as he left the Damante's Barbershop in Shaker Heights.

Richard W. Ahern, an agent with the Immigration and Naturalization Service (INS), refused to comment as to whether they would reopen Brancato's old file and review it, or simply start up new deportation proceedings against Brancato. Agent Ahern offered that if there is a second conviction against Brancato involving moral turpitude, "I believe that Mr. Brancato already has one on him already for gambling and murder in his bulging INS file since 1932. We may reopen his deportation hearings as soon as his conviction is finalized."

A *Cleveland Plain Dealer* article written by Ann Hellmuth on May 16 said:

Frank (Uncle Frank) Brancato, a reputed Mafia leader, denied conspiring to extort money from two Youngstown businessmen when he was arraigned in front of U.S. District Judge Thomas Lambros. Brancato's attorney mentioned yesterday in the Federal Courtroom of Judge Thomas D. Lambros, Brancato denied these charges earlier in Federal Grand Jury on April 28. Terry Brunner, a lawyer with the U.S Justice Department on Organized Crime, describes Brancato as "the brains behind the operation. He did not make the threats himself... but was a moving part behind the plan."

Brancato and two others charged with conspiring to extort money from two Youngstown men, Carmen Semenoro and Michael Romeo, pleaded innocent when arraigned before Federal Judge Thomas Lambros. The three men were charged with threatening the life of William Manus and Richard Eden, co-owners of Diversified Homes Inc.

In a request to the Director of the Federal Bureau of Investigation from the Assistant Attorney General of the Criminal Division, Will Wilson, asked for all electronic surveillance information pertaining to the Brancato and his co-defendants.

FBI Director J. Edgar Hoover forwarded the request to the offices of Cleveland, Baltimore, Cincinnati, Detroit, Miami, Newark, New York and Pittsburgh, asking them to review their files and to forward any

The offices all replied that they had no further information to disclose.

CHAPTER TWENTY-NINE

Carmine Semenoro Murder

According to an FBI file, a reliable and confidential source stated that there were many versions on why Carmine Semenoro got "hit" on the night of September 23 at his home in Warrensville Heights.

The Outfit believed that, after he was arrested on September 10 for trespassing and disturbing the peace, Semenoro started talking to them. It was their feeling that he was now a "stool pigeon" and was talking to the police and possibly to the FBI about local Mob activities, since he was only given a $100 bond. Bedford Height's police indicated that there would be no mention of his arrest in his record.

Another source stated Semenoro was alleged to have a great many enemies in the Cleveland area because of his activities and his association with various women. Any number of these people could have killed him.

Another source told the FBI Semenoro had been arrested in Bedford Heights several weeks earlier on an assault charge after he beat up John Brancato, the ex-son-in-law of Frank Brancato and the son of Frank's late brother John. John Brancato told others that Semenoro was "the most cold-hearted bastard he has ever met."

The Bedford Heights police had released Semenoro before a bail bondsman could post his bail. This same source told the FBI Semenoro had gotten into a terrible and serious argument at Chester's Lounge with John Brancato and stated that the beef between the two men came from Semenoro moving in on a waitress named Linda who had been going out with John.

A few years earlier, to help him in his collection business, it is believed Frank Brancato had arranged the release of Bob Boggess, a young man of thirty-two, from the Ohio State Penitentiary. Boggess wanted to move up in the ranks in Cleveland. Boggess was a very tall, intimidating, strong man who stood 6'2" and a solid 230 pounds of muscle, and as mean as they come. He had a reputation of being a hothead, and carried his .45 weapon with him all the time.

My cousin John Bisco was sitting in the Mayflower Lounge one early morning with Boggess, Tommy Sinito, and Uncle John Brancato. All the men were drinking heavily when Sinito and Boggess started arguing over a stupid matter that my cousin does not recall. Boggess quickly pulled out and aimed his weapon at Sinito and shot his .45 several times over his head, hitting a jukebox near the bar. Luckily, there were only a few other people at the other end of the bar at 2:00 in the morning.

Another story about how Semenoro was murdered comes from an unnamed source who stated that the hit order came directly from Frank Brancato. To correct the situation that many believed was his fault, it is believed Mr. B took the situation into his own hands and met with two men, his son-in-law John and a man who police knew to be a hardened, crazy criminal—Bob Boggess. Brancato gave the order and Boggess was the trigger man.

Boggess later died at the age of thirty-five on October 6, 1973. Many think it was because of his love for excessive drinking, gambling, drug use and women.

After being picked up for questioning, an FBI informant advised them that he had no firsthand knowledge concerning the murder of Semenoro on the night of September 23. His sources stated that, in all likelihood, Dominic Lonardo would be considered a possible suspect; however, his source stated this was not the case. Lonardo was not a close associate of Semenoro, but knew of him slightly. The source continued that the recent indictment of Semenoro, Romeo, and Brancato and others was a bad rap, as far as it included Romeo.

The source said all Brancato did was to introduce Semenoro to a couple of people. This source said Semenoro did not have any highly-placed connections in the New York Outfit, although he was always bragging that he did have such connections. The source told FBI that Semenoro was a loudmouth who used the name of Brancato quite often and names of various other individuals in the city in an effort to impress young women and other people.

FBI reports included the newspaper article from the *Cleveland Press* that spoke of this news that would bring down unwanted heat on the Outfit.

The way Semenoro, who had been described as "no good and a loudmouth" was hit with a double-ought shotgun blast through his front living room window in the early mornings hours, gave the appearance of an ordered hit.

Scalish was angry and incensed that Brancato allowed himself to become associated with Semenoro in the first place. The police felt it was a professional hit, and it became yet another unsolved killing in Cleveland.

An FBI source stated that there were many versions as to why Semenoro was murdered. The feeling was that he was a "stool pigeon" and was talking about Mob activities in Cleveland and New York to the local police and possibly to the local FBI agents.

Semenoro had a great number of enemies in the Cleveland area because of all of his stupid actions. Carmine had been seen at the Highlander Restaurant on Northfield Road, and had caused problems for the owner, Angelo Lonardo, as well.

The informant told FBI agents that, from what he had heard, Semenoro was sent to see Brancato on recommendation of a "mutual friend in New York." The informant said Semenoro got himself into some type of jackpot in New York with a top man and was forced to leave.

Brancato helped his friend get out of the mess with Semenoro as a gesture of friendship to his good friend in New York, whose identity was not known.

Ever since Semenoro arrived in Cleveland, he had not had a steady job. He just hung around Brancato to meet people in Cleveland and to act like a big shot, to appear connected.

Regarding his killing, this source noted that undoubtedly numerous individuals would have what they considered sufficient cause to kill Semenoro or have him killed. The source said he would remain alert in his contacts for any discussion of possible suspects or motives for this gangland-style murder.

Many Mob people in Cleveland were upset with Brancato because of his failure to disassociate himself with Carmine months earlier.

After several months of being in Cleveland, the informant told the FBI yet another theory of how Brancato had contacted his friend in New

York, and that Semenoro had given certain people headaches in the Cleveland area.

His friend indicated to Brancato that Semenoro had no highly-placed contacts in New York, that he was "no good," and had always had a loud mouth and tried to continually brag and use people's names to make an impression and connections in an effort to impress women and people. "He was nothing and they could not care less about what happens to him,"

The informant told FBI agents he had heard from a friend of his that the hit on Semenoro was ordered by someone in New York, and that they sent a hit man into Cleveland from a Family there. The source told agents he had overheard Semenoro state shortly before his death that he had tried to contact his man in New York City on two different occasions, but this man would not take his calls.

When Frank Brancato was picked up for questioning by Warrensville police the day after Semenoro's murder, he told them that he was with Semenoro the night before at a clambake. He said they had a good time and did not know why the murder took place.

Frank told them Semenoro had been in a fight with some college boys at the Balcony Lounge in Woodmere a few weeks ago in which several of the boys got beat up pretty bad; one boy needed fourteen stitches. But other than that, he had no other information that would help them.

On September 25, the Cleveland police notified the Cleveland FBI they had arrested Semenoro back on September 10 for trespassing and disturbing the peace. They had no other criminal record of him and released him on a $100 bond, which Semenoro gladly paid.

The *Cleveland Press* ran an article on September 26 which said:

The possibility of a special Federal Grand Jury appeared remote today as the investigation (continued) into the gangland slaying of Cleveland Mafia figure Carmine Semenoro.

Carl Miller reported today,... Justice Department officials in Washington had decided to await further developments in the investigation of the slaying before calling a jury."

Miller is the head of the government's strike force here to combat organized crime.

Miller was in Washington yesterday discussing the slaying of

Semenoro. Police described the murder as a professional hit and a contract slaying. The Warrensville Police have questioned (Frank) Brancato and Dominic Lonardo, who are currently under indictment for extorting money from two Youngstown businessmen, along with Semenoro.

The Racketeer Influenced and Corrupt Organizations Act (commonly referred to as RICO Act or RICO) is a United States federal law that provides for extended criminal penalties and a civil cause of action for acts performed as part of an ongoing criminal organization. The RICO Act focuses specifically on racketeering, and it allows for the leaders of a syndicate to be tried for the crimes which they ordered others to do or assisted them, closing a perceived loophole that allowed someone who told a man to, for example, commit murder, to be exempt from the trial because they did not actually do it.

RICO act was enacted by section 901(a) of the Organized Crime Act of 1970, enacted October 15, 1970. While its original use was to prosecute the Mafia as well as others who were actively engaged in organized crime, its application has been more widespread.

On October 7, 1970, in Boardman, a suburb of Youngstown, Ohio, the police department notified the FBI that a man who owned a construction company had received a note which was delivered by two teenage boys who were unknown to him. The teenagers told the police that an unknown man paid them $100 to deliver the note to the owner of the construction company, who in turn contacted the Boardman police department and furnished them with the note.

The note basically stated:

Stop playing games, DeNiro, I did not come all the way from New York to play games with you. I am here on business because you will not cooperate with the men that I represent. And if you do not pay the money they are asking for, and you do retract the statement that you made and go to the law, you will be a dead man. Along with you I will hit your family, DeNiro, and anyone else that is near to you. Dynamite doesn't care who is around when it goes off. I will get you no matter what or where, even if you are in jail. Consider yourself lucky that you are given a break.

I will call you on your office phone. Answer it on the second ring, no sooner and no later, understand? We will take it from there. Remember, your life and the life of those related to you and associated with you are in your hands. We are watching and listening very, very closely to every move on your part and your partners and families."

After the FBI examined the contents of the note carefully, they felt that the note had been written by a crank, as all of the information that was contained in this note had appeared in the local newspapers during bond reduction hearings for the subjects. The writer of the note referred to himself as the brother of Carmen Semenoro, which was not true, as Semenoro had no brothers. The FBI noted Semenoro was a known associate of Frank Brancato.

CHAPTER THIRTY

1971

An article appeared in the *Cleveland Press* on January 6, which mentioned:

The indictment of Cleveland Mafia figure Frank Brancato, age seventy-three, was mentioned by FBI Director J. Edgar Hoover in his annual 1970 report on organized crime.

Brancato is a well-known gambler, racketeer, loan shark, prohibition gangster, and is currently charged in Federal Court with conspiring to extort money from two Youngstown businessmen.

On January 27, the *Cleveland Press* had an article which said:

The Highlander Motel stopped being a known mob watering hole in Warrenville Heights on January 19, when a fire originating in the nightclub area routed twenty guests from their hotel rooms in adjoining building.

No one was injured in the fire, and firemen brought the blaze under control within an hour. The Highlander is owned by Angelo Lonardo, who is the brother-in-law of the "Outfit" Boss John Scalish.

After the investigation, the Warrensville Heights Fire Marshal determined that the fire was a result of arson. No one has been charged in this crime at the current moment.

During the late sixties until now, The Highlander has been a major hangout for the area's top hoodlums.

Eventually Lonardo collected about $160,000 on an insurance claim, according to Martin Lax, who had secretly transferred the ownership of The Highlander Motel to Big Angelo Lonardo years earlier. Big Angelo's first direct link to the Seaway Loan Company came on December 30, 1965, when Seaway Company loaned him two identical loans of $93,100.

According to an FBI file dated March 11, an informant said he had heard a Cleveland LCN Family capo had wanted to kill a witness whose testimony could convict him, but he was under orders from his LCN boss not to issue the murder contract. The capo took this matter into his own hands. Knowing exactly where the witness was living, which was located on a first-floor apartment, the capo, seeing his shadow behind a closed curtain in the living room, blasted away with a shotgun and killed the witness. With this successful murder, the capo killed the main witness against him, and after the killing, admitted he had done so to his boss, but nothing was done to him.

This statement was believed to have been regarding the murder of Carmen Semenoro. The capo mentioned was believed to have been Frank Brancato.

On March 11, the Warrensville police were informed by a waitress from Chester's Lounge that she had heard Frank, Nasher, and John Brancato talk about how sad it was that Carmine was hit. Then they all laughed. To her, this meant the men all had something to do with his murder, or they knew about the murder ahead of time, or who could have done it.

The detectives became very excited for some solid information in their investigation and continued to press her for more information on the three men, but the woman told them she was only coming forward because she felt concerned and (because she was) a good Catholic who wanted to pass the information along to authorities who could look into the murder of this poor man without getting herself personally involved.

When the police asked if she would testify to this in court, the woman exclaimed "no" very loudly and all the eyes in the police squad room looked at her. She insisted that she did not want to get killed, and she had a husband and two small children who needed her. The detectives tried to calm the woman down the best that they could, but the young woman did not say another word to them and soon got up and wanted to leave, so they let her go home.

Knowing her full name and address, the detectives brought this new information to their chief and then they all went to the city prosecutor to see if they would have enough to bring the three Brancato men in for questioning or to arrest and then try to prosecute Frank Brancato.

The prosecutor told the police that they needed to push the woman for more information and then to get her to agree to testify and to sign her statement. Then they could have a good case to go to trial, but the detectives needed to be careful and continue their investigation into these allegations. If they were going to nail Brancato this time for murder, they needed to be sure they had all their facts straight before going to trial.

On March 26, a detective from the Warrensville Heights Police Department advised FBI agents that his department had not obtained any further information that would aid them in determining who the murderer of Semenoro was. The detective told the agents that this investigation was continuing and he would immediately advise them if he obtained any other information of value.

On May 28, an attorney from the Cleveland Strike Force advised the FBI that he had reviewed the case and felt that the case against Michael Romeo and Frank Ross would be very difficult to prosecute now in the Youngstown extortion case, due to the fact the main participant in the case against both men was to have been Carmen Semenoro, who had been murdered. The attorney advised that he intended to dismiss the process against Romeo and Ross, but he intended to continue with the prosecution of Frank Brancato as the person who had planned and authorized the extortion of the two men. The prosecutor advised that there was currently no trial date set at this time.

On June 4, an article in the *Cleveland Press* said:

The current gambling operating in Cleveland is estimated to be grossing $300,000 a week and has been successfully broken up by several surprise raids and arrests by FBI agents, in cooperation with the police. Eleven men have been arrested from Cleveland, Toledo, and Akron. Among them were John Blank and his brother James. Both men have been known to work with Frank Brancato in past gambling operations, although Brancato was not arrested in these raids.

Bond was set at $10,000 for each of the eleven men by U.S Commissioner Clifford E. Bruce.

On July 8, the *Cleveland Press* ran an article written by Tony Natale, which reported:

There has been an attempt by underworld crime figures to gain control of the City of Cleveland's rubbish-hauling operation.

The Cleveland Police Department Intelligence unit came across the names of several people who are well-known to police, and some with reported ties with organized crime during their investigation.

The names of these men were then turned over to the Federal Task Force of the U.S. Justice Department for the attempt to muscle in and take over the Cleveland rubbish hauling business.

The Grand Jury is said to have subpoenaed at least twenty-five people in their investigation of labor racketeering in the private rubbish hauling industry. One man who was named is Danny Greene, the ex-waterfront labor boss who organized the Cleveland Trade Solid Waste Guild.

Greene came under criticism earlier this year when several private rubbish haulers complained to the Press that they were being coerced to join Greene's organization.

In the past, Greene has been known to have worked with Frank Brancato from time to time, and (it) has been reported that Brancato, with the "OK" from John Scalish, is the man behind Greene and in turn is giving Greene protection against the independent trash haulers in the city, mainly Mike Frato.

On July 27, the FBI raided a major bookmaking establishment. An informant told them the man that they raided was now closing down his operation and looking for a new place to reopen it.

The source mentioned that he was looking to go into business with Nasher and John Brancato to ensure that he would have protection from this happening again to him.

The game took place every night except on Sunday nights, from 9:00 at night until 6:00 in the morning, and was located in the Harmon Trucking Company building.

The men placed a guard on the rooftop of the building with a rifle for protection, and another guard on the main entrance door, and an additional locked door on top of a long staircase leading to the main room.

In his opinion, the informant told agents he would consider this to be a large-scale operation, with six men operating the crap tables; four on duty at one time and the other two watching the game from the sidelines.

The informant told them there was always liquor and food provided to the customers for a price, from $1 to $10. Poker chips were utilized in the game, and there was no limit placed on bets. The informant personally observed one individual drop $12,000 in one night and stated that the action was heavy like that on most nights.

One of the many FBI files on Frank Brancato pertaining to the extortion case in Youngstown stated that the case against him was currently in a pending inactive status, since the subject (Frank Brancato) was a subject of a different matter currently pending prosecution in the Northern District of Ohio involving an alleged extortion credit transaction and a Hobbs Act violation. It should also be noted that the subject was under investigation along with others in an illegal gambling business matter in Cleveland with file 182-338, as set forth in the details of an anti-racketeering report. The information on Brancato was that he was the major gambling operator in the city of Cleveland, and currently operated crap games at the Harmon Trucking Company in Glenwillow.

On September 15, the Warrensville Police Department was contacted by the Cleveland FBI and asked what was going on with the case against Frank Brancato for the murder of Carmen Semenoro. The police informed the FBI that a trial date for Brancato was set to have taken place earlier on April 26, in U.S District Court set by Robert Gary, Assistant Attorney in charge of the U.S. Task Force in Cleveland, Ohio.

Then, on September 25, 1971, Mr. Gary advised the Warrensville Heights Police Department that the case against Brancato was removed from the court docket for insufficient evidence against him, and no trial date was set at that time. The police told FBI that they had thought the U.S District Court would have notified them at the same time as well.

Here is yet another situation where there was not enough supporting evidence against Frank Brancato, so he was saved from prosecution, a long prison term, or possible deportation once again.

A police detective advised the Cleveland FBI that Frank Brancato was picked up for questioning by the Cleveland Police Department concerning the murder of Anastasio Brettos, who was shot and killed on October 13, near East 9th Street and Captain Frank's Restaurant.

Detectives told agents that Brancato had acknowledged he had talked to his friend Brettos during the early morning of October 13 and had requested Brettos to meet him at Captain Frank's for a late-night bite to eat. During the police interview Brancato stated firmly that, by the time he arrived at the restaurant, Brettos was found dead and police were already on the scene.

On October 26, an attorney with the Northern District Court in Cleveland advised the FBI office that there was still no trial date set for the prosecution of Frank Brancato concerning the extortion credit transaction and the Hobbs Act violation matter, for which he was under indictment.

Brancato's attorney had informed agents that the government had been required to answer certain questions in their filing of particular questions submitted by the defense, that the government had failed to answer and amplify some answers already furnished by the government, and that they could not go on with a trial until these matters were cleared up.

1972

On February 4, 1972, the attorney for the Cleveland Strike Force advised the Cleveland FBI that after reviewing the current evidence against Frank Brancato and Michael Romeo, he had requested the Department of Justice allow him to dismiss the indictments against the two men.

Based on the fact that Carmen Semenoro was now deceased, he felt that the evidence presently available was not sufficient to proceed with the trail against Brancato and Romeo.

The indictments were reviewed once again and dismissed on February 11 by the Government Organized Crime Strike Force. Judge Ben C. Greene in Cleveland, Ohio, signed the dismissal order.

Documented in an FBI file on February 11, the *Cleveland Press* reported:

Charges (have been dismissed) against Frank Brancato of conspiring to extort money in May 1970 from two Youngstown businessmen Richard Eden and William Manus, who are co-owners of Diversified Homes, Inc.

Similar charges against Mike Romeo were also dismissed. Federal Judge Ben Green ordered the charges dropped at the request of the Government Organized Crime Task Force, because of a solid lack of evidence against both men.

The action was approved by the Justice Department in Washington. David Margolis, head of the Strike Force here in Cleveland, declined to comment on the reason for the dismissal.

Informed sources, however, indicated that another key government witness had become reluctant to testify against Brancato.

Another article in the *Cleveland Plain Dealer* on February 12 by Thomas Andrzedlewski reported:

Attorney David Margolis, who is the head of the U.S. Justice Department Crime Task Force on Organized Crime, presented the case to Judge Ben Green, who would later sign the dismissal order.

It is believed David Margolis had relied heavily on the testimony of the late Carmen Semenoro, but with his death, they have no case against either man, plus there was insufficient additional evidence to proceed with the trial of Brancato and Romeo.

On April 14, the Cleveland FBI, in a very successful event, raided the gambling casino run by Frank Brancato at 28555 Pettibone Road in Glenwillow, Ohio.

Brancato was not in the building at the time, and the games were shortly shut down. The FBI was looking into charging Brancato with gambling, a violation of Title 18 sections 894.

Brancato later told an FBI informant that he was highly incensed over the complete success of the FBI raid and that they had such an easy access to his building when he had been paying people $50 a night to keep a lookout for him and to safeguard his operation.

The FBI learned while interrogating the customers in the raid that they heard Brancato had decided to stop or shut down all of his gambling ventures and card games, since there was "too much heat" from the police.

The FBI continued to report numerous spot-checks of Brancato activities by special agents, but failed to reveal any unusual activity.

From this time until September, the FBI has had little information in regard to Frank Brancato and what he has been doing. Yes, he is still a heavy smoker and drinks scotch most nights and he still claims to live with his daughter Bella and her family in Northfield, Ohio, and goes out every morning to get a shave from LaMarca's Barbershop. Then he may go to the IAB Club or Captain Frank's for lunch or to the Blue Grass in Northfield or another restaurant for dinner, and he has been going home by midnight most nights.

It was now late in August of 1972, and Frank Brancato was turning a milestone: seventy-five years of age. His friend John Scalish, along with his sons Joe and Ignatius, known as Nasher, all decided to throw a party for him. Nasher suggested having it on Labor Day.· All the men were in agreement and the planning began.

The event would be held at the Blue Grass on Northfield Road near Rockside Road, a well-known stop for all the men and a safe environment to enjoy the festivities. There was a large party room in the back that held three hundred guests.

Some of the guests in attendance were John Scalish, John DeMarco, Johnny Blank, Angelo Lonardo, John Nardi, and Shonder Birns. Many of the men brought their wives with them. Mr. "B" who always helped his friends and family, became dearly loved by many.

As a highly respected member of the Italian Community, Frank had many friends from the community attended, as well as the entire Brancato family, including all of his eighteen grandchildren. Some of the grandchildren were married, and they were accompanied by their spouses as well.

The guests would all dine on prime rib, chicken marsala, cavatellis, fresh green beans with almonds, baked potato, fresh-baked Italian rolls, and for desert were cannolis and tiramisu and a two-layer cassata cake made by his friends at Corbo's that simply said, "Happy 75th Birthday Mr. B."

The guest were thrilled to attend this happy affair to honor their friend, as they all toasted Frank with champagne several times throughout the night and wished him a very Happy 75th birthday.

My family and I enjoyed the evening with our grandfather very much. It was a memory that we will never forget. We had never seen him this happy, as he enjoyed the guests who attended his birthday bash. Frank was shy man and almost looked embarrassed by all the attention given to him by the people who loved him and cared for him.

As a special present to Frank B, his friends John Scalish, Johnny Blank, John DeMarco, John Nardi, and Angelo Lonardo gave their friend an amazing gift of a brand-new 1972 Cadillac Fleetwood.

John DeMarco even showed up with his wife, as sick as he was, slowly walking with a cane. He did not look like he had much time left in this world, but he would not miss this opportunity to wish his good friend a happy 75th birthday.

Before the entertainment began, a man came out onto the stage carrying several large plaques with him. The man brought up onto the stage the shy Mr. Brancato. The man was there to honor Frank for all of his charitable work in the Italian community over the last fifty years.

The plaque was framed in a rich oak finish that had a very nice facial bust and was engraved with his name under it and the year, 1972, from The *Societa Licata Di Cleveland*. Frank was being honored with "The Man of the Year" award from this Italian Society for his outstanding interest, devotion and in appreciation for his dynamic leadership, personal dedication and total commitment to the society and to his fellow Italians in the city of Cleveland.

This was a very high honor for anyone in the Italian community to receive. All of his five children were given a copy of the bronze plaque that honored their father. I am proud to say that I have my mother's copy of the plaque hanging on a wall at my home.

Next to come, after the wonderful ceremony, was the entertainment for the evening. Without anyone's knowledge, the friends of Frank Brancato had been able to bring in Frank Sinatra Jr. to perform for this wonderful and exciting evening.

Frank Jr. performed all of his father's wonderful hit songs and many of his own versions of other songs that he had made popular over the years. The women in the audience, as well as some of the men, were thrilled to have this young man singing in front of them. After the wonderful concert for Frank Brancato, his children were all introduced to Mr. Sinatra backstage.

The Cleveland FBI was advised of the details of the birthday party by an informant on October 17.

On September 30, the *Cleveland Press* reported that the FBI had arrested ten men for gambling, and they all could face fines of up to $10,000 each, with a prison term up to ten years.

Arrested were Frank Brancato, the reputed leader of organized crime in the area, along with his son Nasher and son-in-law John Brancato, an unnamed grandson of Frank Brancato, along with John Blank and Charles Blank (John's older brother), and several others.

All the men were indicted for violation (of) the illegal gambling statute of Organized Crimes Act, according to Special Agent John Burns.

The agents made a sweeping series of raids in a three-hour period starting shortly after 8 am. Agents confiscated over $15,000 in cash from the Pettibone Club Brancato operated.

The men were indicted for interstate transportation of wagering information on sports games, interstate travel for racketeering, and conspiracy to run an illegal gambling operation.

Brancato was also charged with taking $12,300 in cash and checks and gambling records to keep them from the FBI during the raid.

The indictment stated, "The Pettibone Club was in operation from November 1971 until last April 14, when the FBI here, led by Special Agent John Burns, charged in, broke into the club, and confiscated a dice table, $15,000 in cash and other gambling paraphernalia and records."

The indictments were handed down by the U.S. Justice Department Strike Force on Organized Crime by David Margolis and Roger McRoberts, who supervised the investigations.

On October 11, an article in the *Cleveland Plain Dealer* reported that the ten men, including street boss Frank Brancato, decided to plead not guilty to the gambling charges in Judge William Thomas' courtroom.

On the way into the courtroom, Attorney Giuliani told the defendants, "Don't worry, nothing is going to happen today. You will all be able to go home." All emerged in ten minutes and left the courtroom.

At the arraignment; Attorney Jerry Milano began by telling Judge Thomas, "we have gotten a copy of the indictment. They all understand it and wish to plead not guilty at this time."

The attorneys who were representing the men were Jerry Milano and Elmer Giuliani. Judge Thomas gave each man a $5,000 personal bond and would set the trial date later on.

On October 25, a little over a month after Brancato's birthday party, John DeMarco, the capo and consigliore of John Scalish, died of a heart attack. My uncle Nasher later told us all, after our grandfather had died, that the passing of John DeMarco, his best friend, was very hard on his father.

On December 15, the *Cleveland Press* ran an article about gambling, which stated that a $24-million-dollar-a-year clearinghouse gambling machine was being threatened by known criminals throughout the city, as there was a behind-the-scenes war going on that very few people know about.

Some of the estimated twenty-four gambling operations have been visited by a member of the "organizers," who are asking for a $200-a-week cut from all the operations to ensure their safe operations moving forward, week in and week out.

Some of the men have paid up to the organizers, while others are willing to fight them to keep their money.

Although no threats have been given to these men, they are willing to wait and see what happens to them.

Police are well aware that a power push is being waged, so much so that members of the homicide, intelligence and central vice units are all working together on the investigation.

There are two major types of numbers, or policy and clearinghouse games. A daily drawing takes place where numbered balls are pulled out of a bag.

The clearinghouse game is the most popular game in Cleveland and is based on the final stock quotation from the Wall Street Journal. The people who take these bets are called "writers," and they will often work out of their home or an apartment, a bar, or even a well-known restaurant. Sometimes these were called "wire rooms," where a bank of phones would be set up to take the incoming calls.

The Cleveland police believe that Shonder Birns, Frank Brancato, and fight promoter Donald King are the main men involved with most of these types of policy games at the present time.

In 1972, Frank Brancato took on his last role within the Mafia family as consigliere.

CHAPTER THIRTY-ONE

The Final Chapter
1973

From January until the end of April, Frank Brancato was in seclusion and not seen much around the cities of Cleveland, Akron or Youngstown. Many people thought he was on vacation once again with either Sam Cardinal or Frank Visconti, but only his children and a few trusted people close to him knew the truth of the high-ranking Mafia street boss.

In February, Frank was given a blessing while he was very sick, the birth of his first Great Grandchild, Christopher, who was the son of his grand-daughter Virginia Cerney.

Early in March of 1973, an informant advised the FBI that Frank Brancato would leave Captain Frank's and drive to Bolivar Street, where he would meet up with John Fotos, who would then get into the car with him. He had been seen handing Frank an envelope, which appeared to contain money, and then Fotos would leave as Brancato drove off. Brancato would never enter into the building. He would proceed east to Southgate Shopping Center and enter the Post and Paddock Restaurant, where he would hand this package to the owner, who is believed to have been banking and holding the money for "Uncle Frank."

On March 22, an informant advised the FBI that Frank Brancato was in the company of Angelo Lonardo, John Nardi, Martin Lax, and Joey Gallo prior to the fire that destroyed the Highlander Motel, owned by Angelo Lonardo, back in mid-January of 1971. Brancato and Lonardo implied in a friendly way that they would consider it a favor if Lax did not make any additional attempts to purchase the motel back.

On May 16, an informant advised the FBI that Brancato continued to be seen at the Blue Grass Lounge or at the Post and Paddock Lounge and Restaurant on Aurora Road, and he operated a high-stakes card game inside the Rockside Towers Apartment in building "A" on the corner of Rockside Road and Interstate 271.

The informant said Frank owned the game along with his son Nasher, who ran the games for his father. Nasher had been seen at the games every night, but Mr. B. had not been there in person.

The informant told agents the game was predominantly a progressive poker type of game, in which cards were dealt to each player, and four cards were dealt up the middle of the table. All players used the cards in the center of the table in an attempt to make the highest possible hand. Betting was done progressively, in that the first bettor must bet a minimum of $4 or fold. With five players sitting at the table, when it got around to the fifth guy, he must bet $10 or fold.

The source told agents that the house got 5 percent commission on every pot, and depending on the length of the games, the house got up to $6,000 a week. To the best of his knowledge, there were at least five guys a night in the game. The source also told agents he heard Brancato was now operating a card and dice game in the basement of the Mayflower Motel Tavern on the south side of Broadway east of Interstate 271.

The *Cleveland Press* ran an article by Jim Dudas on August 2, which said:

> *Frank Brancato, the reputed top man in organized crime in Cleveland, is in a federal court with two other men for running a $2,000-a-day gambling operation at the Trucking Company in Glenwillow.*
>
> *The two men named are John Blank and Nick Minniti. (Charges stem from) the April 14, 1972, raid at the Harmon Trucking Company on Pettibone Road.*
>
> *The trial judge is set to be Judge William Thomas. Ten others who were arrested with the three men in the… raid… have pleaded guilty and received fines of $1,000 to $2,500 from Judge Thomas.*
>
> *When the FBI agents raided the operation they confiscated over $10,000 in cash from a dice table.*
>
> *FBI Agent John Covert testified that he went undercover into the gambling club eight times, and each time he used and lost between $50 and $100 of government money in gambling on the dice table.*
>
> *On each night, he personally saw over $2,000 being bet and passing between the house and customers on one dice game.*
>
> *Lawyers for the Federal Strike Force on Organized Crime are*

Paul Corradini and Fred Clervi.

On August 4, the *Cleveland Plain Dealer* ran an article written by B. Vivian Aplin, who wrote:

The conservatively dressed Frank Brancato looked more like a retired old businessman than one of the top men in Cleveland's organized crime as he was convicted in the U.S. District Court of conducting a dice game, after the jury deliberated about eight hours. The FBI claimed "Evidence has indicated that the games netted $2,000 a day for Brancato and John Blank."

On August 4, the *Cleveland Press* had an article which said:

The testimony that clinched a guilty verdict was from the FBI Agent John Covert on how he personally noticed the gambling and the loss of money in the $2,000-a-night... dice game.

Brancato was found guilty. Judge William Thomas announced he will sentence Brancato at the end of August at the earliest, or in December at the latest,... Brancato is looking to possibly receive five years in prison and a $20,000 fine.

The other two defendants, John Blank and Nick Minniti, were acquitted of the charges against them.

The *Plain Dealer* on August 12 reported:

Brancato's attorney, Elmer Guilliani, convinced the judge the government had insufficient evidence, and that the affidavit they used to obtain the search warrant which led to his arrest did not show probable cause.

An accompanying motion asked the judge to acquit him of the gambling charges. Brancato is still awaiting sentencing from U.S. District Judge William Thomas, who said he would rule on the new request soon.

On August 17, an informant advised the FBI he heard that a fund-raising party was now being planned in honor of Frank Brancato, and it was going to be held in the near future at the Blue Grass Lounge. The party was to help raise funds for his defense against the gambling charges currently pending against him.

A source informed the FBI on September 20 that Brancato was now in room 624 in the Heritage House in University Hospital for prostate cancer. He would stay until September 29.

On October 6, a *Plain Dealer* article reported:

Frank Brancato, seventy-six, was fined $5,000 yesterday in U.S District Court in Cleveland for running an illegal dice game at a truck terminal in Glenwillow.

As undercover FBI Agent John Covert testified in court on April 14, 1972, he personally saw Brancato at the cash box where between $10,000 and $15,000 changed through his hands in the time he was in charge of the cash box.

Judge William Thomas gave Brancato eleven days to pay the fine. The maximum penalty for a charge like this is $20,000 and five years in prison. No prison term for Brancato was disclosed to the newspaper.

It was now mid-November of 1973 and the cold winter air in downtown Cleveland was kicking off the cold and frigid Lake Erie shores, telling the city to get ready for yet another cold and snowy winter for the north coast city.

Frank Brancato had been in the hospital on the sixth floor of University Hospital for three weeks now, dying a slow and painful death. His room was located in the corner suite, where it was considered to be private room.

He had no roommates who were patients. He did, however, have a man named Joe who was his roommate. Joe did wear pajamas and wore a long robe tied loosely at his waist, and always seems to have his hand in his right pocket whenever there was someone around Mr. B.

Joe wore hard shoes that looked to be brown Stetsons to me, and not slippers. Joe was never in bed, and he looked way too healthy to be inside the hospital. No, Joe was there to help protect Mr. B., just in case somebody had the wrong idea. Mr. Brancato was going to die fighting, just the way he came into the new world.

Nasher was there every day, meeting and greeting all the well-wishers who came to pay respects to his father. Some men came to discuss business, but most came to bring flowers and to talk with the "old man" one last time.

This holiday season was the worst that I can ever remember having. There was no holiday spirit in our family at all—no celebration of the birth of Jesus, no Christmas tree up in any of his children's homes, nor were they decorated for the holiday season that was ahead for everyone. There was no holiday spirit for the family of Frank Brancato and no presents under the tree in my mother's house, waiting for her children to come over and open up on Christmas morning.

For weeks on end, I watched my mother suffer deeply over the upcoming death of her father. She had lost her mother at the very young age of fifty-five, and now her father was leaving her as well. Mom seemed to cry every day, knowing that her father was not going to be with her much longer. I could tell her heart was breaking and that her love for her father ran deep into her soul, more than what the normal public citizen could imagine or care about.

To them, Frank Brancato was a criminal, a gangster, a terrible man who had killed other humans; a man who had been accused several times to have been a cold-hearted killer and deserved whatever he got out of life. At this time, it was his death that was right around the corner, and not while shooting craps or playing in a game of poker or pinochle.

The day the family had been dreading finally arrived on December 17, 1973, at 11:20 in the morning. Frank's children were all there with him as he took his last breath of air. His sons Joe and Nasher, along with his daughters Ninfa, Bella, and Jennie, all cried and watched the man they loved and called their father die a slow and painful death.

Frank Brancato did not show his love in words to anyone except to his family. He loved them all in his own way and was near and dear in all of their hearts.

This was the day many people in Cleveland, who had great respect for Frank Brancato, lost a mentor and a good friend, but most importantly, his family lost their father, father-in-law, and grandfather. He would soon become a great-grandfather for the second time in early February 1974 with the birth of Christina, John Bisco's daughter, and then in July with my daughter Carrie's birth.

The cancer inside Frank's body spread faster than anyone thought it would. With as much fight and strength as he had left in his aging, weak body, the cancer finally won out, as it almost always does. He had beaten death when he was shot in 1932, in a battle that would have killed a normal man, but this time death won.

For weeks, the Cleveland newspaper reporters had all watched the hospital daily to report any changes in Frank's condition. It was news to the people in Cleveland that the capo and street boss of organized crime in their city was dying. The television channels finally told the city and the world about his death that December day.

Reporters told the public he was a known racketeer, gambler, bootlegger and a killer of men. But to his family and friends, Frank Brancato was always a quiet, soft-spoken, loving, and caring man who was gentle and kind to the people close to him.

Frank, like so many of the other men in his profession, never hurt the average "Joe" down the street. If you were a good citizen, you did not have to fear Frank Brancato, John Scalish, John DeMarco, or any of the other men in their line of business. The people who tried to hurt him or his family were his enemies.

Mr. B. always helped his friends when they needed it. He never raised a hand to hit or hurt anyone in his family. His voice would rise up a little if you made him mad, and you would just stop and look into his face and his eyes that told you that you were going a bit too far. Then he would smile or give you a grin, or a wink or a quick pinch on your cheek that told you he loved you.

The *Plain Dealer* reported on December 18, 1973, "Mass to be Friday for Frank Brancato:"

For forty-three years Frank Brancato (was) reportedly one of the top Mafia figures, who made the headlines with a variety of alleged underworld activities.

Funeral services will be at St. Jude Catholic Church. Joseph Brancato (Frank's eldest son) described him as "a wonderful father" while top law enforcement officials say he was a top man in Cleveland organized crime.

Frank Brancato

Frank Brancato was a prime example of a man who led a dual life, or what we like to now call, "old school" He was a loving father to his family and to many people over his seventy-six years on this earth. He would help anyone that he could—a charming man who had a wonderful smile that would light up your world in an instant; a man who was well-respected in the community, as well as throughout the United States, and a man who enjoyed his life to the fullest.

Frank Brancato also had a dark side that, when he needed to do the job that he had chosen to do earlier in his life, he was able to it without guilt, remorse, and with a determination that others could not understand.

Frank Brancato fought for his life and his freedom to be a free man, day in and day out, throughout his life, just as millions of other American immigrants have done over the centuries before and after him. He worked hard to give his family a comfortable lifestyle, with a roof over their heads and food on the table every night. Frank Brancato lived his life his way, just as the great singer Frank Sinatra told the world in the song he made famous, "My Way," written by Shawn C. Carter, Paul Anka, Francois Claude, and Giles Thibaut:

"The record shows I took the blows

and did it my way."

Frank Brancato fought the United States government for many years as they tried in vain to deport him back to his old home in Sicily, but he won several deportation hearings against him that lasted over the last twenty years of his life.

Frank Brancato was a strong man in body and in sprit, who lived his life to the fullest and always had great pride in his heart. He always held his head up high when many men tried to beat him down, arrest him, or even tried to kill him.

December 19, 1973, was a very cold day as the family gathered up its strength to greet the many friends who would attend his wake. Mr. B. had his great smile on his face and looked relaxed, like he was just resting. There were hundreds of bright red roses over the top of his coffin and large arrangements of red roses at both sides of the gold and mahogany coffin that I was told cost $10,000. The wake was held at Biondo's Funeral Home on Rockside Road. For two days, from two in the afternoon until nine in the evening, an endless row of men and women came to pay their last respects to a man who they all admired and called their friend.

The reception line was ready. First there was Nasher, who knew most, if not all, of the guests and their families; then Frank's other son Joe and his family; Ninfa and her family; Bella and her family; and last came my mother, Jennie, and her family.

The reception line went from the start of the day to the end of day. It was nonstop, with guests who cried and grieved with the family who had lost their dear father and grandfather. We shook hands and kissed many men and women who we did not even know—men like John Scalish, Angelo Lonardo, John Nardi, Johnny Blank, Shonder Birns, and even Danny Greene, as well as many others who were very powerful in many circles.

We proudly accepted their condolences for our loss. Most said that they would miss him. Others related to us that they loved him like a brother, and all had a tear or two in their eyes for our loss.

So tell me this: how could a man who was so dearly loved and have so many friends be labeled as a terrible or evil man in the eyes of so few who did not really know him?

The day of the funeral was December 21, 1973. All of Mr. B.'s family met at Biondo's for the last viewing of his body, along with over sixty friends, before we left for St Jude's Church on Richmond Road.

After the black hearse with Mr. B. as the man of honor, there was a limousine for each of his five children and their families. Then came four carloads of fresh floral arrangements for the cemetery and the church. Many of the extra flowers that did not fit in the four floral cars were sent to a local senior center on Richmond Road. Three cars of flower arrangements were emptied at the church and stayed there for them to enjoy for the upcoming Christmas Mass that was only a few days away.

After a beautiful funeral service for Mr. B., the mourners filed into their cars for the long journey to his last resting place at All Saints Cemetery in Northfield, Ohio.

Outside the church were over one hundred fifty mourners that did not know Mr. B., but wanted to see who showed up for the funeral mass, along with camera crews from all three of the local television stations. All were disappointed, since none of the top criminals came to the funeral mass at Saint Jude Church or the burial service.

The Bedford Heights police gave the procession an escort onto the I-271 freeway south, while the Cleveland Police Department, along with several cars from the FBI, as well as local newspaper and television stations, reported on how large the line of cars was on the ride to the cemetery. Some say as many as one hundred cars or more were in line, while others claimed it was longer than a mile or two in length.

The pallbearers were made up of Mr. B.'s oldest grandson from Joe's family; Frank, Ninfa's oldest boys, John and Frank; Bella's sons,

John and Bill, and Jennie's two boys, Jim and Frank. It was one of the coldest and windiest days so far this winter. There was a fresh four inches of soft snow on the ground from overnight, and wind gusts were up to forty miles per hour, making it so cold that the priest at the graveside service cut it short, since there were so many visitors and the tent was too small to hold all of them.

It was difficult for the Brancato family and friends to say goodbye properly to the man that so many people respected, loved, and admired, considering the weather was so terrible.

In the spring of 1974, Frank's dear wife Virginia, who had passed away in 1955, was moved from Calvary Cemetery on Mayfield Road to be with her love and best friend Frank. They both now rest in peace together next to their five children, who have all passed on.

The Brancato family is all in heaven once again now, playing cards together like they enjoyed doing while living on earth. Most people thought Mr. B. was the best card player; my mother was good, but not as good as her siblings. Others thought Joe or Nasher or even Ninfa or Bella was the best. I have my money on Bella; she was always sharp and had a great poker face that would fool everyone at the table.

Frank Brancato was survived by his five children and their spouses, along with eighteen grandchildren. Before he passed away, Frank was already a Great Grandfather, and now two more great-grandchildren were going to be born the next year. Christiana, John Bisco's daughter, and my daughter Carrie.

On December 22, 1973, the *Cleveland Plain Dealer* ran stories written by Harry Stainer on Frank Brancato titled, "Man Who Beat the Odds on Deportation" and "Brancato Funeral Carries Note of Dignity:"

Maybe forty-five years ago, no one would have given odds on Frank Brancato living through the Prohibition years and the Corn Sugar Wars in Cleveland, but he was seventy-six years old when he died.

Would it have been a good bet that he could have staved off deportation repeatedly by the government, Congressmen and the newspapers that were after him as a reputed Mafia leader?

But he did survive, even after his kidnapping by the U.S. Immigration and Naturalization Service that surprisingly flew him from Cleveland to Boston in 1955 on a one-way trip to Italy. A court overruled this action and Brancato was ordered to be brought back to Cleveland the same day.

In 1937, Clevelanders learned that Governor Martin Davey had secretly commuted his sentence in December of 1936. This sentence was to cause Brancato several problems later with the Immigration and Naturalization Service. His citizenship was revoked and periodically there were attempts once again to deport him to his native Italy.

FRANK BRANCATO'S ARREST RECORD

F.B.I. records on Frank Brancato's arrests with federal ID Number 137835; Cleveland ID Number 29063:

Cleveland, Ohio: Arrested on May 13, 1926, on suspicious person charge; released.

Cleveland, Ohio: Arrested on June 13, 1927, on suspicious person charge; released.

Cleveland, Ohio: Arrested on December 11, 1927, on suspicious person charge; released.

Cleveland, Ohio: Arrested on August 21, 1930, for the murder of Frank Alessi; later found not guilty and released.

Cleveland, Ohio: Arrested on March 8, 1932, on suspicious person charge; released.

Cleveland, Ohio: Arrested April 9, 1932, for perjury. Held in jail until June 2, 1932, when he was found guilty of perjury and sentenced to the Ohio State Penitentiary in Columbus, Ohio, pending his appeal. He was later released on bond until his next jury trial.

Cleveland, Ohio: Arrested on July 28, 1932, on suspicious person charge; found not guilty.

Columbus, Ohio: State Penitentiary ID Number 66919 on April 24, 1933: found guilty of perjury for the Porrello brothers' murders and sentenced to 1 to 10 years in prison. He was discharged from the Ohio Penitentiary on December 2, 1936.

Buffalo, NY, at the INS office ID Number 2544646; registered as an alien on October 1, 1940.

Pittsburgh, PA: Allegheny County ID Number 17141: Arrested May 28, 1945 on a suspicious person charge and discharged on May 29.

Cleveland, Ohio: picked up for questioning on August 25, 1950; questioned and released.

U.S. INS office in Cleveland, Ohio: Number 0707-K-2129 on August 28, 1951, for violation of immigration laws.

Los Angeles, California: ID Number 362369 on October 5, 1956; Registered with the city as an ex-con, given ID Number 40146. Not arrested.

Cleveland, Ohio: ID Number 90341 on July 29, 1957; brought in for questioning and released.

Las Vegas, NV: ID Number 72377 on September 19, 1963; registered as an ex-felon per the county ordinance.

Cleveland, Ohio: June 23, 1968; brought in for questioning in the case of Peter DiGravio murder in Chesterland, Ohio. Released the same day.

FBI, Cleveland, Ohio: ID Number 5041 on April 28, 1970; charged with extortion and conspiracy per the Anti-Racketeering Hobbs Act, Title 18 Section 371. No trial date was set. Later in the year, charges were dismissed.

Cleveland, Ohio: September 25, 1970: Questioned in the murder of Carmine Semenoro.

FBI, Cleveland, Ohio: ID Number 8174 on September 29, 1972; for violation of Ohio gambling laws. No trial date was set.

EPILOGUE

No matter what you may have read in magazines or books or in this book, for our family, Grandpa Brancato was a very well-respected, loving, kind, and generous man. He would always take the time to stop over to our home to visit with my mother and his other children at least once a month, and many times more often. Yes, he was a busy man, but in his business, it was the nighttime that took up most of his time.

I cannot remember a time when I saw him that he did not give us a genuine, loving hug or a kiss. With a smile on his face, he would pinch our cheeks so hard we yelled for our mother to save us. He did love his family, and seemed very proud of all his children and grandchildren.

Grandpa would always give us some kind of gift or another; it really did not matter what it was— it was from him. What I can remember most was the gift of money. It was a shiny silver dollar that could have come from Las Vegas, a brand-new crisp $2 or $5 bill, but they were all very special; they were from him. These bills were printed in red ink, not green or black, and they were called Silver Certificate bills and were only minted for a short period of time. The $2 bill was mostly developed to be used at race tracks across the county, since that was the smallest wager amount that could be bet on one horse. The $5 bill was a special minted edition. I remember we always commented to Grandpa, "Are these real?" He always laughed at us and just told us, "Yes, they are."

Frank Brancato always had a very kind and friendly smile that made people smile along with him. He had many friends across the country who called him "Mr. B." out of respect. He was always a man of honor, and a man who believed in loyalty, and would never betray a trust or friendship.

Frank's other siblings beside brothers Giuseppe and Giovanni, Salvatore, Samuel, then came brother Nunzio, Vincenzo, along with yet a younger brother also name Giuseppe (aka Peppino) who took care of his aging and sickly mother Ninfa (Vecchio) until she passed way in Rome.

Her family decided to bury her in Rome, next to the love of her life Gusieppe who passed away in his mid sixties. Then there were the sisters Antoinetta and Rosaria (known as Sara), then Carmela, Elena, Maria and finally the youngest Angelina (known as Lina). Frank's sister Angelina (Lina) was brutally murdered by her husband Attilio Terraneo at a very young age on June 13th 1959. Sisters, Carmela, Maria, and Elena all passed away in Rome.

The senior Mr. Giuseppe Brancato died within a year of moving to Rome in hopes of curing his painful and debilitating cancer.

Sister Antonietta was the only sister to Frank who came to America and lived after she had married Amedero Casuccio in Italy. In New York, Antonietta passed away in 1987 while visiting with her sister Rosaira who was 88 and came over from England to spend the last few days to be with her very ill sister from England. Rosaria would later pass away in the county of Barrow, In Furness's Hospital in Cumbria, England in February 1989.

His first son Joseph (who passed away in 2006) was born in 1923, and he would marry Dolly Licata. They had three children: a son, Frank, and two girls, Virginia and Isabella. Joe worked as a plumber and pipefitter in the Cleveland area and worked for several years on the Perry Nuclear Power Plant located in Perry, Ohio, with his son-in-law Mike. Joe and Dolly were married for over sixty years before Joe passed away. Dolly is still alive, but is very sick. Joe's daughters, Virginia and Isabella, still live in Ohio, while their brother Frank has a very successful law practice in Kentucky.

Ninfa passed away in 1993. She was second to be born, in 1924. Ninfa met and fell in love with her first cousin, John Brancato, the son of her father's brother John. This was against their Catholic religion and beliefs. He passed away in 1998 in Las Vegas. Both Brancato brothers were very opposed to their marriage of their children, but just like young lovers anywhere in the world, John and Ninfa married anyway. They had six children together. Dorothy was first to be born, in 1946; then John, eleven months later; then came Virginia, Rose (deceased in 1997), Frank, and Joe. Joe passed away October 7, 2012, at the age of fifty. The surviving siblings live in Las Vegas with their families, except for Virginia, who lives in Middlefield, Ohio. Ninfa and John divorced in 1969. Ninfa never re-married.

Isabella, or Bella, was third to be born, in May 1926. Bella, who passed away in May of 2011, would go on to marry John Bisco and have three boys: John, Bill, and Frank. John Sr. was a master upholsterer of fine and very expensive furniture for over fifty-five years. Bella and John enjoyed their retied life together and were married for sixty-five years before we lost Bella. Uncle John still lives in the Cleveland area with his three sons, along with their families and his grandchildren.

Ignatius, or Nasher, who passed away in April 1999, was the fourth to be born, in March of 1929. Nasher married Marie Santa Maria, who was John Bisco's cousin. They had one daughter, Virginia, together. Marie currently lives in North Carolina with Virginia and her son. Nasher was the one who worked with his father the most. He worked at both horse race tracks in Cleveland, the Thistledown for thoroughbreds during the summer months and at Northfield Park for trotters in the fall. Nasher went on to own a very good and popular Italian restaurant known as Heller's on the Westside of town on Dover Center Road in North Olmstead. When Nasher finally decided to retire, he moved to Phoenix, Arizona, with his second wife, Louise. Louise passed away in December of 2012.

Fifth to be born, but the first child to die, was my mother JoAnn (Jennie) Grace, born on January 6, 1931. She passed away on June 4, 1982. We will always remember and love her. Jennie married James Paul Monastra. They enjoyed a large and beautiful wedding, and the reception was a major social event in the city that Labor Day weekend of September 4, 1950. They were married at Saint Dominic's Parish and their reception was at the city's famous Hotel Statler in downtown Cleveland. Jim and Jennie were blessed with four children, two boys and two girls, Jim, Frank, JoAnn, and Karen. My father continued on with his life after Mom's sudden death, and married Rose D'Alessandro in April 1985. Jim Sr. enjoyed his long sixty-five year career as a barber, taking after his father Jim. I am saddened to say that I lost my father and best friend on February 2, 2012, after a short illness, at the age of eighty-two.

Even at my mother's funeral at Fioritto's Funeral Home on Mayfield Road in Lyndhurst in 1982, some of the top men from the city still came to pay their respects to a good friend's loss of a daughter.

"In every conceivable manner, the family is link to our past,
bridge to our future."

~ Alex Haley

Frank Brancato, John Scalish, John DeMarco, Al Polizzi, Frank Milano, Tony Milano—all had several items in common: their proud heritage of being Sicilian / Italian and their undying respect and loyalty to one another. Yes, these men were members of a crime organization and crime family known for its violence, murder, and brutal beatings to their enemies. Not one of these men ever broke their vow of omertà. All of these men died of natural causes, unheard of in many of the other major Mafia cities around America.

Frank Brancato died as a very wealthy man in his heart. He had his children and grandchildren all around him, who loved and cherished him unconditionally for the man that he was and were proud to call them their father or grandfather.

Many people may wonder what happened to all of the hundreds of thousands of dollars that Mr. B. made over the years. Well, that is a mystery to all of his children and to the U.S. government, but he also died as wealthy as he was when he came to America—with only a few dollars in his pocket. He had nothing of value in his name; he leased all of his cars; he had no checking account or savings account, and no life insurance policy to bury him.

I am sure along his life he helped his children financially here and there with cash while he was in his prime and they were growing their families while he was making hundreds of thousands of dollars a year.

He died with no money to be found by the government; he had spent his money as fast as he made it—his way.

ABOUT FRANK MONASTRA

Frank Monastra is the grandson of Frank Brancato. Frank's mother Jennie was the youngest daughter of Frank and Virginia. One of Jennie's hardest tasks in raising four children was desperately trying to keep her father's secret life as a criminal and crime boss from her young children; while his life played out in the daily newspaper thoughtout Cleveland in *"The Cleveland News, Cleveland Press*, and *The Plain Dealer"* starting in the 1930's until his death in

1973.

As children my cousins, siblings and I were always told by our parents that our grandfather was a tire salesman and worked long hours. He always showed us all, how much he loved us when he visited. Grandpa dressed in expensive looking suits and always seemed to drive a brand new car, mostly Cadillac's, which was hard to imagine how he could afford them by only selling tires.

Earlier in 1995 I read "The rise and fall of the Cleveland Mafia" by Rick Porrello. I knew my quest and journey into my grandfather's colorful and highly publicized past must begin. My catalyst to investigate my grandfather's past began while I was in my young twenties when I told myself I would not dig into his past until all of his children had passed on. My research would not begin until May 2011.

I am married to Judy, who is the love of my life and best friend. We are blessed to have three children, along with five wonderful and healthy grandchildren that we cherish, adore and enjoy spending time with. We have two Yorkie's who give us great joy.

I have worked for a major grocery chain in Cleveland, for almost forty years. I enjoy playing golf, but sadly I have not had much time to enjoy the sport lately. I enjoy reading and writing in my spare time, but would rather spend time with Judy, my children and grandchildren.

I would enjoy hearing from you; so if you have any thoughts or comments after reading "Mafia Street Boss"

I may be contacted at: MafiaStreetboss@att.net

(Please no attachments)

I hope you enjoyed your true mafia experience!

CPSIA information can be obtained at www.ICGtesting.com
Printed in the USA
LVOW08s1418121214

418556LV00002B/2/P

9 781621 831365